PHILOSOPHICAL ESSAYS.

PHILOSOPHICAL

ESSAYS.

IN TWO VOLUMES.

By THOMAS GORDON, Esq.

VOL. I.

THERE ARE MORE THINGS IN HEAVEN AND EARTH
THAN ARE DREAMT OF IN OUR PHILOSOPHY.

SHAKESPEARE.

London:

PRINTED FOR THE AUTHOR,

BY C. ROWORTH, BELL-YARD, TEMPLE-BAR.

1808.

CONTENTS.

VOLUME FIRST.

VOLUME SECOND.

═══

ESSAY VI. *Continued.*

CONTENTS.

ERRATA.

ERRATA.

Introduction—Page vii. line 29, *dele* and.
Page   10, line 15, *for* them *read* their.
        30, line 13, *for* of *read* in.
        40, line 16, *after* as *insert* by.
        46, line 3, *dele* the comma.
            line 10, *for* or *read* nor.
        54, line 20-1, *for* the ancient metaphysics and logic *read* of the metaphysics and logic of the ancients.
            line 24-5, *for* that they were *read* as to have.
        55, line 8, *after* ancients *dele* the comma.
            line 22, *after* phantoms *insert* a comma.
        60, line 15, *after* can *insert* now.
            line 30, *dele* the comma after realists, *and insert* one after idealists.
        65, line 3, *read* result.
            line 17, *dele* as.
        70, line 4, *for* reasons *read* reason.
        72, line 10, *for* in *read* on.
        75, line 6, *for* and *read* or.
        99, line 11, *after* things *insert* a comma.
    105, line 22, *for* recal *read* real.
    157, line 1-2, *for* which clearly shews *read* it must be manifest.
    159, line 1, *for* of *read* or.
    229, line 3, *dele* or.
    260, line 13, *for* immediate *read* intermediate, *and after* only *insert* a comma.

for Galvini *and* Galvinism *read* Galvani *and* Galvanism.

CONTENTS.

VOLUME FIRST.

ERRATA;

ERRATA;

OR CORRECTIONS AND ADDITIONS.

VOL. I.

Page   2, line 23, *after* and *add* it is also evident.
    10,   15, *for* them *read* their.
    18,   24, *dele* the comma after ideas and the words or to, *and insert the word* and *instead of* them.
    30,   13, *for* of *read* in.
    40,   16, *after* as *insert* by.
    46,   3, *dele* the comma.
          10, *for* or *read* nor.
    54,   20-1, *for* the ancient metaphysics and logic *read* of the metaphysics and logic of the ancients.
          24-5, *for* that they were *read* as to have, *and after* induced *insert* them.
    55,   8, *after* ancients *dele* the comma.
          13, *after* meant *insert* by them.
          22, *after* phantoms *insert* a comma.
    59,   12, *after* more *dele* the short line.
          27, *after* size *insert* of the figure.
    60,   15, *after* can *insert* now.
          30, *dele* the comma after realists, *and insert* one after idealists.
    63,   23, *for* on *read* in.
    65,   3, *read* result.
          17, *dele* as.
    66,   7, *after* than *insert* either.
    67,   16, *for* but *read* except.
          22, *after* and *insert* they.
    70,   4, *for* reasons *read* reason.
    72,   10, *for* in *read* on.
    75,   6, *for* and *read* or.
    81,   27, *after* but *dele* it.
    87,   2, *after* when *for* on *read* in, *and after* not *for* on *read* in.
    96,   18, *for* in *read* on.
    99,   11, *after* things *insert* a comma.
   104,   31, *after* or *insert* in.
   105,   22, *for* recal *read* real.
   123,   9, *after* and *insert* that.
          10, *for* that *insert* of.
          11, *for* are *insert* being.
   157,   1-2, *for* which clearly shews *read* it must be manifest.
   159,   1, *for* of *read* or.
   166,   15, *for* on *read* or.
   178,   15, *for* on *read* in.
   229,   3, *dele* or.
   233, lowest line but one, *for* electrical *read* elective.
   234,   2, *for* acid *read* acids.
   260,   13, *for* immediate *read* intermediate, *and after* only *insert* a comma.
   279, lowest but one, *after* necessarily *insert* also.
   280,   1, *for* the comma after owing *insert* a semicolon, *and in place of* also *insert* and consequently that OXYGEN and HYDROGEN are identical or the same substance.
          3, *after* and *dele* of.
   283,   29, *for* they *read* these theories.
   284,   17, *for* nature *read* things.

for Galvini *and* Galvinism *read* Galvani *and* Galvanism.

INTRODUCTION.

———

THE observing, collecting, and recording, of physical phenomena and facts constitute the HISTORY OF NATURE. And in the discovery and knowledge, as rationally deduced from the phenomena and facts thus observed and collected, of those pre-established, undeviating, and determinate mutual relations and dependencies which subsist between things, commonly distinguished by the name of the laws of nature, does SCIENCE consist.

SCIENCE is either theoretical or practical; and the practical part of science differs from art, as consisting in the discovery and establishment of rules according to which practice to be successful necessarily must be regulated. In the application of these scientific rules to practice, with dexterity and address sufficient for obtaining by their means the purposes intended, does ART consist.

The ultimate end and object of PHILOSOPHY is the attainment of the greatest possible degree of human happiness, by the enlargement of human power, and the proper regulation of human conduct.

PHILOSOPHY may be defined—*Knowledge of things, and of the powers of nature or physical causes of things, in as far as things and the causes of things are discoverable and determinable from phenomena by human reason; and, consequently, of the laws of nature, or the different modes of operation and different degrees of energy or force with which these causes or powers act for each particular case as influenced by different circumstances.*

From this definition it is manifest, that philosophy furnishes the means not only of discovering the phenomena and effects which necessarily must result from the operations of these different causes or powers of nature, as

influ-

influenced in their respective modes of action and degrees of force by different known circumstances and thereby the means of foreseeing events and providing for futurity, but also of discovering methods whereby these powers may in many cases by human ingenuity and exertion be rendered subservient to man so as to be applied by him to purposes of the greatest utility to him, and which are highly conducive to his comfort and happiness.

Philosophy, in the full and proper acceptation of the term, is of very comprehensive signification, as including every kind of human knowledge acquired by means of *rational* investigation, whether that knowledge respects the laws of physical or of moral action; whether those laws which, by rational investigation from phenomena, have been discovered to regulate the course of natural events, or the actions of inanimated substances; or which, by the same means, have been ascertained to regulate and determine moral conduct, or the actions of animated beings; or as it respects the use and application of the powers of nature, or causes of events, agreeable to their various different modes of action; or the proper application of the laws of nature with regard to the accomplishment of those ends intended to be obtained by their means, and which are obtainable by no other means and according to no other laws :—that is every kind of human knowledge that is not the result of mere observation and memory, or that is not the offspring of the sportings of fancy; so that philosophy comprehends every kind of useful knowledge except that of languages, nomenclatures, geographical, historical, &c. facts; and a knowledge of the rules and practice of many of the arts and sciences without a knowledge of the reasons on which that practice and these rules are founded.

It is upon philosophical knowledge that the well-being, power, and happiness of rational beings principally depends, as their conduct is in every case in a great measure necessarily regulated by the degree of it they respectively possess, and as the degrees of success attending their conduct also necessarily depends upon it whatever the object of that conduct may be, whether the attainment of some physical or of some moral end; whether the applying of the physical powers of nature, as that of gravity, for the attainment of some useful purpose; the applying the principles of mechanics to the construction or improvement of some instrument or machine;

or

or those of astronomy to the improvement of navigation : or whether the attainment of moral good or excellence, or of virtue and happiness in the individual, in the state, or in mankind in general, is the object. In it are included all the sciences properly so called, those of jurisprudence, government, political œconomy, &c. as well as those of metaphysics, morals, and mathematics, and those which are usually denominated, and are often regarded as exclusively physical mechanics, chemistry, astronomy, &c.

But though the extending of philosophical knowledge must on the above-mentioned accounts undoubtedly be an object of great importance to mankind, yet it is not so much so as the establishing of it on a solid and permanent basis by freeing it from any erroneous and delusive principles, from any chimerical entities, any illogical deductions and conclusions, and from any unfounded and visionary theories on which it may in part be established ; since these must necessarily render the knowledge of it not only unprofitable and vain, but also deceitful and prejudicial in a high degree : error and disappointment ever being the inevitable consequences of proceeding on principles unfounded and the precepts of an imaginary philosophy.

As there are many facts from which it may be inferred, so there are many reasons which evince a probability at least of philosophy having been cultivated with much success and of its having attained a very high degree of perfection in some very remote period of antiquity, and in some country now unknown, though most probably situated in the East. That the arts and sciences, and many most profound and enlightened philosophical doctrines, were introduced into Greece either directly from the East, or, in a more corrupted state, through the medium of Egypt, are facts well ascertained. To Cadmus a Phœnician the Grecians were indebted for the first knowledge of letters. Thales of Miletum, the founder of the Grecian philosophy, travelled into Egypt and the East for the express purpose of acquiring the wisdom of the East, and was the first European who predicted an eclipse of the sun :—a fact he must have become acquainted with in Egypt or the East, as not possessing instruments proper for making such a discovery himself. Vetruvius informs us that astronomy was introduced into Greece immediately from Babylon itself by Berosus a Babylonian who opened an astronomical school in the isle of

Cos ;

Cos; and Pliny says the Athenians in consideration of his wonderful predictions erected him a statue in the gymnesium with a gilded tongue. According to Herodotus it was from the Babylonians that the Greeks first learned the Pole, the Gnomon, and the twelve divisions of the day.

Pythagoras the Son of a Phœnician, and, according to some authors, a Phœnician himself, as being born at Sidon in Syria, but according to others a native of Samos educated in Phœnicia, travelled into the East for instruction; some say even into India. Among other profound and sublime doctrines introduced into Greece by Pythagoras were those of the obliquity of the zodiac; that the sun is in the center of the universe; that the earth is round, and people have antipodes; that the earth moves both round the sun and also round its own axis; that the moon reflects the rays of the sun and is inhabited like the earth; that comets are a kind of wandering stars disappearing in the further parts of their orbits; that Lucifer and Hesperus are not, as was then supposed, two different stars, but the same being the planet Venus, and that the movements of the planets are in harmony: meaning, perhaps, that they all harmonize or accord in describing areas about the sun which are proportional to the times in which they are described. The common multiplication table is also ascribed to him; and he either invented or introduced into Greece several geometrical theorems of great importance in that science. He also unfolded the fundamental principles of music, and gave the several parts their proper names. Like the Brachmans of India he and his disciples abstained from all animal food.— Knowledge, both in the sciences and in the arts, was introduced into Greece from the East by many others, both foreigners and natives, besides those mentione d above.

Euclid, the celebrated mathematician, author of the Elements of Geometry, and Data, which are still extant, and of other geometrical works on Conics, Porisms, &c. which are lost, was a native of Alexandria in Egypt, and taught mathematics there under the reign of Ptolemy Lagus; and there it was that all the eminent mathematicians from that time till the conquest of Alexandria by the Saracens were either born or studied. It was there that the philosophers and mathematicians of these times could avail themselves of the advantage of consulting the famous library formed by the Ptolemys from what had been saved out of the wreck of the learning of that part of

the

the East which had been overrun by Alexander and his successors—and that they did so there can be no reason to doubt. That this treasure of oriental wisdom and learning did afford abundance of materials of which Euclid and other compilers of Elements of Geometry could, and probably did, avail themselves seems highly probable at least. And that this library, among its other valuable relicts of the knowledge of the East, contained books on the Science of Algebra there is reason to suppose from that part, still extant, of the work of Diophantus of Alexandria, the only known writer of antiquity on that subject, as in it he treats of algebra, or rather of that mode of calculation which is now called algebra, as a science the fundamental principles and rules of which were then too well known and too well established to require his taking any notice of them.—Diophantus's work consisted of 13 books, but only 6, with part of a 7th, have ever been printed. Regiomontanus, in his preface to his Alfraganus, informs us, that in his time the whole of the 13 books were preserved in manuscript in the Vatican library; and Bombelli, in his Algebra, expressly says, that when Antonio Maria Puzzi Regiano, Public Lecturer on Mathematics at Rome, and he were translating some of these books, *they found that in the said work the Indian authors were often cited, by which they learned that this science was known among the Indians before the Arabians had it.*

About eight hundred years ago the arithmetic as well as the algebra of India was introduced into Europe by the Arabians, a circumstance which soon produced in Europe a complete revolution in arithmetical science, the decimal or Indian arithmetic, and the Indian arithmetical notation—often called the Arabian though the Arabians acknowledge their having got both the notation and the arithmetic from the Indians—being so decidedly superior to the Grecian and Roman arithmetic and notation, as to occasion the arithmetic and notation of these latter to be soon entirely abandoned, and that of the former adopted in its stead; and the Indian arithmetic and notation has ever since in Europe been the arithmetic and arithmetical notation in common use.

The state of astronomical science in India, Siam, China, &c. at present—though it resembles, as was justly observed by the truly ingenious and eloquent but unfortunate Bailli, the shattered remains rather than the elements of a science, as containing many precepts without explications and

many

many periods of which the advantages are unknown—is such as seems to support and confirm this conjecture (which is not new but has been entertained by several eminently distinguished for learning and discernment) of the sciences having in some remote period of antiquity and in some country now unknown, attained a very high degree of perfection; and it seems probable that China—in which the mariner's compass, gun powder, the art of printing, &c. were so long known before they were known in Europe—has not always been inhabited by the same race of human beings it is at present, who seem incapable not only of making any discoveries or improvements in the sciences themselves, but also of adopting and carrying into effect those made by others:—the arts and sciences having remained stationary in that country for many centuries.

But however this may be, it is to be remarked that few discoveries of importance—at least in mathematics, physics, and astronomy—have ever been ascribed to any Grecian who had never travelled into the East or at least into Egypt; and that the sublime truths and profound philosophical knowledge, thus introduced into Greece, were either soon so altered, corrupted, and disguised, by the Grecian philosophers as to be converted into fiction and fable; or were entirely rejected and abandoned by them from the decided preference they gave to hypotheses of their own conceiving, the mere offspring of a too luxuriant fancy, which, though ingenious, and supported by the most refined eloquence, the most artful sophistry, and all the embellishments and allurements of figurative language and a splendid diction approaching in some cases to poetry, as in the philosophy of Plato, had no foundation in the nature of things; and which, having no solid foundation, served no other purpose than to amuse the fancy, mislead the judgment, and involve science in obscurity, mystery, and absurdity. The only part of the philosophical knowledge introduced into Greece which the Grecians seem to have retained, adopted, and naturalized, were those portions of it they had received through the vitiated medium of Egyptian hieroglyphics, allegories, and fables, being that from which in a great degree the Grecian mythology derived its origin. The philosophical doctrines of Pythagoras appear to have been much corrupted and altered by his disciples of the Italic school, before they passed over from Græcia Magna into Greece Proper, where they were soon so vitiated that scarcely a vestige of many of the originals was to be found in the writings of those

who

who pretended to develope, describe, and illustrate them ; while many of the others were so obscured as to be rendered almost unintelligible.

From the doctrines of Parmenidas, the poetical Pythagorean, Plato borrowed many of those highly embellished but obscure reveries in which his philosophy consists ; and in it he seems to have lost all sight of the real Pythagorean doctrines, substituting in their place an ideal system well suited to the purposes of mysticism and superstition, but very ill calculated for enlarging the stock of useful human knowledge, and for investigating and discovering the laws of nature. While the doctrines of his pupil, the mighty Stagirite, who so long with unrivalled sway controuled and directed the opinions of Europe and the schools as to philosophical principles, in place of having had any tendency to instruct and enlighten the world, served only to involve it still more in error, in sophistry, and in endless disputes from which no real knowledge could possibly be acquired. The Romans being abject admirers of the Grecian philosophy, adopted it without scruple or reserve, and without adding any thing of importance to it, or forming any new systems of their own. And in the barbarous ages, as they are called, which succeeded the downfal of the Roman empire, as these corrupt systems of philosophy, founded on fallacious principles, transmitted to them from the ancients, were held in such high estimation as to be regarded as models of perfection ; and as the highest ambition in the way of science was to understand, elucidate, and enforce them ; it was utterly impossible that any foundation could be formed, or any progress made for the acquirement of just principles and sound philosophy.

As the Grecian philosophers nevertheless were undoubtedly men of great ingenuity, of splendid and superior talents, the bad success which attended their philosophical enquiries must in a great degree be attributable to the fallacious mode of philosophizing or manner of conducting the investigations they adopted and pursued, in attempting to spiritualize every thing ; to deduce all knowledge from sources purely intellectual ; and, reversing the order of nature, not from what is known but from what is supposed only ; or in endeavouring, to use an expression of Thales the founder of the Ionic sect and father of the Grecian philosophy who inculcated and practised the doctrine himself, " to make philosophy descend from the

b   " heavens

" heavens to the earth:"---attempts necessarily vain, and which could ter-minate in nothing but hypotheses, delusion, and error.

Some men of strong mental powers and sound judgment, as Roger Bacon, &c. even in what are called the barbarous ages, deviated so far from the hypothetical mode of philosophizing adopted and inculcated by the ancients, as to have recourse in their philosophical investigations to experiment---the oracle of nature ; but these instances were rare ; and the great Lord Chancellor Bacon, Viscount of St. Albans, was the first who had a clear and comprehensive view of the errors and absurdities of the ancient systems of philosophy and of the deceitfulness and inefficacy of the ancient mode of philosophizing.

Since Lord Bacon pointed out the proper mode of philosophical investigation, the great progress that has been made in the sciences comparatively to all that had been done before is truly astonishing, and those have ever succeeded best in the pursuit, in the acquirement, and the dissemination of useful knowledge, who have had the least regard for the doctrines of the ancients, and have deviated most from their mode of procedure. But, though this is the case, the progress has notwithstanding on the whole been but slow, so difficult is it even by the most direct and surest methods to penetrate into the secrets of nature, and trace science to its first principles ; much remains yet to be done, many are the things which seem to be still hid under an impenetrable veil of obscurity ; and what is still more to be regretted, there is reason---from that obscurity and even mysticism which pervades some of the sciences ; from those differences of opinion which still prevail with regard to them ; from the first principles on which they are founded not being in many cases so clear and convincing as first principles ought to be ; and from the reasons and conclusions deduced from these principles, even when denominated demonstrations, being sometimes erroneous, sometimes improbable, and sometimes even contradictory, impossible and absurd---to believe that science is not yet, in every case, founded on so stable a basis as not to admit of being shaken or overturned ; on first principles, facts, and reasonings, so evident, logical, and decisive, as necessarily to preclude all doubt and to impress conviction on every mind capable of understanding them.

The

The insufficiency of the evidence with respect to the justness of the first and fundamental principles of metaphysical science in particular, and the improbability and in some cases even impossibility and consequently absurdity of the conclusions deduced from them, has impressed mankind in general with no very favourable opinion of the soundness of these principles and the justness of the reasonings on which it is established, and has induced many to suppose that metaphysical investigations, however ingenious, must all necessarily terminate in fiction, sophistry, or paradox. And it is from this supposition, or a despair of subjects and researches so intricate, abstruse, and perplexing as those comprehended in this science, the principal objects of which come not within the cognizance of sense, being ever treated in such a manner as to be productive of any knowledge which may with safety, certainty, and utility be relied upon, that that indifference now so generally manifested for metaphysical speculation has proceeded. There are several other sciences besides that of metaphysics to which unsoundness of principle and erroneous theory is justly imputable; and, among others, some perhaps which at present are generally regarded as being established on evidence the most satisfactory and on reasonings irresistible.

To treat of subjects so recondite as those of the following Essays with perspicuity must be no easy task, and perspicuity is all that is aimed at in the stile, other embellishments being the less requisite, that it is the object of these essays rather to establish than to illustrate. Any pompous display of words full of sound and seeming import but in reality signifying nought has, therefore, throughout studiously been avoided; and the author has also—from a dread of being deceived himself, and from having no wish to entrench his doctrines in incomprehensibles and obscurity, and of thereby, perhaps, becoming the unintentional cause of deceiving others—cautiously guarded against the admission of sophistry, of all arguments of a dubious nature, and the use of symbols, except where unavoidable; though he well knows how highly acceptable ingenious sophistry, from its apparent acuteness, pompous pretensions, and seeming to mean more than meets the eye, is to many readers, and with how much admiration and applause it is often received by those with whom obscurity and perplexity of thought pass for profundity and discernment; and that there are no errors so egre-

gious,

gious, no blunders so gross, but an algebraical form, and the finesse of an abstruse analysis, will with some sanction for truth itself.

The intention of the following Essays is not so much to amuse the fancy, to interest the passions and affections, or to indulge in poetic description and eloquent declamation, as to reason consequentially, closely, and conclusively; to address the understanding, and from obvious and certain principles consonant to nature and right reason, to endeavour to remove from some of the phenomena of nature that veil of obscurity in which their causes have been involved, and which hitherto has been deemed impenetrable; to investigate and ascertain some important truths; to give some greater degree of stability to opinion; to trace science to its first principles; and to a certain extent to establish philosophy on the solid and permanent basis of reason and of nature: the object of these Essays being an attempt to research into and discover the fundamental principles of philosophy by a metaphysical analysis of the human mind, and a physical and metaphysical investigation into the nature of things; and, by means of the facts thus ascertained and of rational deductions from them, to endeavour to ascertain that relation which subsists between the human mind and the objects of its knowledge; the foundation of that right it assumes to become a judge of such objects; and consequently the extent and degree of certainty of this knowledge itself; and to establish the facts and fundamental principles thus discovered on evidence as satisfactory, cogent, and convincing, as the nature of things admits.

With this intention it is attempted in Essay I,—First, To investigate the nature, evidence, and necessary consequences of consciousness. Secondly, To point out the distinction between sensation and perception which in metaphysical disquisitions as well as in common conversation are so often confounded together, and to ascertain the difference between them on principles different from any hitherto proposed for that purpose. Thirdly, To investigate and ascertain the fundamental criterion or test of truth with respect to human knowledge, &c. And in this and the two immediately succeeding Essays a refutation of the ideal system of philosophy is attempted, not on assumed instinctive principles and laws of human thought, but on principles founded on and rationally deduced from the nature of things.

In

In Essay II, it is attempted, First, To enumerate the various faculties of the human mind, to distinguish them accurately from each other, and to ascertain the precise province, intention, and use of each; as of memory, judgment, fancy, &c. each of which is separately treated of. Secondly, To ascertain whether or not there actually are in nature any such existences as abstract general ideas, either real or nominal, or as abstract or absolute truths, immutable, necessary, and eternal. Thirdly, if there really is any such thing in nature as any human knowledge acquired by means of pure intellection only, besides what results from the consciousness of the mind with respect to its own sensations, powers, and operations, and thereby of its own existence and identity. Fourthly, if any kind of human knowledge can with propriety and justice be said to have been acquired purely *à priori*. Fifthly, On the facts thus investigated and ascertained, and the reasonings thence deduced, to endeavour to discover and develope principles on which a system of logic founded in nature, or on the *reality of things* in place of on *ideas, fancies, or phantasms*, may be framed and established; to ascertain the source from which all human knowledge is derived, and the means by which it is acquired; and thereby to establish philosophy on the stable and permanent basis of nature and reason.

The objects of Essay III, are First, To attempt a refutation of Mr. Hume's doctrine of Causation and the consequences he deduces from it, and thereby to complete what has been attempted in the preceding Essays, the refutation of the ideal system of philosophy. Secondly, To investigate and discover the characteristic differences, and nature and operation of powers and substances in as far as they can be discovered from their effects. And, Thirdly, from thence, to deduce the GENESIS of matter.

The object of Essay IV is, First, An attempt to investigate and ascertain the nature of mechanic power and action. Secondly, To account for the impressions made in the forms of bodies on percussion when there appears to be no expenditure of power or force on that account, the moment or quantity of motion being the same after the percussion as before it. Thirdly, To account for the impressions or cavities made in soft yielding substances being *ceteris paribus*, as the squares of the velocities of the bodies by whose action on them they are formed. Fourthly, For the loss of motion in the composition of forces, and the generation and gain of it in

certain

certain cases of percussion as that of elastic bodies increasing in geometrical progression. Fifthly, To ascertain what would be the laws of percussion with regard to perfectly hard bodies, if any such there were. Sixthly, To account for the operation of those simple instruments or machines called the mechanic powers. And lastly, To endeavour to decide and terminate that so very warmly and long contested dispute concerning that fundamental principle of mechanics, the ratio of the velocities according to which the forces ought to be estimated and appreciated.

With regard to the remaining Essays as full and distinct conceptions of their intentions and scope are to be acquired only by a perusal of the Essays themselves, it may here suffice to observe that originality of thought and comprehensiveness of views are not less conspicuous in them than in those by which they are preceded; and that the principles of the sciences treated of in them are represented in a very different light at least from that in which they have hitherto been regarded, the doctrines at present generally adopted with regard to the nature and composition of Fire, as formed of a combination of what is called Caloric with Light, and with regard to the nature and causes of differences of temperature, &c. being, in Essay V, rejected; and others proposed in their stead which perhaps are not liable to the same objections which are justly imputable to these: and, in Essay VI, a refutation of the Lavoiserian or Antiphlogistic Theory of Chemistry, as well as of the Stahlian or Phlogistic, and of those which preceded them, and of the Electrical Hypothesis of Franklin, and Magnetical of Æpinus, is attempted; for which other theories of these sciences are substituted, which perhaps may be found to account for many of the phenomena and facts treated of in them in a more satisfactory and rational manner than has hitherto been done; and, rationally and justly, for several facts and phenomena which hitherto have been deemed inexplicable. In Essay VII a proof is attempted of there actually being no such existences in nature as *absolute* space, and *absolute* duration; and, in this and the succeeding Essay, of the whole of the doctrine of infinites being founded in delusion, and therefore necessarily terminating in error and disappointment. And in the last Essay it is attempted in Part 1st to refute the metaphysical and mathematical doctrine of the *infinite* divisibility of magnitude; and the supposed demonstrations of the mathematical definitions of a point, a line, and a superficies;

superficies; to ascertain the true base on which geometrical science rests; and to free it from abstruse, paradoxical, enigmatical, erroneous doctrines, and unfounded prepossessions, though of very great antiquity and sanctioned by general approbation and names of the highest celebrity, by pointing out the true natures of the first and fundamental parts and principles of the science; especially of those fundamental propositions called axioms. In Part 2d of it, it is attempted to prove: First. That the true meaning, intent, and use, of the signs + and − in the science of algebra are not understood. Secondly. To ascertain, point out, and establish, by just deduction, sound reasoning, and pertinent examples, the real meanings, intent, and uses, of these signs in that science. And, Thirdly, To detect many of the erroneous doctrines which have been introduced into this science from a misconception of the proper meanings and applications of these signs, and from other causes; and to point out the means and methods whereby they may be avoided or corrected, and by which the science may be further improved. And in Part 3d, it is attempted to prove, 1st. That the doctrines of the Infinitesimal Calculus, of Fluxions, of Indeterminates, of Limits, and of Increments, are all founded on erroneous principles. And, 2dly, That no discovery ever was or ever can be made by their means:—as necessarily must be the case if the immediately preceding position, of their being all founded on false principles, is established; since it would be absurd in the extreme to suppose the possibility of true conclusions being justly deducible from erroneous principles.

From the above slight statement of the import of the doctrines treated of in this work, it is manifest that if the principles advanced, developed, and maintained in these Essays shall prove to be well founded, satisfactory, and just, they must necessarily effect a revolution in the fundamental and highly important sciences treated of in these Volumes.

The Appendix consists in Geometrical Solutions of the five following famous problems, viz. 1st. The Quadrature of the Circle. 2d. The finding of two Continued Geometrical Mean Proportionals to two Extremes given. 3d. The Duplicature of the Cube. 4th. The Cubature of the Sphere. And 5th. The Trisection of an angle.

Philosophical Essays.

ESSAY I.

OF CONSCIOUSNESS AND PERCEPTION.

1. ALL human knowledge is acquired by means of Sense or mental consciousness, and of inferences thence rationally deduced. And the sum and extent of it amounts to nothing more than a very partial and limited acquaintance with the existence and relations of things.

2. The human mind, of whatever formed, or on whatever depending, is evidently liable to changes in its state, since of such changes every one is sufficiently conscious; and, indeed, to suppose consciousness in the mind, without the mind's being acted upon and affected, or while the state of the mind remained the same, without being forcibly retained in that state by means of external action on it, would be to suppose an effect without a cause. It is however, only, in a state of life and of vigilance that the mind is conscious; for in a profound sleep, a faint, a catalepsie, and in other cases of suspended animation, consciousness, as well as thought, in the mind seems to be suspended for the time; or, at least, we have no proof or reason for supposing the contrary.

3. In the various affections of the mind, as it is variously acted upon and modified, and in the consciousness of these, does sensation consist. The mind, however, is not conscious of sensation only: it is also conscious

B

of

of its own existence and identity, of its faculties of remembering, imagining, reasoning, perceiving, understanding, judging, willing, and acting; of all its internal modifications and operations, or of whatever passes within itself. Consciousness to be known must necessarily be experienced; as it is impossible, from its being merely an affection of the mind, and from each individual mind being conscious of what passes within itself only, to define or describe it in such a manner as to be intelligible to those who either never did or are incapable of experiencing it. The discovery of the proximate cause, or causes, of consciousness in the mind from its being differently modified and affected, and of the manner and means by which consciousness is effected, lies far beyond the reach of human investigation.

4. Consciousness refers merely to what passes within the mind itself; and it is from it that thought, or the action of the mind results: since without consciousness, though itself a passive principle or property of the mind, there would be nothing to employ the mind, nothing to think about, nothing to rouse it to action.

5. That sensations, or those changes of state in the mind from which they result, are the effects of the actions of the bodily organs of sense on the mind must be sufficiently evident, when it is considered that no change of state or impression can be induced in these without a corresponding change of state or impression with its consequent sensation taking place in the mind also as is consonant to every one's experience, and that those changes of state in it with their corresponding sensations, which have been ascribed solely to its own internal operations, may also rationally be deduced from the same cause. The bodily organs, however, are merely the instruments of sensation: it is not the eye that sees, or the ear that hears, &c. Sensation exists not in them, but in the mind; and it is merely to particular sensations in it, from its being particularly modified by the agency of the eye or of the ear, that we give the names of colours, sounds, &c. and since sensations depend entirely on particular states, modifications, or changes of state of the mind, or on privations of these, it must necessarily follow that they cannot exist out of the mind; and that they cannot exist in it, but when and while the mind experiences, and is conscious of these states, modifications, or privations.

When

When the mind is not acted upon, impressed, and modified, by some power, either internal or external, it seems to remain in a torpid, insensible state, without either thought, pleasure, or pain. When the impressions and modifications excited in it are the effects of moderate and gentle action, the sensations thereby produced are always pleasurable, sometimes highly so, unless when the mind is so weak and languid from fatigue or disease as not to tolerate with ease even gentle action. But when they are the effects of action so strong and violent as to endanger the frame and organization of the body, or the regular action of the vital powers, then the sensations produced are always, other circumstances being the same, more or less painful as the actions by which they are produced are more or less violent.

6. But though sensations are in the mind only, yet bodily organs of sense are indispensably necessary for sensation; as sensations cannot possibly be produced in the mind but either mediately or immediately, directly or indirectly, by their instrumentality, and not by them otherwise than by means of modifications induced in themselves: and hence a mind unprovided with these, if such could be supposed, would be entirely destitute of all sensation and consciousness (since no affection, change, or difference of modification could be induced in it) and, therefore, of all thought; and yet it would be a mind, though a mind in a latent or dormant state, as being capable of sensation and thought if it were provided with these, and was acted upon by their means in the proper manner for producing these effects in it. If unprovided with one of these only, as the eyes or the organ of sight, it could by no possible means ever acquire sensations of the same kind with those which are produced in other minds possessing that organ by means of that organ and to which we give the names of light, colour, &c. since these changes of state or modifications in it, of which they are a consequence, could not in that case be effected in it from want of the proper organ: if unprovided with ears or the organ of hearing also, it would likewise be destitute of all the sensations acquired either directly or indirectly by means of that sense; and then the deficiency of sensations would be such as that the mind, though sound in other respects, could not with propriety be regarded as rational, as wanting that necessary information attained by means of the senses of those relations of things which are absolutely indispensable for its

B 2   preservation,

preservation, well-being, and rational action. It is altogether impossible for this deficiency to be supplied by any other natural means. It is not possible for the mind to generate any original sensation of itself, or to acquire it by any other means than those of the bodily organs of sense: one born without eyes can never by any means acquire the sensations of light or colours, or one born deaf those of sounds, &c.

7. Sensations differ among themselves not only as they are excited and produced by means of different organs of sense, those of one sense having no resemblance, common properties, or necessary connection with those of another, as of colours with sounds, &c. But those produced by means of the same sense also differ among themselves, there being different colours, different sounds, different odours, tastes, and feelings, to which, on that account, we give different names, as red, blue, yellow, &c.; and as it is common not only for two or more of those of one sense, but also for two or more of those of different senses, to be excited and produced in the mind at the same time, and seemingly in a combined or compound state, it may be proper to distinguish sensations not only into species, as they are produced by means of different senses, and into the varieties of each species, or according to their specific and particular or individual diffe-rences, but also into simple and compound, according as they are pro-duced in the mind singly or compounded.

8. Since sensation is only a particular species of mental consciousness, it must be evident that *simple* sensations do not admit of being defined or described so as to be intelligible to those who never experienced them, and that they can be known only by being excited and produced in the mind. *Compound* sensations may be intelligibly defined or described to such as are acquainted with the simple sensations of which they are compounded.

9. Besides the differences in sensations with respect to kinds, mentioned above, there are also differences in those of the same kind with regard to each other, as in degree, extent, &c. of which the mind is conscious. And the consciousness of the mind with respect to differences in its sensations among themselves, and with respect to differences in its faculties and opera-tions, differs essentially from that kind of consciousness in which sensibility consists.

10. In the former of these kinds of consciousness the mind seems to be entirely passive, excepting as far as that in certain cases it may be
                                                                    attentive,

attentive, and thereby the distinctness or degree of, consciousness encreased, since it is, if attentive, conscious whether it will or not : and this kind of consciousness seems neither to be attended with nor to be the result of action or reaction in the mind. In the latter kind of these, or that of sensibility, the mind is also conscious, if attentive, whether it will or not; and, if the impression is strong whereby the modification and sensation is produced, whether it is attentive or not: and this consciousness in certain cases seems to be attended with, if not to be the result of, reaction in the mind to the force impressed, or change of state induced ; it is, however, even in those cases so far passive as to act only in consequence of being acted upon.

11. As sensations in the mind, or those changes or modifications in it which they either accompany or result from, are produced by the immediate means of the actions of the bodily organs of sensation on it, in consequence of corresponding modifications or changes in their respective states being impressed upon themselves; so the changes impressed on these organs, and through them on the mind, must necessarily be the effects of some causes, beings, or existences, different and distinct from, and external to, both mind and body; since the mind is entirely passive in this case, and the body acts only in consequence of being impressed or acted upon: and that this is actually the case, we have the evidence of our senses confirmed by our reason under all the various circumstances that occur or can by conceived, or under which experiments can be made for ascertaining the fact. And as there could be no sensations, consciousness, or thought in the mind, without bodily organs, as has already been shewn, so it now appears, that even with these, sensation, consciousness, and thought in the mind could have no existence, without the existence and agency of things external to us. It will afterwards be shewn that these external things, to be capable of acting on our minds through the medium of our bodies, must themselves be corporeal or material, that is, of the same nature with the human body ; and that the mind can be acted upon immediately and directly by no other beings or powers than material agents, as the several parts of the human body, or at least by no other powers or beings, imaginary excepted, otherwise than through the agency of matter.

12. Those particular sensations we denominate pleasure and pain seem

to

to accompany most or all of our other sensations in a greater or less degree; and hence sensations become the cause, and the only cause, of all those actions in the mind we denominate voluntary. And thus as external things are the causes from which all sensations originate, and as sensations are the immediate causes of all voluntary actions, external things must also necessarily be the cause in which that kind of action originates: that they are likewise the cause of all involuntary action is sufficiently manifest.

13. Sensations do not of themselves constitute knowledge, those of a particular kind excepted to be mentioned hereafter. Our knowledge does not consist in sensation, but is founded on it and acquired by its means. Sensation is not knowledge, but that on which it rests, and the instrument whereby it may be obtained. As sensations can exist in the mind only, so the mind at first, as being ignorant of any thing external to itself, and before being deceived into a belief by instruction, habit, &c. of certain of its own sensations existing in things external to it, must necessarily be conscious of their existing within itself only: and they must all also necessarily, from the same cause, seem to it to originate within itself: and if any sensation is excited and produced in it, by any external impression on the body, it must necessarily be ignorant of any such external impression, as well as of the external cause, and of the part of the body affected by it, as being altogether unconscious of body, or of any thing distinct from itself. The above must be the case with all infants; and also would be the case with any adult new created, if such could be supposed, or of any adult perfectly devoid of experience and instruction.

14. Perception is not to be confounded with sensation, as was the case before Dr. Reid wrote. And it is not, as supposed by Dr. Reid and his followers, either an instinct, or a particular faculty of the mind acting instantaneously and instinctively and always attended with an irresistible belief and conviction necessarily arising from the constitution of our nature. Sensation differs essentially from perception, and it also differs essentially from the object of perception; for sensations cannot with propriety be said to be seen or be perceived by the mind, or in any case either to be perceptions, or objects of perception, and far less to be both perceptions and objects of perception at the same time. The mind perceives nothing within itself; even those sensations excited and produced in it,

through

through the medium of the eye, which are those which seem most to resemble their external causes, being nothing but a mere jumble or confused mixture of those sensations we call colours, of which no meaning can at first be understood by the mind, as affording neither vision nor perception to it, in the proper acceptation of these terms, from having no reference real or apparent, of which it is conscious, to any thing external to it. Mr. W. Cheselden informs us*, that the young gentleman born blind, who was couched by him, " when he first saw, he was so far from making any " judgments about distances, that he thought all objects whatever touched " his eyes (as he expressed it), as what he felt did his skin; and thought " no object so agreeable as those which were smooth and regular, though " he could form no judgment of their shape, or guess what it was, in any " object, that was pleasing to him: he knew not the shape of any thing, " nor any one thing from another, however different in shape or magnitude: " but upon being told what things were, whose form he before knew from " feeling, he would carefully observe, that he might know them again; but " having too many objects to learn at once, he forgot many of them; and " (as he said) at first he learned to know, and again forgot, a thousand " things in a day. One particular only (though it may appear trifling) I " will relate; having often forgot which was the cat, and which was the dog, " he was ashamed to ask; but catching the cat, (which he knew by feeling) " he was observed to look at her stedfastly, and then setting her down, " said, 'So puss! I shall know you another time.' He was very much " surprised, that those things which he liked best, did not appear most " agreeable to his eyes, expecting those persons would appear most beau- " tiful that he loved most, and such things to be most agreeable to his " sight, that were so to his taste. We thought he soon knew what pic- " tures represented, which were shewed to him, but we found afterwards " we were mistaken; for, about two months after he was couched, he dis- " covered at once, they represented solid bodies; when to that time he con- " sidered them only as party-coloured planes, or surfaces diversified with " variety of paint; but even then he was no less surprized, expecting the " pictures would feel like the things they represented, and was amazed when

* Philosophical Transactions abridged by Reid and Gray; vol. 6th. part 4th. chap. 2nd. (and 7th.) page 42.

he

" he found those parts, which by their light and shadow appeared now round
" and uneven, felt only flat like the rest; and asked which was the lying
" sense, feeling, or seeing? Being shown his father's picture in a locket,
" at his mother's watch, and told what it was, he acknowledged a like-
" ness, but was vastly surprized; asking, how it could be, that a large face
" could be expressed in so little room, saying, it should have seemed
" as impossible to him, as to put a bushel of any thing into a pint."

15. Sensations are merely the means or mediums by which the mind is
enabled to discover their respective causes, that is external things*, with their
several qualities, and their relations to us and among themselves; and in
this alone, or in the discovery of these, does perception consist; the
cause of the sensation being the *object* of perception, and the sensation
itself neither the cause, object, nor perception. Hence a visual perception, or a perception by means of a visual sensation, and a vision, signify
the same thing, but not the same thing with a visual sensation; as there
may be a visual sensation, without a vision or visual perception; though
there cannot be a visual perception without a visual sensation. Or, there
may be mental sensation and mental representation without mental perception; that is, without the mind's being conscious of that sensation
being a representation, or of its having any necessary connection, resemblance, or other relation, to *anything else;* but mental perception, and
mental sensation attended with a consciousness of this relation, signify,
and are in effect, the same thing: in this case, the sensation and representation are the same, and the perception and consciousness of the representation, are the same; and it this *something else* which is represented
that is the *only object* of the mind in perception, or that the mind perceives.
Sensation, unattended with such consciousness, may be, and often is, an
object of thought; but it is not, and cannot be, perception, or an object
of perception. It is *things* external to the mind that, by being *causes* of
mental *sensation*, become *objects* of mental *perception*. There may be, and often
is, sensation without perception, as in the case of infants, idiots, &c., but
there cannot be, and never is, perception without sensation: and, in every
case, on the distinctness of the sensations must the distinctness and accu-

* Art. 11.

racy

racy of the perception very much depend. Sensations have, and can have no meaning, but as signs, symbols, or indications, of those things by which they are respectively caused ; those of pleasure and pain excepted, which have a meaning independant of that relation, as incentives to animal action.

16. As consciousness refers only to what passes within the mind itself, so perception refers only to things external to the mind. And it is from being conscious of a difference between two sensations, that we infer or perceive a corresponding difference in the external objects by which they are caused. All those sensations which have no reference to things external, and which are always attended with a consciousness of their being in the mind itself, as those of pleasure and pain ; and, indeed, many of the compound ones in which these predominate or prevail in an eminent degree may with much propriety be denominated feelings ; not only to distinguish them from the others, but also as being the causes of all the passions and affections of the mind, and thereby of all its voluntary actions ; these are the sensations alluded to in Art. 8, in which a kind of knowledge of the utmost importance, the knowledge of good and evil with respect to the mind itself consists ; and, by analogy and induction, the knowledge of good and evil with respect to other minds so constituted.

17. Though it is by means of our sensations that we are enabled to perceive external things, yet we could never perceive them by sensation alone without the assistance of thought aided by repeated and varied experience. By the joint operation of the different senses, experience, memory, observation, reason, and judgment, we are enabled not only to discover and perceive them, but also many of their relations with regard to us, and with regard to each other, and thereby many of the powers and properties by which each is particularly characterised, as well as many of those which are common to several individuals of them, whereby we are enabled not only to distinguish them from each other, but also to arrange them into genera and species. To obtain a complete perception of particular bodies, or of all the sensible relations or powers and properties of any one body, it is frequently necessary to employ not one sense only, but two or more or all the senses for that purpose ; and that not after one manner only, but in various manners : thus, if a pin pricks me, I may feel pain only ; to perceive, by

means

means of touch, the figure &c., of the instrument by which it is produced, I must handle it in various ways; and to perceive its colour, local situation, &c. I must see it and the things contiguous to it: by the means of the sensations furnished by the sense of touch we are enabled to perceive extension, figure, magnitude, solidity, motion or rest, divisibility, hardness or softness, roughness or smoothness, fluidity, gravity, &c.; also the supposed properties of heat and cold, in things external to us. By means of those furnished by the sense of sight, we perceive the supposed properties of colours in external things; and by their means, aided by touch, experience, and observation, we learn in time, through the sensations furnished by sight only, to perceive also, the extensions, figures, motion or rest, relative local situations, &c. of external things. By means of the sensations furnished by the senses of smell, taste, and hearing, we are enabled to perceive these supposed properties in external things, we call them odours, tastes, and sounds, with many of their necessary relations.

18. Our senses of touch and taste give us information of external bodies only when they are in contact with the particular organs of these senses; of bodies at a distance they afford none. Yet by means of the sense of touch alone, aided by experience, reason, and instruction, a person may discover and perceive a very great variety of bodies external to him, and also many of their respective relations, or powers and properties. This is sufficiently evident from the acquirements, in these respects, of many persons who have been born and continued blind; as those of Professor Sanderson of Cambridge, &c. By means of the sense of taste, independent of that of touch, it is impossible for us to perceive the size, figure, hardness, softness, &c., of the sapid substance: and, indeed, these qualities in any substance external to the mind cannot be discovered or perceived by means of the senses of taste, smell, hearing, and sight, either separately or jointly, without the co-operation and assistance of that of touch aided by experience and observation, &c. Of any bodies but such as are sapid the sense of taste can give us no information at all. The sense of smell, of such only as are odoriferous; of hearing, of such only as are sonorous; and of sight, of such as are coloured only; or at least of those bodies only to which we attribute these properties of possessing colour, smell, &c. By means however of experience, founded upon these senses,

in

in conjunction with that of touch, &c. we are soon enabled to acquire in many cases a tolerably distinct perception of the nature of the bodies from which the sapor, the odour, the sound, or the vision, proceeds; and even in some cases to judge in some degree of their relative local situations and distances: thûs, we are soon enabled to perceive, that these particular tastes with which we are affected are those of an orange or an apple, &c. those particular odours, are those of a rose or a violet, &c., those particular sounds, are those of a flute or a violin, &c., and those particular visions, are those of a house or a mountain, &c. Of the distance and relative situation of these objects, or of certain of the causes of these sensations in us, our senses of smell and hearing, even after much experience, afford us in many cases but very indistinct information, and that information often very limited as to distance.

19. By means of the sense of sight alone, we are enabled, after we have learned, by means of our other senses, experience, &c., the things our visual sensations severally signify and represent, to perceive bodies even at a considerable distance from us, and these not of one particular kind only, as odorous, sonorous, or sapid, but almost of every kind. It at once in a manner introduces the whole material world to our acquaintance. Every thing in nature that is possessed of taste, smell, or sound, that is palpable to us by means of contact, bodies perfectly diaphanous, perfectly black, and that are perfect reflectors, excepted, are spread out before us, and are rendered sensible to us by means of sight, though at a distance: and though this sense furnishes no sensations but those of colour, yet by means of it we are enabled to put visible marks on such bodies as we discover by means of our other senses to possess the qualities of hardness, softness, smell, taste, &c., so as these bodies may be known afterwards, by sight only, to be possessed of these qualities. The knowledge we acquire by means of this sense is not confined to one or a few objects in contact with us or near us, but includes all objects, if there are no intervening obstacles, within our visible horizon; even the sun, planets, and fixed stars. It is by means of this sense, that we direct our course in walking, riding, &c., as it is by means of it that we perceive the colours, and thereby the form, size, number, motion or rest, relative distance or local situation, &c. of all the bodies surrounding us, within the full range of our vision, and that in a

manner

manner all at once, whereby we are enabled to direct ourselves properly to the place to which we wish to go, and to avoid in our way such bodies as might obstruct our progress or prove injurious to us. This acquired talent we possess of distinguishing the relative situations, &c. of things by means of sight, may, in some degree, be regarded as a kind of practical Geometry.

20. When any particular thing, as that which we denominate a house, or a mountain, acts on the mind through the organs of sight, the mind is particularly affected by that action, which affection we call sensation; and when, from the experience of this sensation frequently repeated by means of the same cause under various circumstances, the mind, by a process of reasoning, is enabled to discover that thing by means of which it is produced, that thing so discovered by the mind is said to be perceived by it, or to be an object of its perception: and that particular sensation by means of which it was discovered is then particularly marked and distinguished by the mind, as that particular sensation whereby that particular thing has been, and now at any time may be discovered, perceived, and known, when it may again excite and produce that sensation in the mind; since that sensation, in as far as it can be produced directly or indirectly by means of that particular thing only, and, therefore, can indicate it and nothing else, must be a just and perfect representation of that particular thing with respect to the human mind; and thus it is, that we perceive and become acquainted with the various things our several sensations respectively signify and represent. Whenever we have discovered the object we give it a name, which name, in many cases we apply to the sensation also, especially the visual one, by means of which it was perceived, and which we have now adopted as a true and just representation of it; a practice which, along with that of applying the names of sensations to the external things or objects by which they are respectively produced, as when we speak of heat in an ignited body, and thus give the same name to both cause and effect, has contributed in conjunction with the ideal system of philosophy (the fundamental principle of which is, that the mind perceives nothing but what is within itself), to throw a mysterious veil of obscurity over metaphysical investigations, as tending to confound sensation with perception, and sensations with the objects of perception, and thereby to
support

support and corroborate the principles on which that system is founded, as well as the doctrines deduced from them.

The ideal philosophy, or that system of metaphysics which makes all the objects of perception and of real knowledge to consist in forms or images to which the names either of ideas, or of species, or phantoms, have been appropriated, and which inculcates that nothing is perceived by the mind but what is in the mind that perceives it, seems to have derived its origin from Plato; at least he appears to have been the first who made use of the term idea, and though he admits that all things consist of matter and form, and that the matter of which all things were made existed from eternity without form, yet he represents *ideas* as the only *objects of perception* and of *true knowledge,* and as those things concerning which all science is employed. Ideas, according to his doctrines, are self-existent, eternal, immutable, immaterial, and independent beings, which existed before things, and which are the patterns of things. The latter Platonists, however, who differed in opinion in this respect from their master, represent them as not existing of themselves but in the Divine Mind. The doctrine of Aristotle and the Peripatetics was, that the mind has no perception of things themselves, but only of certain images, forms, or what he calls species of things, which emanate and fly in all directions from material bodies, and entering the mind by means of the organs of sense, produce in it perceptions of which these images or species are themselves the only objects. These he distinguishes and distributes into three kinds or classes: the first of these he denominates sensible species; these according to modern phraseology are ideas of individuals or particulars. The second kind he calls intelligible species, being the same with what are now denominated abstract general ideas. And the third kind phantoms; that is, ideas of beings formed by the imagination out of the other kinds. It would appear from what Plato says on the subject of perception, in the seventh book of his Republic, that in perception his ideas also proceeded from material bodies, and by the same process as that supposed by Aristotle produced it in the human mind, they being the only objects of it. The doctrines of Democritus and Epicurus with regard to perception were nearly the same with those of the Stagirite; and all of those differed in little from that of Plato, except in the names and in the origins of the ideas or species.

There

There were no other theories or doctrines with which we are acquainted with respect to perception and the objects of human knowledge till Des Cartes published his system; according to which all perception and knowledge is purely intellectual, even in its origin, all being the result either of mental consciousness or of innate ideas coeval with the mind; the existence of ideas proceeding from material bodies or external existences being expressly denied. The next theory was that of Malebranche, which represents the objects of human thought and perception as the ideas of things in the Divine Mind, which ideas the Deity, from pervading all space and being intimately present to every human mind, can and does impress on and make known to every human mind in as far as is proper for answering the end and intention of their creation. Mr. Locke, in his justly celebrated Essay concerning the Human Understanding, published in 1689, after having with complete success and effect refuted the Cartesian doctrine of innate ideas, lays down the following fundamental principles, viz. First, That there are no objects of mental perception but ideas. Secondly, That all ideas originate in mental sensation and mental reflection. And, thirdly, That knowledge consists in nothing but *the perception of the connection and agreement, or disagreement and repugnancy of any of our ideas.* And these he regards as truths that admit not of doubt or dispute, and which every one will grant on reflecting on what he experiences in his own mind; and on this basis he erected a system of metaphysics, supported by so many interesting and valuable facts, and by such profound, just, and conclusive reasoning, that it soon attained such an ascendancy over all other systems as to be generally adopted; and no suspicions were entertained with respect to the validity of its fundamental principles till such time as the doctrines it inculcates had been carried by Bishop Berkeley and Mr. Hume to conclusions repugnant to common opinion, and leading to scepticism: the first of those writers regarding and representing *perception* as the effect of *ideas* projected into the mind by spirits; and the other as the effect merely of a natural instinct, whereby the mind is deceived into a belief that its own *sensations, or impressions and ideas,* are *things* external to it, and that when it is *conscious* of the former it *perceives* the latter. When, for the first time, a refutation of the ideal system, which under different modifications had reigned from the time of Plato without a rival, and with an indisputed title

* See vol. 3 of Hume's Essays, pp. 230, 231.

in all the schools and among the learned, was attempted, and a system of metaphysics unfolded which regards perception as a particular faculty, or rather instinct, of the human mind; which represents the material world, or external things, as the immediate objects of this faculty; and which maintains that we are, *independent of all reasoning*, necessitated by the constitution of our nature, or by a law of thought or of the human mind, to believe in and take for granted the existence and qualities of external things, as manifested to us by this faculty, or constitutional instinctive power of the mind.

This system was made public in the year 1764, in a work intitled " An " Enquiry into the Human Mind on the Principles of Common Sense, by " Thomas Reid, D. D. Professor of Philosophy in the King's College, Aber- " deen." This work has been succeeded and supported by several others on the same subject, and on the same principles, by Dr. Reid himself, and by other authors of great respectability, in which this system is maintained with much zeal and ability, at the same time that it has attracted very general attention, and on the whole been well received and approved of by the public. But though this is the case, and though the conclusions in which the ideal system terminate, as deduced by the ingenious and acute Bishop Berkeley, and the no less ingenious and acute Mr. Hume, seem to confute themselves and the system from which they result by their seeming incongruity and absurdity, as in the case of that inference deduced from it by Bishop Berkeley of all material things; even our own bodies, the houses in which we dwell, the earth we inhabit with all its furniture, the sun, planets, and fixed stars, and, indeed, the whole choir of heaven, being nothing but the baseless fabric of a vision, having no existence but in the ideas, or what are called the perceptions of the mind; and that by Mr. Hume of there being nothing in nature besides ideas or perceptions, not even spirits or a mind to perceive them; yet so great is the predilection for the ideal system, especially for the doctrines of Mr. Locke, and with so much ability, so much eloquence, and such ingenuity and subtility of argument have Berkeley and Hume supported their respective doctrines, that that system and those opinions have not yet been abandoned, even by many of those who have adopted many of Dr. Reid's doctrines, as the late ingenious Professor Robison of Edinburgh, who in his Elements of Mechanical Philosophy,

published

published only a few years ago, regards external things as mere phenomena, or appearances or affections of the mind only, and which have no existence but in the mind.   With respect to such of the learned as could never reconcile themselves to the substitution of assumed instinctive principles for reasoning, and the concise and commodious method of resolving every difficulty, and accounting for all phænomena and facts, the reasons of which are not understood, by means of opinions or judgments deemed, without proof, to be instinctive and denominated principles of common sense, or to a system erected on such a basis, the doctrines of Dr. Reid could have little or no influence ; and the attempted refutation thus failing of the effect intended with respect to them, they could have no reason or inducement, on account of that attempt, to abandon the ideal system, or relinquish the metaphysical opinions they had adopted in consequence of it.

These facts and considerations have induced the author of these essays to attempt a refutation of these doctrines of Bishop Berkeley and Mr. Hume, or to prove—that which the unlearned have ever taken for granted, and have always regarded as neither admitting of doubt nor of proof, as being so evident of itself that nothing more evident can be conceived to prove it by— the reality of nature or created things, or of existences, or substances and attributes, external to and independent of the human mind, whether perceived by it or not, in a manner more in detail than has hitherto been done, though he is of opinion that he has already refuted these doctrines, and the principle on which they are founded, of the sensation, the perception, the idea, and the object of perception being the same ; and therefore, of all objects of perception having no existence but in the mind itself that perceives them, and none even there, when not perceived by it, in a manner which may perhaps appear to some sufficiently satisfactory, in having pointed out the distinction between a sensation and a perception, and between either of these and an object of perception ; and in having also pointed out the real manner and cause of mental perception, and that neither by representing it as the effect of an instinctive faculty, operating by a blind fatality, and yet in all cases unerringly ; nor as the effect either of mere consciousness and pure intellection, or of innate ideas ; nor as the effect of ideas, species, or flims, which either emanate from external bodies, and so enter the mind ; or which, being independent of bodies, are either projected into the

mind

mind by spirits, or impressed on it by the immediate agency of the Deity; but, by representing it as a *necessary* consequence of the agency and operation of the natures or qualities of the external things perceived on the senses and understanding, especially the reasoning faculty of the mind, and of the mental inferences and conclusions thence necessarily resulting; and by giving, in a rational deduction of effects or necessary consequences from their adequate causes, the mental process by which this fact is established, and thereby clearly and conclusively proving that mental perception is a deduction by just reasoning from facts and phenomena, or is a necessary consequence of such a process. With the above mentioned intention, the following observations and reasonings are submitted to the consideration of the Reader.

21. The proof of the existence of mind, and of our own existence, rests in the first place on our consciousness of it, and it surely could not possibly rest upon a more solid foundation, or on more satisfactory evidence, since it seems scarcely possible for any one seriously to doubt it, and since no evidence more satisfactory can possibly be conceived. We are conscious not only of existence, but also of self-existence, or of existing as individuals, each possessing many powers, &c. forming one whole or self, as having a unity of feeling, of action, &c. and we are conscious not only of present, but also, by means of remembrance, of past existence, and thereby of identity.

Convincing as this evidence is, it does not stand unsupported, but is corroborated and confirmed in many cases by other proofs as valid as mathematical demonstrations, as resting on the same basis—the testimony of sense, experience, and observation. Thus each person, besides his own consciousness, has also the evidence of the senses, &c. of others for his present existence; and for his past existence and identity, he has not only that evidence, but also that of certain artificial remembrancers as pictures, written testimony, &c. or of two or more of these; and indeed, in certain cases, these may be justly inferred from reason and circumstances; thus, if a person goes to bed in the evening, sleeps through the night, and waking finds himself in the same chamber, &c. in which he lay down, and that it now is morning, he may reasonably conclude that he existed while asleep, though unconscious of it, and in that place, and that he is the identical person who lay down there to sleep; and hence, forgetfulness, and even unconscious-

D

ness,

ness, does not *necessarily* imply either want of identity, or of prior existence.

22. As the proof of the existence of mind rests upon consciousness, so that of the existence of external things, and of their various powers and properties, or their relations with regard to us, and with regard to each other, is founded upon perception and inferences thence rationally deduced. It has already been observed*, that the changes of state impressed upon the bodily organs of sense, and through them on the mind, must necessarily be the effects of some causes, beings or existences, different and distinct from, and external to both body and mind, since the mind is entirely passive in the case, and the body acts only in consequence of being impressed or acted upon; and since changes of state in the bodily organs and in the mind, which do not originate in themselves, could not possibly take place, and are inconceivable, without the agency of external things, as they would otherwise be effects without causes. Bishop Berkeley having, as he supposed, expunged from nature the universe and all created things, but ideas and spiritual beings—by means of rational deductions from the assumed but unfounded premises, that nothing can be perceived by, or known to the mind, but what is within the mind that perceives or knows it—was thereby necessitated to contrive some theory, suited to the then circumstances, whereby he might account for mental perception, and having now but two species of objects or agents remaining in nature to have recourse to for that purpose, there was no alternative but to employ either the one or the other; and, of consequence, either to personify ideas, or to endow them, like the monades of Leibnitz, with activity and intelligence fitted to produce the end intended; or, in imitation of poetical fiction and machinery, to employ spirits to propel ideas as required, and of the kinds required for answering the intended purposes of perception into the human mind. It was to the last of these expedients that he gave the preference. He has, however, clogged his theory with an acknowledgment which appears to me sufficient of itself to confute and invalidate it entirely, viz. that ideas thus projected cannot enter human eyes, and through that organ the human mind, but when the eyes are open; so that, like rays of light, they cannot penetrate through

* Art. 11.

the

the eyelids; and from this it is presumable they could not enter the eyes though open in the dark, or even in day light in any other form than that of uncoloured light, without first having been projected on something external, and being by it refracted before entering the eyes.

For the existence of external things, we have not the evidence of one of our senses only, but of all of them, and often of two or more of them in conjunction and at the same time; and not of the senses of one person only, but of those of all whose minds and bodily organs are in a sound and healthy state; and this evidence corroborated by that of reason, or by those rational deductions from the various phenomena of sensation in which perception consists, perception of the things themselves, whereby the fact is established with all the certainty that our nature and the nature of things admits of. That all our knowledge, that resulting from consciousness in the mind of its own operations, alterations, and existence excepted, is ultimately derived either directly or indirectly from sense, and that sense in most cases affords that evidence which is most to be relied on, and which admits of no appeal, will afterwards be attempted to be proved. But it is not from sense alone that we in every case infer, perceive, and prove the existence, the powers, and the properties of external things. It is not immediately from our sensations we infer the solidity and extension of material bodies, though it is by means of these we discover or perceive them; thus it is from that effect which the ivory ball I hold between my finger and my thumb produces in preventing them from coming into contact, however much I may incline it, and from the distance between my finger and thumb, that I rationally infer the solidity and extension of the ball, and not from any sensations the touch of it then excites in me. And, if I place the ball between other two material bodies, or such as produce in me the sensation of solidity, one in each hand, and if I cannot in the dark, or with my eyes shut, bring these bodies close together by all the force that I can apply, so long as the ball or body is between them, I rationally and necessarily conclude that it is the ball or intermediate body that prevents their coming into contact, and not any sensation, or what they call perception in my mind, since in this case I can have no *immediate* sensation of any kind from that intermediate body, as neither touching it, seeing it, smelling, tasting, nor hearing it; and hence infer, that that body not only has an existence independent and out of my

mind,

mind, and of every other mind, or that it exists otherwise than in sensation or perception, but also that it possesses those qualities we call solidity, hardness, limited extension, and therefore figure, and that these qualities actually exist in the body itself perfectly detached from, and independent of every mind, and every mental sensation and perception whatever. In like manner, it is not immediately from our sensations, but either from casual experience or from experiments made for the express purpose of ascertaining the fact, that we infer and perceive that those bodies we denominate luminous, sonorous, and odoriferous, do not act upon our organs of sense immediately, and thereby produce the sensations in our minds we call colours, sounds, and smells, but by means of a medium; as, from placing some opaque substance between the luminous body and our eyes, and from our being thereby deprived of the visual sensation it produced in our minds, as well as from the distance of the luminous body from the eye, we infer, that in producing the sensation, it must act on the organ of sight by means of a medium proceeding from it; which medium we call light or rays of light. Also from placing a bell within the exhausted receiver of an air-pump, and a rose within a glass phial closely shut, and thereby depriving ourselves of those sensations of sound and of smell, which these produced in our minds, we infer that the bell, or any other sonorous body, cannot produce the sensation of sound but through the medium of the air; and that the rose, or any other odoriferous substance, cannot produce in our minds the sensation of smell but through the medium of an effluvia proceeding from it to the organ of smell. Also from these and other experiments, as by viewing objects by means of a mirror, or of a Gregorian telescope, &c. we infer that visual appearances, sounds and smells, exist neither in the bodies producing them, nor in the mediums by means of which they are produced, but in the mind.

23. These attributes or qualities, modes or manners of being, relations, &c. we call powers or properties of bodies, as solidity, extension, magnitude, figure or form, number, proportion, place or relative situation, motion, rest, attraction, repulsion, &c. exist not in the mind by which they are perceived, and only while they are perceived; for then the mind would perceive them of itself, and by themselves as independent existences subsisting of themselves, and might not only conceive them, but actually perceive them without

out the aid of external objects, or of external senses, or though it had never been furnished with these; but on the contrary, they either subsist in, or constitute subjects or substances external to the mind; which subjects or substances cannot possibly subsist, or exist independent of them; for, take away these qualities, and with them they also vanish. If external things did not possess those powers and properties which, from their effects, &c. we know they actually do possess, we could not possibly realize our conceptions with regard to them: thus, if they possessed not in reality solidity, extension, mechanic power, gravity, elasticity, divisibility, figurability, mobility, &c. it would be impossible for us ever to form a house, a ship, an organ, a mill, or a chronometer, &c. of them, though we could imagine, and indeed were possessed of a perfect conception of the manner in which it might be accomplished, were we possessed of external things having these powers and properties to operate with. But, that they do actually possess them, is a fact which cannot admit of doubt or dispute, since daily experience proves that we can by their means, and a knowledge of the qualities they possess, realize our conceptions, and with entire certainty and success employ them for the accomplishment of ends proposed, or the attainment of particular purposes, as the grinding of grain, the spinning of yarn, the measuring of time, &c. by forming them into machines suited to these intentions; and, hence it is manifest, that external things are, not only with respect to us, but also with respect to one another, what they appear to us to be. Modifications, modes or accidents, relations, &c. though they cannot exist of themselves, are entities since they actually do exist, and since, if they did not exist, they could neither be perceived or conceived by the human mind. Under the terms qualities or attributes of things, I include both the powers and properties of things. Powers of themselves have properties, but properties of themselves have not powers. Accidents, modes or manners of being, as figure, motion, &c. have properties, but not of themselves powers. Relations may be powers, or properties, or both; as things may be related by powers or by properties, or by both. Relation must be between two or more things, and is often determined by means of another thing adopted as a standard. Relations, modes, &c. exist in the nature of things, perfectly independent of our comparisons and perceptions of them, since our perception and knowledge of them is merely the result of experience

and

and reasonings founded on those sensations produced in our mind by the action of the external things themselves in which they subsist, and of which they are the relations, modes, &c., on it. Things which of themselves may have an absolute existence, have as to other things a relative existence only. We, or sentient beings, have only a relative knowledge of the existence, &c. of things, as we know them only from the sensations they excite and produce in us; but though they have only a relative existence with respect to us, yet they have an absolute existence independent of that relation, or at least in as far absolute as having no dependence on that relation; for though that relation, or those sensations which they excite and produce in us, and whereby they are made known to us, had never taken place, yet the things themselves or those powers, &c., whereby these sensations might be excited, if there had existed sentient beings proper for exciting them in, might notwithstanding exist: the existence of external things does not depend on our perceptions of them; but *our perceptions* on the *existence of external things.*

Plato is of opinion that there is reason to suspect the existence of matter from the appearance of our dreams: and the modern idealists represent those things that are generally regarded as material external existences as mere ideas of the mind formed of the same stuff that dreams are made of: but if matter exists not, or if there are no material external existencies, and we have notwithstanding sensations, ideas, thoughts, &c., all must be a dream. The fact however is, that, if there were no external existences, we could have no dreams. For, that those sensations or appearances which the mind is conscious of in waking reveries, deliriums and dreams, as well as in memory or remembrance, are only the effects of trains of sensations and thoughts, which owe their origin to things external to the mind, must be sufficiently evident, when it is considered that it is of things of which we have previous knowledge only that the mind is conscious of in these cases, either in the state in which the mind first felt or perceived them, or as variously modified and combined by the imagination. No person who never saw nor heard of a diamond or a pine apple ever dreamed of these things; the polarity and attractive and repulsive powers of the magnet; electrical phenomena, and gunpowder with its surprising effects, &c. were never dreamed of till their actual existence in nature was accidentally discovered.

24. The

24. The attributes of bodies are either real or apparent. Those of solidity, extension, magnitude, figure, divisibility, numerability, motion, rest, relation, proportion, the powers of attraction and repulsion, and the various powers whereby bodies excite the many different sensations of pleasure and pain, heat and cold, of colours, sounds, sense, and tastes, &c., in animated beings are real, or they actually exist in the bodies themselves, independent of any mind or mental sensations whatever; as must be sufficiently evident from what has been already advanced, as well as from the relations and actions of external things with respect to each other, and from the manner in which we are sensibly affected by them. But those properties of bodies we denominate their colours, sounds, scents, tastes, hotness and coldness, are not real but apparent only, as having actually no existence in the bodies themselves; and they are also merely relative, as these powers in the bodies which produce them can produce them only in such beings as have such organs of sense as the generality of mankind have. Bodies are of themselves colourless; and owe the appearance of being coloured, merely to the sensations of the being in whom that appearance takes place. In the absence of light they are colourless even to such beings however perfect their senses, to a blind person they are colourless under all circumstances; and to a jaundiced person they all appear yellow; so that colour exists only in sensation and in relation. The same holds with respect to flavours, tastes, sounds, and heat and cold. A body from possessing the power of producing in our minds the sensation of colour, or of sound, &c., or of any particular colour or sound, &c., thereby acquires the property of appearing to us of that particular colour, &c., or of yielding that particular sound, &c., the mind in these cases transferring its own sensations to those bodies from which the causes producing them respectively proceed; whereby these sensations, by being thus in a manner rendered external to it, seem to the mind itself actually to exist in these bodies, and hence these bodies become coloured, sonorous, &c., with respect to it, and by that means objects of its perception by means of the senses of sight, hearing, &c. This process, whereby the mind transfers the sensation to its cause and thereby renders the cause an object of thought and perception, is acquired mechanically in early childhood; and we very soon become so insensible of it from habit, &c. as in many cases not to be easily convinced

that

that it actually takes place, or that the apparent colours, sounds, tastes, and smells, of bodies, have in fact no real existence in the bodies themselves. Sensations in the mind, whatever they may indicate or represent, must at first appear to the mind as possessing no meaning, and as existing in the mind only, as in the case of the adult who was couched, mentioned Art. 14; and it must require time, experience, the employment of the other senses, instruction from the nurse, &c., and much practice, before the habit can be acquired of readily and insensibly transferring the sensations to their respective causes, so that these causes, or the bodies from which they proceed, may be perceived and known by their means; and thereby the meaning and intent of these sensations understood. This habit, however, from constant practice soon acquires such strength as to induce many to think that the sensations or phantasms of their own minds are actually external existences possessing all those attributes these sensations are known to indicate: and from hence arises the belief in spectres.

25. The mind cannot possibly voluntarily transfer its sensations to things external, or have any conception of their being so transferred, till such time as it has acquired some perception and knowledge from its own experience and instruction from the nurse, &c. of the existence of such things; nor can it till then possibly conceive its sensations as existing in any other way than within itself; but after it has learned and acquired the habit of perceiving and knowing external things by means of its sensations, it must necessarily, if it transfers those sensations whereby it perceives and knows them at all, transfer them to the things themselves whereby they are respectively excited and produced in it, since this is not with regard to it a matter of choice, but a necessary result of those laws whereby perception by means of sensations takes place; thus when any particular object, as the candles which burn before me, or the painting which is above the chimney-piece of the room in which I sit, excite and produce a visual sensation in my mind, they cannot do it but when the rays of light proceeding directly from them enter the pupils of my eyes either directly or obliquely; or, in other words, can do it only when the pupils of my eyes are directed towards them, and then it is impossible for me not to experience those sensations, or not to have a visual perception or vision of these objects; but it is also equally impossible for me, without either reflecting or refracting the rays of
light

light by means of which they are immediately produced in their passage from the objects to the eye, to transfer, even mentally, the visual sensations or visions they respectively excite and produce in my mind to any other place or parts of the room than those they severally occupy; so that if it is not the objects themselves that we perceive or see, in cases where the rays of light pass directly from the objects to the eye, we at least in these cases perceive the direction in which they lie, or their respective bearings, and in so far their local relative situations; and, if we transfer these sensations at all, we must necessarily transfer them in those directions, or to the sites of the objects themselves, whereby they are respectively produced, that is to the objects themselves, since it is altogether impossible for us, under these circumstances, to transfer them to other places, or even to transfer the sensation produced by any particular part or portion of any object from that particular part of the object in which the power producing it resides to any other part even of the same object; or, other circumstances being the same, to alter the dimensions, &c., of any part relative to those of the other parts of the object. Thus it is only the petals of the rose which lie on the table before me, that are, by means of the visual sensations or appearances the rose produces in my mind, tinged red, or appear red to me, the leaves and stalk of it being by that means tinged green, and the colours of the surrounding objects being no way affected by those of the rose; so that the visual sensations or colours it produces have no tendency to tinge any thing but the rose itself, and the different parts of the rose are by this means differently coloured according to the different sensations or colours these parts respectively excite and produce, the parts differing in powers and thereby in colours being thus accurately defined and distinguished. This transference of the sensations, after the external objects respectively producing them are known, seems, in a certain degree, to be a natural consequence of the manner we employ for discovering the site of any object by means of vision, by directing the pupils of our eyes from different places and under different circumstances towards that which in all these cases produces the same visual sensation in us; that is toward the same object, till we discover that point in which all the rays of light proceeding from it to our eyes from all these different places centre, and thereby the site of the object, or object itself; and, from the same sensa-

E   tion

tion being always produced under all the variety of different circumstances and in so many different places by means of something always centering in that point in which the object is situated, from the sensation taking place only while the pupils of the eyes are directed towards that point or object, and from its being produced as often as we please to look at or direct the pupils of our eyes to that point, and never can be produced by directing them to any other point, the mind is induced to suppose that the sensation itself is actually situated in that point, or in the object; and the mind becomes further confirmed in this opinion when it discovers by means of its sense of touch, that the external thing or object situated in that particular place is actually possessed of the form or figure, the state of rest, or of motion, &c. indicated by the visual sensation of it. And this effect, in a certain degree, seems to be the necessary result of that reaction or resistance to change of state which always take place upon impulse, wherebythe organ, and perhaps even the mind itself, must in this case react with equal force on the particles or rays of light which impress it, and in a direction contrary to that in which it is impressed, so that the sensation must by this means seem to the mind to proceed from the organ to the object. It is on this principle of reaction alone, that the upright appearance of the external visible object to the mind when the picture of it on the retina of the eye is reversed can be rationally accounted for. The reaction in this case, or what is the same thing, the vision operating in the same right lines, or precisely in the same directions, but inversely, as the action, the directions or lines of vision must necessarily recross each other at the same place or point, and at the very same angles the rays of light crossed each other at entering the eye, and thereby each particular line must necessarily fall again on the very same particular points of the object from which the rays proceeded producing the visual sensation; so that the picture on the retina inverted from the rays crossing in the eye must on this account necessarily give an upright vision.

26. In vision we often, indeed, transfer the sensation or visual appearance of the cause or object to places where it really is not from this reaction, or from our always transferring it in the same right line but contrary direction to that in which the rays producing it enter the eye; thus, when the rays of light are inflected or reflected on their passage from the object

to

to the eye, so that they do not proceed from the object to the eye in one right line, but by means of two or more making angles with each other, from our transferring the sensation according to the last of these lines only, or in the contrary direction to that in which the rays act upon and impress the eye, the object must necessarily by that means appear to us to be situated in that direction, though that direction may be different, perhaps even contrary to that in which it is really situated ; as in the case when we view any thing in a mirror, &c. We soon learn, however, by means of our other senses, experience, and reason, to correct the visual deception thus occasioned.

27. This reaction which either occasions or is the effect of sensation, has not hitherto been taken notice of. Vision, or visible perception, cannot take place in any other manner or in any other meaning or sense than that described above in human beings, or in beings whose sensations and perceptions depend on and are the result of being acted upon. With respect to a being possessing spontaneous perception the case would be perfectly different. And hence it is that when we look *directly* at a visible external object we may in some measure be said actually to see it, or to have a visible perception of the thing itself, as by this means we in a manner throw the mental vision it occasions on itself. And on the same principle we may on touch, or sensible contact, from the reaction, be said in some measure actually to feel, or to have a sensible and tangible perception of the object itself : in either case there is not a mental deception. Whether this reaction is the cause or the effect of sensation, or if the cause, how or by what means it should produce it, it is perhaps impossible for human beings ever to discover ; but however this may be, it is certain that on the suspension of this reaction from the organ of sensation, and thereby the mind being restored by that means to the same state it was in before being acted upon or impressed by external agency, the sensation instantly vanishes or ceases at the same time, (though the reaction is in some cases long of restoring the mind to its former state after the external agency has forbore to act upon it), and that the attention of the mind is always exerted in a direction precisely opposite to that of the action by which the impression is made on it : a manifest indication of reaction in the mind. From the

continuation of the sensation, however, for some time after the forbearance of the external action on the mind, it is obvious that the continuance of the sensation does not depend on the continuance of the external action but on the continuance of the reaction it occasions, and that it is no way conducive to the sensation but as occasioning the reaction in which it either consists or by which it is produced.

28. Though the visual sensation may be thrown on the object by this reaction, even before the mind has acquired any knowledge of their being external objects, the mind in that case cannot possibly have any knowledge or conception of that circumstance, as being then conscious of its own sensations only, and having no conception of any thing else; this reaction, as being a necessary effect of the action, is altogether independent of the will: it is action, but it is involuntary action.

29. The sensations of the mind seem to depend on or to be the effect of mechanic impulse in a very great degree, if not entirely. This is sufficiently evident with respect to the sense of hearing, since the pulsations of the air on the organ of hearing, which produce the sensation, can be nothing else but mechanical, and of this the sensation itself in some cases gives us information. That this is also the case with respect to the sense of touch must likewise be sufficiently evident. In certain cases of inflammation, &c. of particular parts of the body, the cause of the inflammation, &c. seems to be chemical, but the pain or the sensation resulting from it seems, nevertheless, from the impetus, pulsation, or repercussion which always accompanies it, and from the mind's not being chemically affected or altered otherwise than in modification by its means, to be the effect in this case as well as in others of mechanic action or impulse merely. The sensations of taste and smell seem to be the same; for though the saliva, &c. may combine chemically with the aliments, and thereby render them more proper for exciting these sensations, yet neither that which produces the sensations of taste, nor that which produces the sensations of smell by acting upon the respective proper organs, can produce these sensations from acting upon them otherwise than mechanically: for if they acted upon them chemically the organs themselves would thereby be altered or destroyed. That the sensation of sight is also effected by the same means must be evident from the

same

same reason of its not being effectable by means of chemical action without destroying the organ, even if chemical action without being accompanied with mechanical could be supposed capable of producing it.

30. The sensations produced in our minds by means of the senses of hearing, smelling, and tasting, indicate their respective external causes, and in most cases with sufficient accuracy for our immediate recognoscence of them on the sensations being excited in us, but they neither resemble them, nor of themselves enable us to form any conception of any of their real qualities of solidity, magnitude, figure, &c. or of any of their apparent properties, except that particular apparent property each respectively denotes; or, indeed, of any thing besides, except perhaps that those of sounds may in some cases resemble and thereby represent motion, or the modes of action by which they may be produced. Those we acquire by means of the sense of touch, though they do not resemble their external causes, enable us to discover or perceive many of their real qualities, as their solidity, hardness or softness, size and extension in various and different directions, &c. whereby the mind is enabled to form mental conceptions, imaginations, or images of their particular figures, &c.; also to perceive their apparent properties of heat or cold, and their modes of motion or rest, &c.; and by these means they not only indicate the respective causes, but also the respective figures, &c. of these causes. Those we acquire by means of the organ of sight not only indicate but also actually resemble their several external causes in many respects, in as far as they truly and accurately represent their respective figures with those of their several parts, and all those parts situated, proportioned, and adapted to each other, as they actually are in the several causes or external objects themselves, with their respective states of motion or rest, &c. whereby the mind is enabled not only to perceive the external objects themselves producing them, but also the several particular parts of which each object is formed, and after it has learned by the aid of the sense of touch, reason, experience, &c. to know the meanings of its visual sensations, these sensations by that means become with respect to the mind visions, visual perceptions, or pictures —of which the mind itself furnishes the colouring—of their respective external objects or causes, as these sensations are faithful representations of these objects, except with respect to the colours with which they tinge them, the

objects

objects themselves possessing none, and that they are in this case, though solid bodies, represented rather by diagrams or pictures than by images of them, though the mind from experience, &c. of the real qualities of external objects is soon enabled to give solidity, &c. in its own imagination to these representations of them, or at least to conceive them as just representations of solid objects with respect to form, proportion, and relative situation among themselves. Thus the visual sensation produced in my mind by means of any particular house resembles that house not only in its figure, but also in having walls, a roof, doors, windows, columns, capitals, cornices, a pediment, dome, &c., and each of these directly of the same figure with its corresponding one in the house itself, and the whole of these parts bearing the same proportions, and having the same relative situations, to each other in it, that they have of the house itself; and if it did not thus resemble that particular house, it could not occasion the perception of that house in my mind, though it might, by exciting a sensation in my mind which resembled it in no respect, indicate its existence, provided it invariably excited the same sensation; and if its qualities could be discovered by other means, it also might be known from experience, &c. to indicate a house possessing these particular qualities. It is not necessary for our having adequate perceptions of external things, that the sensations they produce in our minds should in all cases, or by means of all the senses, be resemblances, pictures, or images, and thereby representations of them; all that is required in most cases for that purpose being only that the same sensation shall always be excited and produced by the same thing, so that it may indicate that thing and nothing else. It by no means follows as a necessary consequence, that, because those sensations of the mind which are commonly regarded as qualities of bodies, and have been called secondary qualities as colour, sounds, &c. are mere phenomena or appearances or affections of the mind only and have no existence but in the mind, external things, or those bodies of which they are the supposed and imputed qualities are also nothing but mere phenomena, and have no existence but in the mind. But on the contrary, from these phenomena the actual independent existence of things external to the mind, though not in every respect as actually perceived by the sentient being as not possessing those *apparent* qualities furnished to them by the mind, follows as a necessary consequence, as has
already

already been proved by rational deduction and inference; and as may at any time be experimentally ascertained, since these phenomena can be excited and produced at pleasure in the mind, by making external things act on it through the medium of the organs of sense, clearly evincing and proving, in a manner the most satisfactory and conclusive, that these phenomena are effects necessarily depending on external existences; and, consequently, that if external things existed not, these phenomena could not possibly exist; and that since these phenomena do actually exist, their causes or external things must necessarily exist also.

31. If by seeing, hearing, touching, smelling, and tasting bodies, perceiving in them, by means of these senses, properties which they do not in reality possess, as colours, sounds, &c. is meant, we can in no case with propriety be said to see, or to hear them, &c. these visual, auditory, &c. appearances and effects we ascribe to them not existing in them, but in our minds. But, if by seeing, hearing, touching, &c. bodies is meant, the perception of the existences of the bodies themselves and of those qualities they respectively in *reality* possess, and their *real relations,* or the effects they produce in us and in each other, with their relative local situations, sizes, modes of motion or rest, &c. then we may with the strictest propriety be said actually to see, hear, taste, smell, and touch them; for, to see any particular thing, and to perceive that thing and its real qualities by means of sight or of a visual sensation—to hear any particular thing, and to perceive that thing and its real qualities by means of hearing or an auditory sensation—to taste, smell, or touch any thing, and to perceive it and its real qualities by means of these senses—must signify and be the same thing. It is not the colours, sounds, sapors, scents, or feelings of the objects we see, hear, &c. or perceive, but it is the objects themselves, with their respective powers and properties, that we perceive by means of these sensations they produce in us of colours, sounds, sapors, scents, and feelings, or by means of the senses of sight, hearing, tasting, smelling, and touching; that is, it is the things themselves that we see, hear, &c. by these means; taking seeing, hearing, &c. in their proper signification as relative to things external to the mind. To throw a visual sensation, of which the meaning is not understood, even on that thing which occasions it, is not to see or perceive that thing. But to have a visual sensation, of which the meaning is understood,

is

is actually to see, or to have a sight or *visual perception* of that thing which
the *visual sensation* is known to indicate and represent, and not to see or have
a sight or visual perception of the visual sensation itself, or of that which is
in the mind;—the mind is conscious of sensation, but perceives it not;—
even when the thing or object appears to the mind to be situated where it
really is not, from its being perceived by means of reflection, as when we
view an object in a mirror, it is not the sensation, but the thing itself that
is the object of its perception.   Though external things do not actually possess colours, sounds, scents, &c. of themselves, yet they possess those powers whereby they produce those sensations to which we give these names in
our minds; and though they are really of themselves colourless, tasteless,
&c. yet they are not so relatively to us and other animated beings; for,
from their possessing those powers which produce them in our minds, and
from that habit of the mind of transferring its sensations to those things
which respectively occasion them, and that in such a manner as even to deceive itself, those things appear to us to be, and with respect to the effects
they produce in our minds, actually are, with respect to us, possessed of
those properties we call their colours, tastes, &c. and hence it is that we value them accordingly, or according to their respective supposed colours,
tastes, &c. though it is more properly, according to their respective powers
of producing those sensations to which we give these names in our minds.
For a thing which appears to us of any particular colour, as red, blue, &c.
though it may be of itself absolutely colourless, is yet relatively to us actually tinged or coloured with that particular tint it appears to us to possess
by or through the sensation or colour it has produced in our minds:—the
same reasoning is applicable to our other sensations of sounds, tastes, &c.
and hence we may with some degree of propriety be said actually to see,
hear, taste, &c. properties in bodies which, of themselves or independent of
the sensations and operations of our minds, they really possess not. Things,
whatever their real natures may be, are, with respect to us, what they appear to us to be;—the sensations they produce in us, and the appearances
they exhibit to us, being the same. Objects are known to us by means of
our sensations only; and what they, and the states of our minds and mental
faculties make them, such must we receive and regard them; and the
knowledge thus acquired, or by means of sense, is real relative to us, whether
                                                                        our

our senses represent things to us as they really are, or as they exist absolutely and independent of that relation or not.

32. Our senses are sometimes, however, apt to deceive us, especially when we employ but one of them at a time, and particularly that of sight, from the rays of light being often inflected, refracted, or reflected, without our knowledge, in passing from the object to the eye; from the differences of the angles which the rays of light proceeding from the same object make on entering the eye according to the distance of the object from it, and from various other circumstances. That of hearing also in cases of reflected sounds, as in those of echoes and of ventriloquism. And indeed, those of touch, smell, and taste, also in certain cases. And in many cases our senses deceive us from the mind, body, or bodily organs of sense, being in an imperfect or diseased state: thus a person in the jaundice sees every thing yellow; and in many cases of extreme weakness from want of nourishment, &c. in cases of fevers, and of madness, all the senses bring us wrong information. In these last cases, the deceptions cannot be corrected or removed without curing the diseases, or remedying the imperfections by which they are produced; but in the former, the errors or deceptions by means of one sense may be, and generally are, detected and corrected by means of one or more of the other senses, experience, observation, and reason; the different senses serving mutually to correct the errors of each other, and even one sense under different circumstances the errors of that sense under others.

33. Since the appearances then which external things exhibit to the mind through the medium of its sensations must depend as much at least on the state and nature of the mind itself, and on that of its bodily organs, as on the natures of the external things themselves by which the sensations are produced in it; and since the same thing must on this account produce different appearances in minds differently constituted or circumstanced, and those appearances must necessarily represent or signify different things or causes to these different minds, though all proceeding from the same thing or cause, whence that thing must actually become, with respect to each, a different thing from what it is with respect to the others, it is manifest that no individual can have any certainty, without some other criterion to judge by than that of his own perceptions only, even though they may carry conviction to his own mind, that his senses represent external things to him

F   such

such as they really are, or that they bring him a faithful and just report with respect to them; and this being the case, that it is necessary for him to have recourse to some other test or criterion for determining whether his senses represent or report things justly or not.

34. That sense of things which is common to mankind in general may be denominated the common sense of mankind with regard to things; and those whose senses are affected by things in the same manner that the senses of the generality of the human race are, or whose senses bring them the same information with respect to things that the senses of mankind in general do, may be regarded as possessing common sense, and as being, in as far, capable of judging justly of things:—their senses being thus proved to be in a sound and entire state, or to be such as are common to the generality of mankind, as giving the same report with respect to things that the senses of others in a state of health or that are sound in body and mind give. And an appeal to this common sense of mankind, is in every case the only proper and just criterion for determining whether the senses of individuals are in a sound and healthy state, and report truly or not. It is this common sense that forms the basis on which all human knowledge and all rational and just belief rests; and it is this common sense that is the only test and criterion of truth in the last resort when an appeal is made to experiment and the senses.

35. Those to whom the objects of sense appear different from what they do to the rest of mankind, or whose senses bring them different information respecting things from those of others, have ever been regarded either as diseased or disordered in their senses, as in cases of jaundice and hypocondria; or as being deficient in or devoid of common sense, as in cases of folly and of mania; and it is particularly to be remarked, that if we allow the premises of those who have the misfortune to be thus affected, we often find, in the case of maniacs at least, their reasoning to be acute and just.

36. That this common sense constitutes a test or criterion, and the only one whereby the individual may judge with safety and certainty of the justness and accuracy of the reports of his senses with respect to external things, is a fact which does not admit of doubt or controversy, as being fully established by experience; for if that was not the case, and the common

mon sense of mankind was erroneous, false, and deceitful, it would, contrary to what actually happens, be impossible for them ever to realize their conceptions in the adapting of means to ends in any of the purposes of life; —as in legislation, in political arrangements, in the conducting of commerce and manufactures, in the construction of machines, the cultivation of the soil, &c. or to conduct themselves with any degree of prudence in the common occurrences of the day ; for in that case, mankind in general would not only necessarily be incapable of realizing their conceptions, but would also, like those who are mad or in drink, and whose senses thereby deceive them, be liable to walk into the fire, into the sea, or over precipices, without being sensible of the danger attending it, or of the real nature or consequences of these things. And thus, then, is this system of metaphysics established on a principle of common sense, as the basis of all rational investigation and all human knowledge, and as the only criterion of truth and well-founded belief; but a common sense very different from that of preceding metaphysicians.

ESSAY

ESSAY II.

OF THE MENTAL FACULTIES, AND KNOWLEDGE; INCLUDING PRINCIPLES OF LOGIC.

———

1. THE human mind, whatever the nature of its elements may be, is evidently possessed not only of sensations and consciousness, but also of powers and action, as is sufficiently manifested by this consciousness, and by the observance of the phenomena exhibited by the human body in moving and acting as influenced by the mind; and the sensations, consciousness, and powers of the mind, are all evidently innate. The infant, indeed, at first, may be conscious of little or nothing besides sensations of pleasure or pain, though they may be attended with those of hunger, touch, taste, smell, sound, light and colours, and with the exertion of powers of the mind whereby it, seemingly spontaneously, alters its own state of modification and thereby that of the body by inducing action in it, from its being entirely ignorant of the meaning of those sensations and actions; but, notwithstanding this circumstance, no doubt can possibly be entertained of the sensations, consciousness, and powers of the mind being innate. Mental powers, however, like all other created things, being nothing but secondary causes, forming one link only of that connected chain of causes and effects proceeding from and depending on the first cause which forms the course of nature, cannot possibly act spontaneously and at random, but must act necessarily according to the decrees of providence, or to those modes and laws established by their Creator for their regulation, and therefore only in consequence of being acted upon and excited; in the first instance, either by the immediate agency of things external to the mind on the organs of sense

and

and the sensations, &c. thence proceeding, or by the agency of associated trains of sensations, &c. thus produced; and afterwards, by the action of the mind itself on itself, as thus induced to act through the medium of its own thoughts. The human mind, however, must very soon become conscious of its own action, as well as of its own feelings. As a child, even before birth, must necessarily, from the action of external things on its mind, have experienced sensations and motions in itself, it seems highly probable that it may, even prior to that period, have been conscious of a power to move itself, &c. Sensation, and a consciousness of power and action in itself, seems not, however, to take place in the fœtus till several months after conception. But though there is sufficient reason for believing that sensation, consciousness, and the powers of the mind, or the means by which knowledge may be acquired, are innate, yet there is no good reason for supposing that knowledge itself is innate; but, on the contrary, convincing proof that it cannot be so—indeed, that there actually are no such things in nature as innate ideas is a fact that has been established on evidence and reasonings so full and satisfactory by the sagacious Mr. Locke as to require no others to support it.

2. In the exercise of power in the mind and in the consciousness attending it does thinking consist; so that thought is the action of the mind attended with a consciousness of it. This power of the mind as it is variously directed and diversified acquires different names; which diversities are respectively called faculties of the mind, and their effects the operation of it. These faculties are those of memory, contemplation, imagination, reasoning, understanding, judging, volition or willing, and that of producing bodily action, or the motive faculty of the mind with respect to matter. Consciousness attends each and all of these faculties, or modifications of this power, and therefore cannot properly be regarded as one of them, more especially as being itself rather a passion or property than a power of the mind. The sensations and faculties of the mind cannot subsist as separate independent existences, or abstracted from each other or from the mind, or that in which they reside, no more than motion or modes can from matter or substance: they are merely attributes and modes of the mind, and therefore possess not any extension, &c., independent of that of the being of which they are the attributes and modes.

Simple

Simple sensation in the mind, the effect of external action merely, is not of itself thought—it only excites it. Though the external senses are known to improve much in many respects by means of exercise, and on the contrary to become duller, &c. when long unemployed, yet it is probable the feelings of the mind in infancy, and even in the fœtus in the latter months of gestation, may be as acute or even acuter than during any other period of life. The mental faculties however seem to be in a very weak and imperfect state, and even are almost imperceptible in the fœtus and new born infant; for their improvement, something they seem to owe to the growth and improvement of the body and bodily organs, but still much more to exercise, experience, and cultivation; as is evident from how much the faculties may be numbed, impaired, and even in the living subject almost obliterated, if deprived by any means of exercise and cultivation : so that even *they* can be regarded as innate in a certain degree, or in a very imperfect state, only.

3. It is the nature of consciousness, or it is essential to it, since the modifications of the mind being different the corresponding sensations depending on them must necessarily be different also, to discover and distinguish each modification, and privation of modification, or change of state in the mind; and thereby not only to distinguish one state of mind from another, but also to discern those particulars in which they differ; and hence it is in consciousness, or in the consciousness of these differences, that the discernment of the mind consists; and it is by means of these differences in its sensations, aided by experience, observation, and reason, that the mind is enabled to discover and perceive differences in things external to it.

4. It does not seem to us possible that a substance or being which is conscious and intelligent could be formed out of substances or beings that are not so, more than out of nothing; or that consciousness and intelligence can be the effect of arrangement and organization, even though all the operations of these beings, when formed, cóuld be accounted for from their organization, and the action chemical and mechanical of external things on them: but we must not pretend to limit the power of the Almighty, though we may rest assured that no power less than His can be capable of creating such beings; and of what, and by what means they

are

are created, lies far beyond the reach of human comprehension to investigate and discover.

5. Changes of state in the mind with the corresponding sensations and thoughts resulting from them are never produced but either by means of the direct or indirect, mediate or immediate, agency of substance, matter, or external things acting on it through the instrumentality of the bodily organs of sense; by means of sensations with their corresponding perceptions; or by means of thoughts, or actions and inferences of the mind, being so associated together by habit, &c., as that the one cannot be excited and produced without its inducing the other. These associations and their consequences are also ultimately the result of external causes, or of these sensations and thoughts or changes of state in the mind having been frequently excited and produced at the same time or in immediate succession by their proper external causes from similar associations among themselves, and by other associated circumstances, in the manner described in detail by the ingenious Dr. Hartley in his Observations on Man, to which with pleasure I refer the reader for information on this subject.

6. That faculty of the mind whereby it revives or recalls sensations and thoughts it has formerly experienced is denominated MEMORY. The term memory is also applied to the casual recurrence of these unsolicited, or unaccompanied with mental exertion. It is, and has hitherto been, the prevailing doctrine, that remembrances are only sensations, or sensations with their corresponding perceptions revived; and in many cases this is really the fact, provided these revived sensations are attended with a consciousness of having been experienced before; but we often have remembrances of sensations, thoughts, and external things, or at least we have remembrances of having experienced, known, or perceived, certain sensations, thoughts, and things, of which we have no present sensation or perception. Of this innumerable instances may be produced; thus, every one must have remembered to have experienced particular pleasures and pains, and must remember not only the particular kinds, but also the nature of each kind, though perhaps not very distinctly, without experiencing these sensations or similar pleasures and pains at the time of this remembrance; and every one must also remember a great many things which neither consist in sensation, nor admit of being represented by sensations. Remembrance

brance seems often to depend more on the associated circumstances, or
on the known connection between the present thought or object of thought
and the thought or object of thought sought or remembered, than on any
other causes; as it is this connection, or these associated circumstances, that
either recall it or lead to the remembrance of it; or it is sometimes perhaps
in these, or in this known connection, that what is called the remembrance
of the thing consists. Remembrance whether voluntary or involuntary
seems to depend in a very great degree if not entirely on association. The
mind cannot produce secondary sensations in itself without having a remembrance of the primary, nor otherwise than by means of associated circumstances; though sensations that may in some respects be regarded as secondary, as being similar to others experienced before, and as not being produced in it by the agency of the same external objects, or the instrumentality of the same external organs of sense by which the primary were, are
often produced in it involuntarily by the agency of things external to it on
it, as too rapid a flow of the blood, &c., as in dreams resulting from indi-
gestion, obstructions, fever, or other cause producing this too rapid flow
of the blood, and perhaps an unusual and rapid flow of the animal spirits
also, whence these dreams or these sensations, often more vivid than the
primary, proceed; which spirits in these cases seem to follow the trains and
tracks they have been most used to:—a sensation produced by the same
agent, or by means of the same organ of sense, cannot with propriety be
called secondary though similar to one which has been experienced before.

7. There are several different kinds of memories, as memory depends
upon different circumstances, constitutions, and habits; the two most re-
markable of which are, first, that kind of memory which perhaps may be
called a consequential memory, that revives or recalls the remembrance of the
thing sought gradually, slowly, and patiently, by tracing it through a long
connected series of thoughts, or a successive train of consequences, or of
circumstances or occurrences which either immediately preceded or succeeded it, especially those of cause and effect: a species of memory
which though slow and but ill suited to the acquirement of languages and
to the current occasions of the day, is yet, as being well adapted for retaining a long train of connected circumstances, or of causes and consequences necessarily following each other, in many respects well adapted for
investi-

investigation and discovery. And, secondly, what may be called a recollected memory, or that kind which revives or recalls the thing sought readily and quickly, principally by means of things and circumstances that were associated with it by cotemporary or co-existing relations, and by means of words, signs, and other artificial remembrancers. This is the kind best adapted for acquiring languages, for forming the poet and the orator, and for the general occurrences of life, as the possessor of it acquires not only a greater command of expression, but has also at all times a much wider range and display of objects of thought with their co-relations presented to his mind, and these not only well suited to the amplification, embellishment, and illustration, of any subject, but also for regulating the conduct in life, as affording extensive information as to the then state of things. It is those only, I imagine, who possess such a memory, or who remember readily and almost instantaneously as required not only the thing or the event sought, but also all the circumstances connected with it at the time, who can with propriety be said to be recollected; and that by the term the recollection of any thing, the immediate and collected remembrance both of that thing and of the circumstances with which it was then attended should be understood, and by recolletion in general the immediate remembrance of things and of the state of things, or of an extensive display of objects of thought with their mutual relations at the time; or cotemporary with the thing referred to. The most perfect kind of memory however consists in a happy coincidence of both these kinds in the same person; and indeed in every case they are in some degree, or more or less, mixed and blended together in the same individual.

The profound Mr. Locke, to whom the world is in many respects so much indebted, and to whom every writer on metaphysics must in particular be under many obligations, was the first I believe who had the sagacity to discover that the sensations and thoughts of the mind have no existence but when and while the mind is conscious of them, and that when it is unconscious of them they cease to be*. That this is really the fact there can be no doubt, since sensation is only a mode of consciousness, and since thought, or the action of the mind, cannot take place without altering its

* Locke on the Human Understanding, book 2, chap. 10. sect. 2.

state,

state, and thereby inducing in it sensation and consciousness; indeed, they no more exist in the mind when it is unconscious of them, than articulate sounds or words do in the organs of speech when they are not in the act of uttering them. These organs are not possessed of any stock of words, or of any repository for them; but only of a power of acting so as to utter or pronounce them when acted upon by the mind for that purpose; and this power of pronouncing them is artificially acquired by imitation, practice, association, &c. In like manner the mind possesses no store of sensations and thoughts, nor any repository of them, but only a power of acting so as to excite, generate, and produce them as required; or, more properly, to revive or generate sensations and thoughts similar to those it has formerly experienced, by inducing similar actions or changes of state in itself with those by which these former sensations and thoughts were produced in it: a power which seems to depend on association and habit in a great degree, and to improve much by exercise. Sometimes no exertion of this power or faculty is capable, however much the mind may incline it, of presenting to it certain sensations and thoughts it has often experienced, from the thoughts it is then occupied with not being associated with and thereby leading to them, though these same sensations and thoughts will not unfrequently present themselves when not sought for, and even in opposition to the will: the effect of unforeseen and unexpected association, or of external causes, as from external objects acting on the mind which are associated with these, or from flows of the animal spirits in trains and in tracks in which they have formerly proceeded, whereby similar sensations and thoughts have been produced in the mind.

8. The mind is capable not only of reviving sensations and thoughts it has formerly experienced, but also of retaining the same thought in itself for a shorter or longer time, as it inclines by meditating on it or contemplating it. This faculty of the mind is named CONTEMPLATION, and consists either in ATTENTION to what it experiences or perceives at present, or in REFLECTION on what it has formerly experienced or perceived; as attention refers to what is *present*, so reflection refers to what is *past*; and as CONTEMPLATION in the mind usually, though not always, refers to what passes within itself, so CONSIDERATION in the mind usually refers to things external to it. Attending to or reflecting on one thing, or one part, quality,

or

or mode of a thing, in preference to or without regarding the others is named ABSTRACTION, and may be truly regarded as such, in as far, but in as far only, as the mind abstracts its attention or reflection from the others or other parts. The very earnest contemplation of any object or subject is INTENTION in the mind.

That modification of thought or faculty of the mind whereby it can alter or modify, mutilate, arrange, and combine its recalled or remembered sensations or thoughts, so as to make them represent and indicate things differing in several respects from those things by whose agency they were originally produced, and which they then indicated and represented, is denominated FANCY: if the things thus indicated and represented have no real and known external existence in nature, they are, as having no existence but in thought and the mind, called either IMAGINATIONS or CONCEPTIONS of the mind. The mental sensations and thoughts thus formed are respectively called either the one or the other, as they either indicate and represent images or pictures of things having no known prototypes in nature, or the actual existence of which seems impossible; or as fancy aided by reason indicates and represents the manner and means by which a thing may be made or done, or a truth may be or is discovered. It is the knowledge of present and past that constitutes the materials of fancy, out of which it forms mental representations, and predicts with respect to futurity;— fancy including both imaginations and conceptions of all kinds. Sensations are not only extended in *duration* as being of more or less permanency, but are also extended in *space,* since they are divisible or consist of parts, which they could not possibly be if not extended; and their particular extents, &c. except in cases of imagination, depend' under similar circumstances on those of their respective causes; thus the sensation produced by and representing the full moon exceeds in extent that produced by and representing the new moon when first perceived, in the same proportion as the full exceeds the new moon; and as they admit of division, so they also admit of addition, and these in an almost infinite variety of ways, so as to produce an almost infinite variety of representations. It is in the fancy or that power of the mind whereby it not only divides sensations or representations into parts, but also combines these parts again, whether representing the same or different objects, so as to form a wonderous variety of

representations

representations that imagination or the mental formation of images or pictures of things having no known prototypes in nature consists; thus does it form
that mental representation called a centaur, by a combination of the muti-
lated mental representations of a man and of a horse; and it is in the same
power, only differently applied and directed, that the conception of the
mind consists, or that whereby the fancy aided by reason forms representations to itself by means of a mental process from facts already known,
antecedent to trial or direct proofs of the manner and means by which a
a thing may be made or done, or a truth discovered; or of the possibility
or probability of any thing, and a mental representation of the thing
itself as it will appear when done, if a thing admitting of mental representation.

9. It is exclusively to such visual and tangible sensations as are revived
or recalled by memory or association, or by any other means than by the
immediate agency of the external causes or objects which they are known
to represent and resemble in certain respects, whether altered or modified
by the imagination or not, that the term IDEA should, in my opinion, be
appropriated; and, indeed, there would be no occasion for employing that
term at all, was it not for distinguishing between the different immediate
causes by which the same sensation or mental representation of the same
external thing or object may be produced in the mind, and thereby
between the judgments or opinions formed by the mind with respect to the
object or thing represented; as whether it has a real or imaginary existence,
or whether the mind actually perceives it or has a visual representation of it
only, &c. as when the sensation or representation is produced by the
immediate agency of the thing represented on the external organs of sense;
and the mind, by means of a process described in Essay I. acquires a conviction of its actually perceiving the thing itself; which is not the case when
the same sensation and representation is induced in the mind by any other
means, as it is then convinced it is not the thing itself that it perceives,
but only a mental image, picture, or representation of it that it is sensible
of; and hence it is convenient and proper to distinguish between these by
denominating the representation in the first case the PERCEPTION of
the thing, and in the second the IDEA of the same thing; and for distinguishing between things real, and things imaginary or which are formed
by

by the imagination out of representations of things real though having no existence of themselves except as sensations of the mind. Both perceptions and ideas refer to external things only—real or imaginary—and all ideas depend, as being either recalled or revived sensations, or modifications of recalled sensations, either upon memory alone, or upon memory and imagination jointly.

10. Both in the idea, and in the perception, of any particular thing by means of a visual sensation attended with a knowledge of its being a visual representation and resemblance of that particular thing, as possessing the same form, parts, and proportions of those parts among themselves, with the thing itself, we may with propriety be said to have a vision or sight of that particular thing; but though we have this vision or sight with respect to it in both cases, yet as we cannot by means of it in the former case, the perceptions of it by means of the other senses and the other circumstances of local situation &c. being wanting, discover whether that of which we have a vision or sight *then* exists, or *where* situated, &c. we cannot with propriety be said to perceive the thing:—we *see* it, but nevertheless *perceive* it not, in the proper acceptation of the term perception of a thing. We cannot, indeed, with strict conformity to truth, be said to see the external thing itself in any case; and we have as distinct a vision of it when we have only an idea of it, or see it in idea only, as when we perceive it and think we actually see the thing itself, provided the visual sensation, and the knowledge of its being a representation of that particular thing, is the same and equally vivid and distinct in both cases; and the only difference between them is, that in perception the mind virtually throws the sensation or vision on the object or thing itself, so as exactly to fit it, or nearly so, if not at a great distance, and at any rate so as in all cases to appear to the mind exactly to fit it; and that the mind, in the case of perception, is led by a knowledge of the existing circumstances to a knowledge of the site, &c. of the object, and of the object's being the efficient cause of the visual representation or picture of it in the mind, of which the mind is then conscious; and though we have a vision or sight in both cases which resembles it in many respects, as in form, &c. yet as that vision is in the mind only, it is not in either case the thing itself we see:—this is evident from our having an equally vivid and distinct vision of it in idea when we are satisfied it cannot possibly be the

thing

thing itself that we see, as in perception, when we think we actually see the thing itself; also, from viewing any thing in a mirror, or by means of a Gregorian telescope, in which an opaque body interposes between the eye and the object, so that it cannot possibly be the object itself we then see. Yet we may in strict propriety be said to perceive the thing itself, when we can by means of vision, or a visual sensation, aided by our other senses, &c. become acquainted not only with its form and size, but also with its actual existence, state of motion or rest, relative situation, &c., and when we actually throw the visual sensation it produces on itself.

11. A visual sensation, as was proved in Essay I. is neither a vision or sight, but in as far as it may be a true and just representation of that thing by which it is or may originally have been produced, and without being attended with a knowledge of its being so, and then it is of that thing only that it is a vision or sight, the sensation itself, or confused jumble of colours, by the instrumentality of which this is effected, being otherwise of no meaning. Except in certain cases of feelings, as of pleasure and pain, hunger, thirst, ease, fatigue, &c. and in certain metaphysical investigations with respect to the mind itself, it is always, after the mind has acquired the habit of readily and instantaneously recognizing and knowing the meaning of its sensations, the EXTERNAL THING itself, or that which is represented, and never the IDEA of it, or the sensation whereby it is represented, that is the IMMEDIATE OBJECT of the mind in THINKING. The mind, indeed, in thinking, often becomes, from habit, in a great degree, if not entirely, unconscious of its sensations, those I have distinguished by the name of feelings excepted, and attends only to the external things represented by them, and the end or object proposed.

12. None of our senses furnish us with images, pictures, or IDEAS, of the feelings of pleasure, pain, hunger, ease, &c. but only with the sensations to which we appropriate these names; and these, though revived by any other agency than that of the external causes by which they were first produced, would, notwithstanding this difference in their causes, experience no alteration in their nature, but be, from their own natures as well as from their having no resemblance or reference to any thing external to the mind, merely sensations in the mind, differing in nothing from the similar ones it had experienced before, except perhaps in being attended with a remembrance

brance of having been experienced before. Our senses of hearing, taste, and smell, furnish us with sensations, but with no images, pictures, or IDEAS. Revived sounds, tastes, and flavours, are only revived sensations ; and these sensations furnish us with no images or pictures of their respective external causes. Except certain sounds as associated with words, revivable by means of the vocal organ, there are few of the simple sensations produced by means of hearing, of taste, or of smell, or of pleasures and pains—those accompanying the passions excepted—or of hunger, fatigue, &c. that the mind has a power of reviving at pleasure. Thus I *remember* to have experienced the pains of a burn, a wound, and the toothach, though I experience none of them at present, and am *incapable of reviving* them by any means merely mental.

13. What are called IDEAS of the sensations of tastes, sounds, and flavours, of pleasures, pains, appetites, &c. are in reality nothing but remembrances of them, and these remembrances of them are seldom, if ever, similar, or similar but fainter sensations ; and, indeed, unless when a similar sensation happens to be produced directly or indirectly by some external cause exciting the senses or thoughts associated with it, and thereby the animal spirits, they are seldom or never attended with sensations of any kind, but are merely thoughts or remembrances of having experienced certain particular sensations of the kinds to which the appellations of pleasures, pains, tastes, sounds, flavours, &c. are appropriated, and that without having any distinct recollection, and far less any feeling or sensation of them at the time of remembrance, unless perhaps some faint recollection with respect to the degree of their intensity. We can have a remembrance even of the visual appearance of an object, as of a particular house, from a recollection of the component parts or associated circumstances, without our having a distinct or perhaps any visual sensation or idea of it at the time ; we can remember its dimensions, number of apartments, windows, doors, columns, &c. and the orders of architecture according to which they are formed, as well as the materials of which they are constructed, &c. ; we can also remember the construction, and the several parts of any instrument or machine we have seen, with its manners of acting, and the principles on which it is formed, without our having any distinct visual sensation or idea, or perhaps any idea or visual sensation at all, at the time, of this machine or its parts.

14. There

14. There may be numberless thoughts, and objects of thought, consciousnesses, sensations, feelings, and even conceptions, which cannot with any propriety, when remembered, be called IDEAS, as having no reference or any resemblance to any thing external.

15. It is only those objects of thought that are possessed of magnitude and figure that can be represented in sensation as images, pictures, or representations; and it is only in those visible representations of magnitude with certain of their modes and relations revived or recalled by memory, whether modified by the imagination or not, that IDEAS, in the only definite, precise, and determinate signification of the term can consist; and hence there may be numberless thoughts and objects of thought revived or recalled, which, though remembrances and knowledge, can with no propriety be called IDEAS. Of this kind are all those revived thoughts and objects of thought, respecting the operations and faculties of our own minds, which some have denominated ideas of reflection, and others spiritual ideas; and hence also there can be no ideas, mental representations, or visible or tangible sensations, of what comes not within the cognizance of our senses, and the independent existence of which is only inferred, as of virtue, vice, infinity, eternity, immensity, absolute impossibility, necessity, equality, justice, &c. or of power or cause of any kind, except in as far as we may give the name of cause to the material instrument by means of which any change may be effected : of these we may form a conception with respect to the possibility or probability of their existence, but of themselves as independent existences, if such they actually are, we can form no IDEA. Though some of our sensations, as the same colour, &c., may virtually be applied to a great number of different external things, yet that colour or sensation does not by that means become general. All our sensations are particulars ; as particular pleasures and particular pains, particular colours, particular sounds, &c., and all things representible in sensation being also particulars, it must be manifest, that we can have no general sensations ; and having no GENERAL SENSATIONS, that we cannot possibly have any GENERAL IDEAS, or revived mental representations of what has no actual existence.

16. It has been usual to represent not only some of the thoughts, but some of the sensations of the mind as abstractions from things external to the

the mind, and to denominate them ABSTRACT IDEAS: thus, the thoughts and judgments of the mind respecting attributes, modes, or relations, without regard to their subjects, as the thoughts and judgments of the mind with respect to the relations of order, number, equality, action, motion, cause and effect, proportion, power, truth, justice, virtue, vice, &c., when considered without any attention being given to the things themselves of which they are the attributes, modes, or relations, have all been regarded as mental abstractions from these things, and as mental representations or ideas of these attributes, modes, and relations, and therefore been called ABSTRACT IDEAS; and, in the same manner, some of the sensations of our own minds have generally been regarded as abstractions from external things, when considered by the mind apart from the real qualities of those external things in which they apparently seem to subsist, as colour and smell in a rose, taste and touch in an apple, and sound in a bell, &c. as if they had actually belonged to and subsisted in these things before being thus considered by the mind; and, when so considered, they have not only been regarded as mental abstractions from these things—though it is manifest that mind cannot abstract from things that which in reality they actually possess not—but also as mental representations or ideas of these apparent and supposed properties of external things, and on these accounts they also have been denominated ABSTRACT IDEAS. The mind possesses a power of contemplating or considering any one attribute, mode, or relation, of external things, and even of itself, without giving any attention to the other attributes, modes, or relations, of these things, or to that in which these attributes, &c. subsist; but it possesses no power of abstracting these attributes, modes, or relations, from the things in which they subsist, or of making them actually subsist of themselves either in reality, or in idea or mental sensation and representation, as separate independent beings; or of making them, if attributes and modes of external things, exist in the mind; or, if attributes and modes of the mind, exist in external things:—thus the relations of equality, justice, virtue, &c., as well as the particular attributes and modes of things, subsist in the things only of which they are the relations, attributes, and modes; or in things only; and they cannot subsist otherwise or abstracted from things, and be made to exist either in the mind as ideas, or out of it as independent beings. We

do not abstract figure from substance when we apply the figure of any particular substance to any other particular substance that possessed it not before, and then consider it when so applied ; as when we delineate the figure of any particular body in the form of a diagram on the substance paper by means of the substance ink, and then consider it ; and, more especially, when the mind considers it in the form of a diagram on the retina of the eye. And as modes cannot subsist of themselves or be abstracted from that in which they subsist, so neither can attributes or relations of modes subsist of themselves, or abstracted from the modes of which they are the attributes and relations ; and consequently from those things in which the modes themselves subsist :—thus that property or relation of equality which subsists between the three angles of that particular mode of existence we call a plain triangle and two right angles cannot possibly be abstracted from that mode, or from plain triangles ; nor can it by any means be made to subsist in the mind, either in reality or as a representation or idea or in any thing else that is not formed of triangles, though the mind may have a knowledge of the fact of such a relation subsisting between these figures or modes of existence in the nature of things. The mind having discovered this property in every plain triangle, whose properties it has investigated, is hence led by induction to conclude that this property is general, or holds with respect to all plain triangles whatever, however much they may differ in other respects among themselves, and this conclusion, JUDGMENT OR FACT discovered, has been denominated and regarded as an IDEA, and an ABSTRACT GENERAL IDEA—*abstract*, as being formed by the mind by abstracting that property from any of the particular beings possessing it ; though it can be only by its being *considered apart* from the other properties of that in which it subsists, since it is impossible to abstract from any thing that on which its subsistence depends, or which is essential to it, without destroying that thing :—*general*, as being rendered so by being thus abstracted ; though it is not easy to conceive how its generality should depend on its being abstracted in place of subsisting in and being common to many particular beings, since it can not be abstracted from those particular beings without destroying that generality it derives from being common to them all :—and *an idea*, because the property thus abstracted exists in the mind only ; though it is impossible to conceive by what means it could exist or
subsist

subsist in the mind, either in reality or in idea, unless the mind was formed of triangles and right angles; and though there can be no *idea*, or mental representation, of what is unrepresentable, and the very existence of which independent of those things of which it is a property, is in the nature of things impossible. The existence of some of these supposed ABSTRACT GENERAL IDEAS, or of the properties they are supposed to represent and express, is besides impossible from these properties being inconsistent and incompatible, as that *abstract general idea* of a triangle given by Mr. Locke, viz. " An idea of a triangle that is neither obliquè nor rectangle, neither " equilateral, equicrural, nor scalenon, but all and none of these at " once *."

17. Bishop Berkeley, after quoting the above definition or general idea of a triangle as given by Mr. Locke from his Essay, says in his Treatise concerning the Principles of Human Knowledge, Introduction, sect. 13: " If any man has the faculty of framing in his mind such an idea of a " triangle as is here described, it is in vain to pretend to dispute him out of " it, nor would I go about it, &c." The Bishop, however, throws no new or additional light on this abstruse doctrine of universals,—when he tells us, sect. 15, " It is I know a point much insisted on, that all knowledge and " demonstration are about universal notions, to which I agree," and " when " I demonstrate any proposition concerning triangles, it is to be supposed " that I have in view the UNIVERSAL IDEA of a triangle; which ought " not to be understood as if I could frame an idea of a triangle which was " neither equilateral nor scalenon nor equicrural. But only that the parti- " cular triangle I consider, whether of this or of that sort it matters not, doth " EQUALLY STAND FOR AND REPRESENT ALL RECTILINEAL TRIANGLES " WHATSOEVER, and is in that sense universal. All which seems very plain, " and not to include any difficulty in it"—since it is sufficiently manifest that no particular triangle can be universal, or can represent and include in itself all different kinds of rectilineal triangles whatsoever, and since there is no less difficulty in conceiving universality in a particular substance or in a particular figure than in a particular idea, the existence of it in either being equally impossible. It seems truly surprising that persons of so great discernment and sagacity as Mr. Locke and Bishop Berkeley

---

* Locke's Essay concerning Human Understanding, book 4, chap. 7, sect. 9.

should

should have been so much deceived by the ideal hypothesis as to have allowed themselves to have been betrayed by it into definitions so palpably absurd as those given above of an abstract general idea of a triangle.

18. So far is the mind from possessing any power of abstracting attributes, modes, and relations from all substances or subjects, even in thought, that it is not so much as capable of conceiving them thus abstracted, either as subsisting in the mind as thoughts or ideas or as separate independent beings subsisting of themselves; thus we cannot conceive of attributes and relations otherwise than as the attributes of substances and as the relations of things related : nor can the mind form any conception of modes, as of motion or figure, &c. without substance, though it can consider an attribute, relation, or mode, without considering or paying any regard to the thing in which it must either in reality or in imagination necessarily subsist to be conceived. The mind may consider the modes of action of any power from the sensible phenomena of its effects, the modes of motion of particular beings, and thereby the modes or laws of motion in general with respect to all beings of that particular kind, the relations of particular numbers, and of particular magnitudes to each other, the moral, political, and religious rights and duties, the passions and affections, events and circumstances, without any regard to those particular beings in nature of which they are respectively the attributes, &c. and draw conclusions or judgments from such considerations, and thereby discover truth, and acquire knowledge, which may be general in as far as it may respect several particular beings; but the things thus considered exist not in the mind, the passions, affections, and powers of the mind excepted, nor out of the mind as separate independent beings, nothing respecting them existing in the mind but the knowledge of such attributes having an actual existence in things, the judgments thence deduced, the truths discovered, and the knowledge thus acquired; and these do not exist in the mind as representations of any thing external or internal, or as ideas, or any otherwise than as judgments of it, and as truths and knowledge with respect to the attributes, relations, and modes of those beings to which these attributes, relations, and modes belong.

19. The considering of one thing or of one attribute, mode, or relation, without considering at the same time other things co-existing with it, does not abstract that thing from these others, either in reality or in thought;
for

for although the mind, being conscious that it cannot contemplate or consider more than one thing at one time with distinctness and accuracy, directs its attention principally or exclusively to that thing, or to that substance, whose power, property, mode, or relation is the then object of its investigation ; yet in doing so it abstracts not, since this preferring of one thing to others as an object of its attention or reflection can with no reason or propriety be regarded as abstracting that thing, substance, quality, or mode from the others. It is not the mind's attending to and considering certain things in preference to others, or what has been called abstracting them, that can make these things general. The generality does not depend on the thoughts and operations of the mind, but on the natures of the things themselves ; and the *generality* of any thing in particular, whether it is an attribute, relation, or mode, or the modes of a mode, as those of motion, as conceived by the mind is merely a mental inference by induction, from its having discovered that it holds with respect to all the particular beings whose properties, &c. it has considered or investigated, and this generality holds or is applicable to those particular beings only of which this particular thing is an attribute, relation, or mode : with respect to the mind it is nothing but a mere inference or thought. The mind by means of experience, observation, and reasoning, discovers or perceives the existence of certain relations in things, as those of agreement, &c. but even then these relations have no existence in the mind as ideas, abstractions, or any thing else ; it is the knowledge thus acquired only that exists in the mind, the conclusion from the premises that such particular relations do exist in things, or the knowledge of the facts or truths with regard to their existence, &c. thus discovered and ascertained. As these inferences or thoughts which have been called abstract ideas, intelligibles, and universals, possess not magnitude or figure, are altogether incapable of subsisting of themselves as separate independent beings, and are not cognizable by our senses, it must be manifest that they can not be represented in sensation or idea, and therefore that, though thoughts of the mind, they can not, though revived or recalled by memory, be *ideas* properly so called ; and not being ideas, that they can not be ABSTRACT GENERAL IDEAS.

20. I must acknowledge it seems to me truly surprising that it should never have occurred that what in metaphysics and logic is regarded and
represented

represented as the abstraction of attributes from substances, and of substance from attributes, is in reality nothing but the abstraction of the attention of the mind; and that the abstracting of the attention of the mind from some or all of the qualities, except one, of certain beings should ever have been regarded as abstracting that one quality either from that being, or from the other qualities or attributes, modes, or relations, of that being; and that this quality should, in consequence of this abstraction of the attention of the mind from the other qualities of the being in which it subsists, become an IDEA, and an ABSTRACT AND GENERAL IDEA. Yet such is the fact, these abstractions have universally been thus regarded, and on this basis rests the whole doctrine of abstract and general ideas, of universals, dialectic, and the logic of the ancients and of the schools, or what has been called pure speculative science, which not being acquired by means of *experience*, and being totally independent of *natural things* which are of themselves *mutable*, is conversant only about *ideas*, universal, necessary, and *immutable truths*, or *things purely intellectual* engendered in the mind by the mind, without requiring or receiving any external or foreign aid, *abstract general ideas*, sometimes denominated by them intelligibles, sometimes the pure essences of things, and sometimes logical universals, being the foundation on which the whole of the systems of the ancient metaphysics and logic are erected; which, however erroneous, they clothed in the garb of probability and of truth with so much dexterity, eloquence, and address, as to render them so plausible and even convincing as to have so far imposed upon the most penetrating and profound of the moderns that they were induced implicitly to adopt them, among whom we must include even the sagacious Locke, who has researched deeper into the human mind than any other—according to whom general natures are nothing but abstract ideas, general and universal the creatures of the understanding, and those abstract ideas the essences of genera and species * ; there are no other known essences of things but the essences of sorts, or those abstract general ideas which form these essences; nothing is essential to individuals, and real essences are unknown to us † ; and it is to these abstract general ideas or essences of sorts that he applies the term *nominal essences*, as they

* Locke's Essay on the Human Understanding, book 3, chap. 3, sect. 9, 11, 12.
† Ditto, book 3, chap. 6, sect. 2, 4, 9.

are

are distinguished by their respective names from one another, as well as from the real essences of individual things which are unknown :—and such is the profound veneration for antiquity, and blind deference for the authority of names that have acquired celebrity, that doctrines founded on and deduced from these principles are those that are still most in repute, and most generally adopted.

21. The precise meaning affixed to the term *essences of things* by the ancients, can not now, from the obscure indefinite manner in which they treated of these essences, and the differences of opinions among themselves with respect to them, be easily ascertained. Whether by essences they meant the elements of things, and by these elements atoms, as the doctrines of Leucippus, Democritus, Epicurus, and others of the ancients seem to indicate; or whether they meant types, intelligible natures, or ideas, which have a certain and stable existence, and are the patterns of things, which are immaterial beings, eternal essences, uncreated, antecedent to and independent of things, existing in the Divine mind not as sensations, perceptions or modifications of it, but subsisting of themselves, and capable of being detached or of emanating from it, and of impressing matter with all those various different forms and modes which exist in nature or among created things; which seems to have been the opinion of Plato: or whether by essences were meant the forms of things, as distinguished into species and phantasms without the substance, or the *potential* without the *actual* existence of things, which seems to have been the doctrine inculcated by Aristotle,—who represents logical universals or the essences of genera and species as substances or substantial existences, which kind of substances he calls secondary substances, to distinguish them from individual substances which he calls primary substances, and which he says are more substances than secondary—and was that adopted by the schools, notwithstanding the many absurdities it involves. Indeed, the doctrines of the ancients respecting Philosophy, are in general (a few dogmas attributed to Pythagoras excepted) so much the offspring of conjecture, imagination, and perverted reason, so unfounded, vague, and visionary, that the only inference that can rationally be drawn from the few glimpses of science and truth that are sometimes discernable through the haze of eloquent and ingenious misrepresentation, metaphor and mysticism, in which they have enveloped them, is, that there

seems

seems actually to have existed, as I have had already occasion to observe in the Introduction, in some very remote period of antiquity, some nation, where situated it is not now easy to determine, though probably in the East, among whom the sciences and real philosophy had acquired a great degree of maturity and perfection, and from whom, though not perhaps directly, the Greeks had derived many of the arts they possessed, and all the scanty portion of real philosophical knowledge to be found in their works, some geometrical discoveries only perhaps excepted. We have, indeed, from the striking difference, and even contrast between the sublime truths promulgated by Pythagoras, and the philosophical doctrines proposed, adopted, and inculcated by the Greeks and Romans, every reason to believe that the Greeks and Romans were the corrupters, in place of the discoverers and improvers of real philosophical knowledge; especially Plato, who has embellished reveries, mysticism and absurdity, with all the charms and allurements of the most elegant and refined eloquence, and thus formed a system under the name of philosophy the most irrational that can well be conceived, but possessing much seeming sublimity, and admirably adapted for pleasing congenial spirits, and for affecting and operating upon the weak and the visionary.

22. It may often be useful to substitute the word *meaning* for the word *idea* in metaphysical writings, since by the idea of a term or expression, nothing can with propriety be understood but the meaning of it; the word *knowledge* may also in many cases with much propriety and advantage be substituted for the word *idea*; thus, in the language of Logicians, to furnish ourselves with ideas, can properly mean only to acquire a knowledge of things.

23. The too general, vague, and improper use which has been made of the term IDEA, in substituting IDEAS not only for the feelings, sensations, perceptions, thoughts, opinions, judgments, remembrances, &c. of the mind, but also for all the objects of thought, and all the objects of human knowledge, and thereby for things themselves or external existences with their relations and modes of being, for passions and affections, for virtues and vices, for powers, properties, and facts, in a word for every thing in nature, real or fanciful, the faculties of the mind perhaps excepted, has been productive of effects highly prejudicial to the investigation and discovery of

truth

truth and the advancement of science; and, from making all the objects of thought to be ideas, or to be regarded as that which this mode of expression represents and indicates them to be, has naturally led to the adoption of those opinions on which those systems of metaphysics which necessarily terminate in an imaginary philosophy and the belief of an ideal world have been erected; which, though so ingeniously and artfully contrived and though buttressed up with so much strength and acuteness of argument as seems to have imposed on the authors themselves, as resting on such a foundation and leading to such conclusions, necessarily refute themselves, independent of any direct proof of the reality or actual existence of things external to the mind, or of their repugnancy to the real natures of things. By some, the word notion, which in its proper meaning seems to be synonimous with conception, or rather with indistinct conception, has been substituted for the word idea, and has been used with the same, or nearly the same, unwarrantable licence of signification.

24. In investigating the natures of things, among the observations that first present themselves to the mind is that of their *natural* arrangement into sorts or kinds; from perceiving that many individuals or particulars possess certain qualities, or powers and properties, which are alike or of the same kind in each, and which therefore are common or general to them all; and which, by distinguishing them from all other individuals possessing not these, forms them into a sort or kind, separate and distinct from all other individuals and all other sorts or kinds; or that many individuals *naturally* agree, or are alike in possessing certain qualities, however much they may differ from each other in other respects, and however much from all other sorts or kinds of things that possess not those particular qualities which connect them as one class or species, and which characterize and mark them with sufficient accuracy and precision as a distinct sort or kind distinguishable from all other sorts or kinds. Indeed, there are no facts better ascertained, or of which we have clearer evidence, as our daily observations are almost constantly furnishing us with intuitive experimental proofs of them, than those of the assortment of things into kinds—that these assortments actually exist in nature, altogether unconnnected with and independent of human ideas and conceptions—that they are the workmanship of the Author of nature, and not the offspring of the human mind as a de-

I

vice

vice for facilitating human converse—and that all human knowledge with respect to them is ultimately derived from and founded on the natures of things themselves.

I must again observe, as the doctrine is of importance to science, that these common or general qualities are so far from being ideas or general ideas, or abstractions, that even our acquired knowledge of most of them does not so much as admit of being represented in IDEA, as consisting merely in perceptions, conceptions, and remembrances of them ; and those qualities that in this case seemingly do, are only sensations in our own minds, as particular colours, &c. which we virtually transfer to the various individuals by whose agency they are excited and produced, and from this circumstance alone are apt to regard them as ideas, or to mistake them for mental representations of things external. And that these general qualities of things can not be abstractions, whether abstract natures or notions, must also be sufficiently evident, when it is considered that they cannot be abstracted or separated from each other, or from the other qualities of the things in which they subsist, without the destruction or annihilation of these things taking place, and thereby of themselves ; and that, though this were possible, either in reality or in thought, it could not be effected without destroying their generality, since that generality consists merely in their pertaining to or being the qualities of several individuals differing among themselves in other respects :—and hence also it must be manifest that they cannot be distinct independent beings, immutable, necessary and eternal. And since these general qualities are neither ideas nor abstractions it must be manifest that the general terms by which they are expressed, in place of being signs of ideas, must signify either these qualities themselves, or the aggregates of the individuals or particular things possessing them which form the several sorts or kinds of things which these qualities or combinations of qualities characterize, distinguish, and determine.

25. That GENERAL TERMS actually denote and signify either general qualities, or those aggregates of individuals possessing them which form the several sorts or kinds, or genera and species of things, and neither ideas nor abstractions, the descriptions of these things or sorts, or the definitions of these general terms, evidently evince :—so that GENERAL TERMS are not
the

the signs of GENERAL IDEAS, but each general term signifies either a particular sort of things, or a particular quality or combination of qualities, peculiar to that sort as belonging to all the individuals included in it, and to no others; and in as far as these terms are applicable to particular sorts or kinds only, or to the particular individuals included in them, in as far are they particular in their respective significations. Thus, a triangle has been described and defined to be a plain figure having three angles and three sides, or a plain surface comprehended by three lines; so that the term triangle signifies either the three angles, and thereby the three sides including them whereof the figure is formed, and from whence it is therefore denominated; or it signifies either any *particular figure* possessing the properties of having three angles and sides and no more;—or all figures or plain surfaces whatever that are possessed of those properties of being bounded by three lines and having three angles, however much they may differ from each other in other respects; nor are these differences, as whether the surface is great or small, black or white, &c. of any consequence with regard to the justness and adequacy of the description or definition, since the qualities included in it are fully sufficient to characterize, arrange, determine, and distinguish the figures possessing them from all other figures: so that there is evidently one settled meaning which limits the signification of the word triangle, and there is evidently no keeping to the same definition, or to the term expressing it, without keeping also to the same meaning:—thus when a triangle is mentioned we can be at no loss to know what is meant, though no particular kind of one may be specified, when we know that all that is essential to such a figure is the being possessed of three angles, and being included in three sides, and no more; and that it is indifferent what the size, or what ratios the particular angles or sides of the figure bear to each other, as be they what they may it must still be a triangle if possessed of that only essential quality of containing three angles and sides and no more, as we know from the definition of the term that it signifies or denotes any figure, be it what it may, and therefore all figures, possessing these essential qualities.

The above definition—which is at the same time both general and particular, as being common to all figures possessing these qualities, and at the same time applicable to each in particular, however different in degree or in kind they may be from each other, or whatever their several sizes, substances, colours, &c. may be, and whether oblique or rectangle, equilateral, equicrural, or scalenon—neither expresses, nor is, either an abstraction, or a sensation, or an idea, as it neither expresses, nor does or can consist in any mental, or visible or tangible representation, or can exist any otherwise than as an object of thought unrepresentable in sensation or idea, or as the knowledge and remembrance of properties which have been discovered to appertain to certain figures, and to no others, and to which the name or term triangle has, on that account, been exclusively appropriated*. That the TERM TRIANGLE, of which the above definition expresses the meaning and which on account of its referring to properties which are general or common to many particulars is with much propriety denominated a GENERAL TERM, is a sensation, idea, or mental representation, no one it is presumed, though some may be inclined to regard it as the essence or nominal essence of that species of figures the term denotes, can be so absurd as to suppose.

26. About the end of the eleventh century of the Christian æra, the Nominals first made their appearance, or those who regarded logical universals, or the essences of the several sorts of things as consisting in their several names only; or who made the sorting of things to consist merely in the artificially distinguishing certain portions of them from others by means of different names appropriated to those different portions of them respectively for that express purpose, without any regard being had to the particular natures or qualities of things themselves; and who, therefore, admit of no essences, or real characteristic and distinguishing qualities of sorts or kinds but their names or nominal essences, and represent the distinction of things into sorts, or into genera and species, as having a NOMINAL but no REAL existence in nature. The difference of opinion thus produced with regard to the nature of logical universals soon divided the learned of those times into the two famous sects of the Realists, or Idealists and the Nominals, and was the cause of long continued and violent disputes in the Schools,

---

* It sems strange to me that so acute a reasoner as Bishop Berkeley should draw from the same premises, the definition of a triangle, conclusions the very reverse of those given above. See his Treatise on Human Knowledge, Introduction, sect. 18. Though most brute Animals are capable of distinguishing their own species, that of mankind, &c. from others, and of learning the meaning of proper names, yet none of them seem capable of comprehending the meanings of general terms.

which

which however subsided on the revival of literature, when the nominal doctrine, though never entirely abandoned, sunk for long into oblivion. It was in some respect revived by Mr. Locke, according to whom nothing being essential to individuals, and real essences unknown to us, the essences of sorts or logical universals can be nominal essences only.

27. This doctrine has, however, of late been revived on a much wider base, or more extended plan than formerly, as not satisfied with substituting words for ideas, or what was supposed to be ideas, logical universals, the doctrines of the more modern Nominals substitute them also for things themselves or real existences, making substances, relations, faculties, and thoughts, all depend upon language. The Idealists, or Realists as in their writings they stiled themselves, substituted the natural signs for the things signified, and thus treated of ideas, or revived mental representations of things, as if they actually were the things represented, or real substantial existences with their attributes. The Nominals of the middle ages substituted one kind of sign for another, or words for ideas with respect to logical universals, and then treated of these artificial signs called general terms, as if they actually were those common or general attributes in things which they are employed to signify or express. But the Nominals of our time treat of words and language not only as if these artificial signs had been invented and applied before the things signified by them were known, but also as if they were actually the only causes and the only objects of human knowledge, and thence deduce many doctrines perfectly inadmissible, as being contrary to experience, and altogether inconsistent with nature and reason. Thus we are informed by the Abbé de Condillac, "that we think only through the medium of words."*—This is making thoughts depend on words, and not words, or the invention and applications of words as artificial signs, upon thoughts; or is treating the subject as if there were no other objects of thought but these artificial signs, and the mind was not only incapable of thinking of things themselves, but also of thinking through the medium of any signs but those particular artificial ones appropriated to the purposes of language.— That " the art of reasoning is nothing more than a language well ar- " ranged"*—as if reason depended on language, or rather on the proper

* Doctrines of the Abbé de Condillac, as quoted in Lavoisier's Elements of Chemistry, as translated by Ker; Preface, pp. 1 and 2.

arrangement

arrangement of language only, and not language and the proper arrangement of language on reason. And the author of the Diversions of Purley tells us, that " What are called its operations" (operations of the mind) " are " merely the operations of languages*."—A proposition which seems to me so obviously erroneous, so contrary to consciousness, experience, the real nature of things, and all rational and just deductions from them, as to require no particular refutation ; and his assertion, that " the greater part " of Mr. Locke's Essay, that is, all which relates to what he calls the " composition, abstraction, complexity, generalization, relation, &c. of " ideas, does indeed merely concern language†," I must acknowledge appears to me equally erroneous. To render that part of the Essay in any degree conformable with nature and truth it must, I imagine, be supposed not to concern signs of any kind, but the things signified by them, or substances and their attributes ; that is, neither ideas nor words, but those things which the ideas there treated of represent, and those things that are there erroneously called ideas, and are treated of as such.

28. Words must not assume the characters of ideas, or revived mental representations, or be substituted as such ; and far less those of the things or real substances they are employed to signify or express, or be substituted as such ; as reasoning on such a supposition would necessarily lead to and terminate in absurdities more gross and ridiculous than those even of an ideal universe founded on an ideal philosophy. We may be and often are deceived in our reasonings by means of words, or rather the abuse of words, from employing them without knowing their proper meanings, or the things they respectively properly signify, or by giving different and improper meanings to the same word ; but it is not to marks without meaning, or to ideas or words merely as such, or to them as signs, further than as they give true reports or are conformable to the things signified by them, but to things and facts themselves that we are to trust in our reasonings and judgments as the only stable and valid foundation of human knowledge, which, as it respects created things and inferences rationally deduced from these only, can necessarily have no truth or certainty but what it derives from the natures and relations of things.

* ΕΠΕΑ ΠΤΕΡΟΕΝΤΑ, p. 70.
† Ditto, p. 53.

29. The

29. The doctrine of the associations which take place in the thoughts of the mind, first treated of by Mr. Locke and afterwards more copiously by Dr. Hartley, which forms a very important and interesting branch of metaphysical science, has hitherto been named the doctrine of the association of IDEAS, though it might with much more propriety have been denominated the doctrine of the association of THOUGHTS, as not only ideas, but feelings, sensations, passions, and affections, the consciousnesses, perceptions, conceptions, and remembrances of things, both of such as possessing magnitude and figure are cognizable by sense, and admit of mental representation; and of such as possess not these and do not admit of being thus represented, as of arguments, reasons, judgments, volitions, relations, truths, &c. are all capable of being associated together, and generally are so in groups of two or more at a time. The associations which take place in the thoughts of the mind are originally results of corresponding associations having taken place among the causes or the objects of these thoughts, whether these associations are between internal causes or objects of thought, or between external causes or objects of thought, or between internal and external causes or objects of thought; and sometimes they are the result of the corresponding actions and associations of external causes on the mind of whose agency the mind is altogether ignorant; and when this is the case, it is not these external causes which are the objects of thought, or the immediate causes of it, but the sensations which these causes occasion on the mind.

30. Thoughts by being repeatedly excited and produced in the mind at the same time, or in immediate succession, or which are otherwise associated together by means of corresponding associations among the causes producing them, whether these causes are internal or external, become in time so linked together by that means in the mind, that one of them cannot be produced without its inducing the others, or without that which induces the one inducing the others also; so that the mind cannot think of any one of the objects of these thoughts without thinking on those of the others at the same time; and by its frequently thinking of them thus associated together this association becomes still more rivetted and permanent, and the mind acquires a greater facility, certainty, and promptitude in reviving

reviving or recalling the one by means of the other :—it is thus that agents or efficient causes are in thought as they are in the nature of things associated with their effects ; and also that the mind, from the natural association between the cause and the effect, associates its own feelings, thoughts, passions, and affections with things external to it, in such a manner that we cannot think of the one without its instantly introducing the thought of the other ; thus whatever external being or agent, real or imaginary, has been the cause of feelings of pleasure or pain, or of good or evil real or supposed with respect to us, becomes by these means so associated in our thoughts with those feelings they produced in our minds, and with the thoughts, remembrances, passions, and affections, hopes or fears, desires or aversions, &c. resulting from them, that the thought of the one cannot be produced in the mind without its instantly inducing that of the others also ; and not unfrequently without exciting at the same time feelings sometimes similar and sometimes different from those which had been originally produced by those beings, causes, or agents.   From the mind's thus habituating itself to associate the remembrances of these original feelings with their causes, and to brood over the enjoyments or sufferings thence experienced, new feelings are thus produced often more impressive and affecting than the originals, and sometimes exquisite in the extreme.   Hence the origin of those hopes and fears, desires and aversions, affection or detestation, esteem or contempt, &c. which the mind is induced to entertain for the beings, causes, or agents which are capable of generating such feelings in it as it has already experienced by their agency.   The mind also of itself, by means of its faculty of fancy, often associates together in thought objects of thought which are not so associated together in nature ; and hence imaginary hopes and fears, the dread of spectres, the supposed association of spirits with darkness, &c.   Those false and delusive judgments or opinions with respect to the associations of things are sometimes founded on false deductions from facts or phenomena, but more frequently on false intelligence, whether derived from the testimony of others or the reports of disordered senses in ourselves.

31. Every succeeding thought of the mind is a necessary result either of some new excitation with its consequent sensation, or of an association with

the

the preceding thought; and this being the case, it is probable that those trains of thoughts which have been by some supposed to be in all cases the result of corresponding trains of action in the animal spirits, may in most cases be the result merely of associations among the thoughts themselves. The supposition of there being animal spirits or a nervous fluid is however not a mere gratuitous assumption, since the existence of such a fluid, whatever its nature may be, is clearly evinced by many of the phenomena of mental action; and if sensations or ideas are ever produced in a successive train, without the mediation of thought, or of any external agency of which the mind has any knowledge — as seems to be the case of the musician, &c. as mentioned by Mr. Locke—it must be by means of such a train of action or flow of animal spirits; though these can neither be the objects nor the *immediate* causes of the trains of thoughts they produce, from the mind's being altogether unconscious of them and their mode of action, but those sensations or ideas of which they are immediate causes by the modifications they produce in the mind; and that such trains of sensations and ideas with their consequent trains of thoughts result from such causes, as the phenomena of intoxication, delirium, reveries, and dreams, give much reason to believe, there being in sleep, &c. no other operative causes, association of thoughts excepted, than such flows of animal spirits for producing these effects; external objects having in that case no influence on the mind.

32. The mind being entirely passive in the reception of feelings, and feelings themselves being entirely passive—except in as far as they are stimuli or excitements capable of producing *involuntary* mental action, or mental action even antecedent to and independent of thought and the will, if the feelings induced are acute or violent; as well as of producing thought and through it influencing the will, and thereby occasioning *voluntary* action also, in cases where the feelings are not so acute or violent, or when the effect of the first shock is a little subsided, after such as are violent or acute have been experienced—it is manifest the feelings of themselves cannot be capable of associating themselves together, or even of exciting or producing any new ones, otherwise than through the medium of thought, and through that medium only by means of acquired associations of thoughts resulting from corresponding associations, real or fanciful,

among

among their causes. It must also be evident that those sensations which are accompanied with little or no feeling, as those which form the sensible perceptions and ideas of things, from their being still more passive in their nature than even the feelings, as being altogether incapable of exciting or producing mental action otherwise than by means of thought and the will, cannot possibly associate themselves together, or be associated together in thought otherwise than by means of thought, or of corresponding associations among their external causes. When this is considered, and it is recollected that there are innumerable thoughts which are neither sensations, nor ideas as not being representable in sensation, which are not only capable of being associated together but of associating themselves together; and that ideas as not being separate independent beings but mere modifications of mind, can possess no inherent powers, and, therefore, cannot be capable of any relations, associations, or modifications, but what they owe either to corresponding relations, associations, or modes, really existing in and among their respective external causes, or to fanciful associations among those, as conceived or imagined by the mind in thought, the impropriety of denominating these associations the associations of ideas in place of the associations of thoughts must appear obvious and glaring; the doctrine of mental association being evidently much more applicable to the associations of thoughts than of ideas.

33. That faculty of the mind whereby it forms conclusions or decisions with respect to things, events, and circumstances, as deduced from the experience of its own consciousnesses, not only with regard to its own existence and identity, and the existence of its sensations, powers, and operations, but also with respect to the differences and agreements of those among themselves, on being conscious of two or more separate, distinct feelings, sensations, perceptions, ideas, thoughts, or remembrances, in itself at the same time, when such actually take place in it, whether accidentally produced by external agency, or purposely by the agency of the mind itself, and thereby the mutual relations among external things they may respectively indicate or represent, is denominated the JUDGMENT, or judging faculty of the mind; and the discernments or conclusions of the mind from the comparisons of things together are called the judgments of the mind with respect to the things compared, whether internal or external. In

comparing

comparing and judging the mind seems to be passive, except in as far as attention may be concerned, since the consciousness or discernment of the agreements or disagreements, and other relations of the sensations or thoughts among themselves, is immediate, antecedent to, and independent of thought and the will; and, if the meanings of these sensations are known, these sensations thereby become either perceptions or ideas of certain known external objects, and hence the relations of these objects or things among themselves, are also by this means immediately perceived and known, and the judgments respecting them immediately formed.

34. Judgments obtained by what has been regarded as pure intellection, or the immediate comparison and discernment of the relations of two ideas, remembrances, or thoughts, with respect to each other, without the intervention of any third, have been denominated intuitive judgments, and have been supposed to possess the highest degree of certainty human nature admits of, and to convey the completest conviction to the mind. But no judgments are purely intellectual, but those founded on the consciousness of the mind with regard to its own existence, and the existence of its sensations, its identity, powers and operations; and no judgments are intuitively obtained but those by means of PERCEPTIONS, or of sensations which result from immediate external agency or direct experience or experiment, whether accidental or intentional, on their being compared together without the intervention of any third; and are those that possess the greatest possible certainty, and afford the completest conviction, those resulting from the consciousness of the mind with respect to its own powers and operations, &c. excepted: for the comparisons and judgments formed of things external to the mind by means of ideas, or remembrances, or conceptions, are and must be in general very inaccurate and erroneous, since our ideas, remembrances, and conceptions themselves with respect to things are commonly so, as being defective and indistinct in a very great degree; and so sensible are we of this, that we seldom trust to them entirely, but in all matters of importance, and where correctness is required, appeal to direct experiment, by applying the things themselves we wish to compare together to each other, and on the perception of them so applied, correct the errors of our thoughts, ideas, remembrances, or conceptions with respect to these things and their mutual relations, and thereby form judgments with re-

K 2   gard

gard to them, which admit not of doubt or hesitation.   The mind, in these
cases of experimental perception, may without much impropriety be said
to perceive the external things themselves, on whose practical or experimental application to each other the judgments are formed, since it
actually possesses a power, partly natural and partly acquired, of applying
really or virtually the visual sensations excited and produced in it, by the
agency of the things thus applied together to the things themselves, and
that in such a manner as exactly to fit them if they are at no great distance
from the eye, and in all cases, or whatever the distance, so as to fit them apparently at least; at the same time, that the perceptions and judgments formed
by means of vision in these cases, may be and generally are corroborated
and confirmed by those formed by means of the other senses, as of touch, &c.
That intuitive experimental judgments with regard to things are actually
founded on, and are conformable to the real natures of things, the relations
and actions of things among themselves, independent of those sensations
by means of which they are perceived, sufficiently evince; and if conformable to the real natures and relations of things, they cannot possibly
be false and delusive; and hence it is that the human mind has recourse
in all doubtful cases, as the dernier resort, to immediate direct experiment,
or experimental perception, as the only criterion that safely can be relied
on, for determining the truth or falsity of its judgments.   There are numberless intuitive judgments which are not experimental, but there are
none strictly experimental which are not intuitive, or the result of immediate perception and discernment or of the bare inspection of the
things compared together, whether we regard the external objects themselves, on which the experiments are made, or the sensations and perceptions they then produce in the mind, as the things compared together; as
it in effect comes to the same purpose, since the latter must necessarily be
correspondent and conformable to the former: and hence it is that these
agreements and disagreements among the things themselves, thus discovered, are said to be manifest to sense; that we always regard the experiment as made with the intention of forming a judgment, with respect
to the natures or relations of the external objects or things themselves,
and not with respect to those of the sensations they produce in the mind;
and that we regard the judgment thereby formed, not only as respecting

ing the external objects only, but also as being founded on, and having its truth proved and ascertained by means of the external things themselves.

35. But though the knowledge thus acquired is the knowledge of things, or of the natures and relations of things, and must therefore be founded on and derived from things themselves; yet as it is merely sensitive knowledge, or only a knowledge of things as represented to the mind by the senses, such as they appear to us through the medium of our senses, and such as can be acquired by means of sense only, it must rest entirely on the evidence of sense, and of inferences rationally deduced from it; that is, things being with respect to us whatever our senses make them to be, we can have no other evidence for our knowledge with respect to them, or even for their existence, than that of sense; and on this account it becomes necessary for resolving our doubts, with regard to the natures and relations of particular things, to make a direct appeal to the senses, by presenting the things themselves to their inspection in every dubious case where it can be done; that is, to have recourse to experiment and experimental perception, as an effectual and infallible means of ascertaining and determining the existence and natures of these things relative to us, and their relations among themselves as they appear to us, since the consequence must be that every one whose senses are in a sound state, who witness the experiment must necessarily draw the same conclusion from it; and therefore such a conclusion as being founded on common sense, the only test we as individuals have for the fidelity of our senses and the justness of our perceptions, cannot be denied, and which neither requires nor admits of any other proof, since it is impossible there can be any thing more evident to prove it by. It is on experimental proof that all our knowledge is founded, and it is from it that all other kinds of proof must necessarily result, and necessarily derive all the validity they possess; that knowledge and those truths respecting the mind, founded on immediate consciousness only, excepted. Experimental intuitive judgments are the only axioms, the only first truths, and fundamental principles on which all just reasoning and all science is established and rests; even those with respect to the mind not excepted, as being founded on reiterated experience, which is allowed to be experiment.

36. All

36.   All human knowledge, except what respects the mind itself, which knowledge is very limited and scanty indeed, has its origin and foundation in the natures and mutual relations of external things, as discovered and perceived through sense, by means of experience, observation, and reasons; and all our enquiries, except those concerning the mind itself, have a reference to, and terminate in, the natures, or powers, properties, and relations of things external and extrinsical to the mind; and in our successful investigations of these, those respecting the mind excepted, does all our real knowledge consist.   For, knowledge is only the perceiving, understanding and remembering of the beings, natures, and relations of things; and thereby the modes and applications of them best adapted for obtaining by their means such ends as may be intended, or for giving to rational beings that dominion over them whereby they may be subjected to their use, and rendered subservient to their purposes.   Though the mind discovers and perceives the beings, natures, and relations of things, only through the instrumentality of sense, or of its sensations, and ideas, yet knowledge consists not in the discovery of the natures and relations of ideas, or in the perception of the agreement or disagreement, connexion or repugnancy of ideas, but in that of the natures and relations of the things of which they are the mental indications or representations;—not in that of the instrument, medium, or means, whereby the natures and mutual relations of things are discovered, but in the discovery of the natures and mutual relations of the things themselves; not in the discovery of the agreement or disagreement of the signs, but in the discovery of the agreement or disagreement, &c. of the things signified by them.   It is not the discovery of the length or breadth of a sensation or an idea, or the ratio, or proportion of one idea to others, or the moment or impulse of ideas, or their elective attractions, that the mathematician, arithmetician, mechanic, and chemist have in view, in their respective investigations and experiments, but it is the discovery of the lengths or breadths, ratios and proportions, moments, and attractions of the things themselves, on which the experiments are made, by applying them to each other, or by bringing them within the sphere of each other's action, for the express purpose of ascertaining these facts in particular, as well as their natures and mutual relations in other respects.

37. Even those judgments, opinions, and conceptions, which have been

called

called ideas of reflection, from having been formed on reflection from facts retained in the memory, have their origin and source in the natures of things, and not in the mind, since the mind of itself is altogether incapable of producing any of those simple sensations by means of which these facts were first perceived and ascertained from which these judgments, &c. are deduced.

38. The mind, however, is capable when excited by motives of exerting faculties of its own, whereby knowledge may be obtained that is new to it, and which could not otherwise have been obtained; but though this knowledge is discovered by the exertions and faculties of the mind, it is notwithstanding founded on the natures and mutual relations of things, and real knowledge only in as far as it is conformable to these. But though it has its foundations in the natures of things, it may yet be said to be, in a certain degree, the production of human invention or mental ingenuity; especially if it is the discovery of scientific principles, or of modes of practice, which before either did not or were not known to exist in nature;--as the conceptions and inventions of a chronometer, steam engine, spinning mill, new form of government, &c. That these conceptions and inventions, though they may, in some respects, be regarded as creatures of the human mind, are yet founded on nature, or the known mutual relations of things, must be evident, when it is considered that they consist merely in the discovery of methods of combining and applying things and powers already known in manners different from those hitherto used, and which are effectual for producing the ends proposed. It is said of Brindley the engineer, that when he had any new project in contemplation, he used to keep his bed for some days, with the windows of his chamber darkened, that his attention might not be diverted from thinking and contriving in what manner it might be accomplished or carried into execution. In this case, as having no opportunity of making actual experiments, by means of external things suited to his purpose, he had evidently nothing to have recourse to, but the thoughts of his own mind; and of these it is evident that none could be of use to him, but remembrances and recollectons of the natures or mutual relations of external things or substances, and of the various ways in which the powers they respectively possess operate; that is, that in this case he must necessarily have recourse to

his

his previous knowledge of things and the natures of things, since without knowledge of things it must be utterly impossible for him to effect the end or object proposed to be effected by their means, and that with it nothing further is requisite for him, than to discover the most proper methods of modifying and combining them, and of applying those powers they possess for producing of that end; so that even in this case, where no immediate recourse is had, or can be had, to external things, yet the whole originates in and is founded on them and their mutual relations, and the discoveries made or knowledge thus acquired is real or not, as it shall be found in actual experiment to be comformable or not to the real natures of things, or as it may or may not prove when reduced to practice to answer the end proposed.

39. Since all human knowledge is founded on, and respects only natural things with their relations and inferences thence deduced; and since the natures and relations of things can be learned only by means of experience and observation, and rational deductions from these, it must be evident that human beings can possess no knowledge, but what is derived either directly or indirectly from experiment. It is indeed to experience we are ultimately indebted for all our knowledge, since without it sense, reason, and existences, could be of no avail:—a child acquires knowledge, as well as facility and expertness in different motions, actions, and operations, gradually as it advances in life, partly from its own experience, and partly from that of others, by means of imitation, instruction, &c. and in time from its own intellectual resources, or rational deductions from what knowledge it has experimentally acquired. A child, after having experienced pleasurable and painful sensations, and not sooner, as before experiencing them it could have no conception of either, and far less of their future effects with respect to it, necessarily acquires, from the beneficial and injurious effects with respect to it experienced by their means, a liking and desire for the former, and an aversion and dread of the latter; and on the good and evil thus experienced, and the perception of the causes producing them, does the regulation of its future conduct in life very much, if not entirely depend. Were human beings to come into this world full grown, and with the faculties both of body and mind in the most perfect and mature state, they would yet, for want of experience and practice be

mere

mere infants, with respect to knowledge and judgment; at the same time that they would be much worse qualified for acquiring knowledge by these means, and much more liable to injure themselves and each other, from the many erroneous judgments which in that case would necessarily be unavoidable;—it is on experience and practice, and on knowledge acquired by that means, that maturity of judgment, if the senses and mental faculties are entire and sound, must necessarily in a very great degree depend.

40. For the purpose of disclosing our judgments with distinctness to others, we are obliged to make use of language, that is of certain *artificial* combinations and arrangements of certain *artificial* signs, to which, by common consent for mutual advantage, certain particular meanings have been appropriated and annexed, and of certain *artificial* modes of combinations and arrangements invented and adopted for the purpose whereby these signs are formed into words and sentences, and thereby become capable of expressing the meanings of our thoughts, so as to enable us to communicate them to each other in a manner sufficiently intelligible. The signs whereby thoughts, or rather the meanings of thoughts, are rendered audible or visible, and thereby in some respects objects of sense, are either certain articulate sounds, or certain written characters, or marks, denominated letters, and, on being properly combined and arranged, words and sentences, which have no *natural* connexion either with the thoughts, with the things to which the thoughts refer, or with the meanings of the thoughts they are designed to signify.

41. Words have been arranged and divided into two classes; viz. 1st. Those that are significant of themselves, as having each an independant determinate meaning. And 2dly. those that are not significant of themselves, or which have no meaning, but when combined with words significant of themselves. The words comprehended in the first of these classes are signs of things, beings, or entities; that is of substances, whether mental or corporeal, and of their attributes and relations. It is things themselves, or real existences, that are expressed or signified by them, or that are to be understood, as the real and only proper signification, meaning, and import of these signs, words, or names, and not ideas, or representations of things in the mind;— they are the signs or names of the things

L   signified

signified or named by them, and not of the sensations or ideas whereby these things were discovered, or are mentally represented; for particular perceptions, ideas, remembrances, and judgments, as such, have not names, and are, in language, discovered only and distinguished from each other by the names of the particular external things perceived, remembered, and judged of by their means, and which they severally indicate or represent.

42. Those doctrines, which make significant words, or the names of things, whether substance or attribute, contrary to compact, their original intent and real meaning, the signs of IDEAS, and not the signs of THINGS, by thus substituting ideas for things, lead to reasonings, which being founded on false principles cannot but be productive of false conclusions, and such as must necessarily inevitably terminate in the total exclusion of being from the universe.

As not treating of grammar, I can have no occasion to take further notice of the words comprehended under the second of these classes than to observe, that though they may perhaps have been originally significant of themselves, or may be derived from words significant of themselves*, (though etymological evidence, far more satisfactory than what has hitherto been adduced, may be required for establishing this opinion) it can answer no good purpose to suppose that they are, on that account, as used at present significant of themselves; especially since they could not now be rendered such without altering their nature, and destroying their meaning, intent, and use.

A judgment expressed in words is called a proposition; a proposition, therefore, is a sentence expressive of some judgment of the mind, with regard either to the relations, or the natures and attributes of certain things, or to the manner in which a thing may be made or done, as either experimentally discovered and perceived, or as conceived by the mind. As it is necessary to compare two things, at least, together, for the discovery and ascertainment of the attribute or attributes, or of their mutual relations, concerning which the particular judgments are formed, so it is necessary in expressing that judgment, or in forming it into a proposition, to make use of two words or names; the one expressive of the thing or things, the attri-

---

* See ΕΠΕΑ ΠΤΕΡΟΕΝΤΑ, or Diversions of Purley.

butes

butes or relations of which to certain other things, have been discovered and ascertained, and the other of the attribute or relation thus ascertained. These are called the terms of the proposition, the first of these being called the subject, and the other the predicate of the proposition; the first being that of which the other is the attribute or relation, as predicated, or affirmed and denied by the proposition. In order to understand the meaning of a proposition, it must be necessary to understand the meanings of the terms or words of which the proposition is formed. The determination of the precise meanings of terms or words not understood, or imperfectly understood, by means of other words or terms, the meanings of which are accurately known, is that in which definition consists; and definition, or the defining of the terms of a proposition, when definable, is absolutely necessary for its being understood by the persons to whom it is addressed, when these persons are unacquainted with the meanings or significations of these terms. Since the simple consciousnesses, feelings, sensations, passions, affections, and operations of the mind, and perceptions and ideas of external things, by means of sense, or of mental sensations, cannot possibly be known, without being experienced, it must be evident the terms expressing or signifying these, cannot possibly be defined, or have their meanings determined by means of other terms or words, there being no way of making these terms intelligible to those who never experienced the mental feelings, perceptions, and operations signified by them, but by exciting and producing these feelings, perceptions, &c. in their minds, by means of their respective proper causes or objects. After the meanings of the terms expressive of the simple sensations, &c. are understood, terms expressive of combinations of these, or of compound sensations, perceptions, &c. may be defined, or have their meanings determined by means of those expressive of the simple sensations, &c. of which they are compounded. For the discovery of the indefinability of terms expressive of simple sensations, &c. and for the important distinction between those terms that are definable, and those that are not, the world is indebted to Mr. Locke. A definition of any definable term is only a description and enumeration of the essential powers and properties, or attributes and relations of the particular thing signified by that term, by means of other terms known to be respectively expressive of these several powers and properties, &c. Definitions of mo-

tion,

tion, place, cause, &c. are only descriptions of what we have experienced or perceived from the motions of things, and their relative situations, &c. which descriptions are intelligible to those only who have also experienced and perceived motion, &c. in things; and to those they will be intelligible, though they may never have perceived the precise modes of motion, &c. then described.

43. REASON, as a faculty, or as the reasoning power of the mind, is that faculty whereby the mind investigates and discovers existences, substances, powers, properties, modes, relations, truths or facts, events, and circumstances, that were before unknown, either by means of direct experiments purposely made, or by means of deducing inferences or conclusions which are necessary results from existences, truths, and circumstances previously known. This it effects by properly selecting, arranging, methodizing, and comparing together the several objects suited to that purpose; and in these operations it brings the consciousnesses, remembrances, perceptions, and fancies of the mind to its aid. This is a faculty of the first importance, since it is to it we are indebted for the greatest part of our knowledge, and since without it, we could not possibly regulate our conduct in life, or be capable of forming or of executing any design for the protection or preservation of our existence, or the promoting of our well being or happiness, for the prevention of evil, or the attainment of good, or, indeed, for the attainment of any end or object whatever. Without it, consciousness, sensations, and external objects or existences could avail us nothing, since, nevertheless, we must in that case necessarily be altogether devoid of perception, and incapable of distinguishing one external object from another, and, indeed, be altogether ignorant of there being any such existences, as must be manifest from what was advanced in Essay I. in which perception is proved to be the result of a process of reasoning. This faculty, like others, improves much by exercise, and, happily, by means of culture, is capable of improvement in a superior degree. It is the improvement of this faculty, or the attainment of the right use of reason, that is the aim and object of the science of logic; and it is on the knowledge of its admitting of being improved, that it is founded.

44. This science, which must have originated in reason uninfluenced by art, professes to investigate and ascertain principles from which it deduces
unerring

unerring rules for the exercise and application of human reason in the successful investigation and attainment of truth, knowledge, utility, and happiness, or to instruct human beings how to think, to judge, and to reason, with accuracy and precision; and hence it has been represented as the grand engine for the discovery, the improvement, and the perfection of all the other sciences, and for the proper and beneficial regulation of human conduct. But it has not hitherto attained to such a state of perfection as to give it any just claim to these high pretensions. The systems of logic proposed and taught by the ancients, and adopted in the schools, if we may judge from their effects, have had a tendency the very reverse of what they professed, or to that mentioned above; for, as serving no other purpose than to bewilder, perplex, and mislead the judgment, they produced nothing but disputations without meaning and without end from which nothing useful or valuable was to be learned; and those of the moderns have been too much contaminated with the logical doctrines and the ideal philosophy of antiquity to afford just conceptions with regard to the powers and properties of the human mind, and the real natures of things, or with regard to those things by means of which, and about which we reason, to admit of their attaining that degree of perfection they otherwise might have done. The boasted and highly celebrated rules of antiquity for the attainment of the right use of reason, and which have been represented as unerring guides to truth, knowledge, and wisdom, are altogether inadequate to the ends they are intended to answer, as not being deduced from just principles founded on nature and reason, as pretending to define what is undefinable, to deduce realities from phantoms, or from abstract general ideas having no real existence in nature, and to reason justly by the mere sylogistic arrangement of terms.

45. To discover the several sorts or kinds, or genera and species, into which the Author of Nature has distributed and arranged natural things, as well as the several individuals which are comprehended under each particular genus, or species, respectively, has ever been one great object of human reason; and in the discovery of these, and the appropriating of names to each, as discovered, does the science of ontology properly consist; that is, in the discovery both of these qualities of things, which are
general

general or common to many particulars, whereby they are connected into
one genus or species, and of those qualities of them which are particular
and distinctive, or whereby they are distinguished from each other or
characterised as individuals.   The ancient metaphysicians and logicians, in
this case, as in others, inverted the natural and only successful method of
investigation, in endeavouring to determine the genera and species of
things previous to accurate experimental discoveries of their several
powers, properties, and relations, as individuals; and in inculcating that
the qualities of particular things are only deducible and discoverable from
genera and species; or that an acquaintance with the genera and species
of things, is necessary before an acquaintance with the qualities of particular
things can be acquired:—the consequence of which has been, that genera
and species have often been fancifully arranged before those qualities, on
the generality of which the arrangements into genera and species are
founded and determined, have been discovered or ascertained in these particular cases.   Agreeable to this principle, except where the distinctive
qualities were so strongly marked and palpable that they could not be
overlooked, they arranged things into genera and species on very slight and
erroneous grounds, as on supposed analogies having no foundation in nature,
ascribing to particular things, previous to any real proof of these particular
things being actually possessed of these attributes from any superficial or
apparent analogy, all the attributes they attached to the genus to which
they supposed them respectively to belong; in place of accurately and
experimentally investigating and ascertaining the qualities of things,
whereby they might be correctly arranged into genera and species, and
each justly referred to the particular genus and species to which they
respectively properly belong.   On this unsound and flimsy foundation,
however, does the whole fabric, the stupendous superstructure of the
ancient dialectic and school philosophy, the fruitful source of so much
error, absurdity, and dispute, in the world, rest.   " The Platonists consi-
" dering science as something ascertained, definite, and steady," says
Mr. Harris (*Treatises*, p. 341) " would admit nothing to be its object,
" which was vague, indefinite, and passing.   For this reason they excluded
" all individuals, or objects of sense, and, as Ammonius expresses it, raised
                                                    " themselves

" themselves in their contemplations from beings particular to beings
" universal, and which from their own nature were eternal and durable."

" Consonant to this, was the advice of Plato, with respect to the progress of
" our speculations and enquiries, to descend from those higher genera which
" include many subordinate species, down to the lowest rank of species
" those which include only individuals. But here it was his opinion that
" our enquiries should stop, AND AS TO INDIVIDUALS LET THEM WHOLLY
" ALONE; because of these there could not possibly be any science."

46. It is on the same principle and the same authorities that the author
of a treatise lately published on Logic, in a work deservedly in high repute
(*Ency. Britannica*), informs us " that all the aims of human reason may
" be reduced to these two: First, to rank things under those universal
" ideas to which they truly belong; and, secondly, to ascribe to them
" their several attributes and properties in consequence of that distribution.
" In the sciences our reason is employed chiefly about universal truths, it
" being by means of them alone that the bounds of human knowlege are
" enlarged. Hence the division of things into various classes, called other-
" wise genera and species. For these universal ideas being set up as the
" representations of many particular things, whatever is affirmed of them
" may also be affirmed of all the individuals to which they belong. The
" steps then by which we proceed are manifestly these; First, we refer the
" object under consideration to some general idea or class of things; we
" then recollect the several attributes of that general idea; and lastly,
" ascribe all these attributes to the present object. The determining the
" genera and species of things is, as we have said, one exercise of human
" reason; and here we find, that this exercise is the first in order, and pre-
" vious to the other, which consists in ascribing to them their powers, pro-
" perties, and relations." The principles of logic above unfolded being to
be found in every treatise on that science, my only reasons for selecting
them from this in preference to others are the peculiar prespicuity of expression with which they are developed, and my wish to delineate them in the
most distinct and advantageous points of view. That these doctrines however, notwithstanding the very favourable and plausible appearance they
here assume from the very clear methodical manner in which they are exhibited, are erroneous, nugatory, and delusive, no doubt I imagine can possibly

bly be entertained, since even a very slight observation of natural things and natural phenomena, or of those created things which form nature and compose the universe, must necessarily convey entire conviction to every sound and rational mind not only of those things being arranged into kinds or sorts, or genera and species, and that not according to the ideas or or fancies of man, or to the names he affixes to them, but according to their respective characteristic and distinctive qualities, in conformity to the will of their Creator in endowing them with these qualities; but, also, that the genera and species according to which things are thus arranged in nature, cannot possibly be discovered otherwise than by means of an accurate investigation of those qualities in the *individuals*, on which these natural arrangements into *genera and species* are founded and constituted.

47. The very imperfect classification of individuals and of their qualities by this erroneous mode of investigation and procedure, they denominated induction; and the propositions expressive of the genera and species, and of their common or general qualities, they denominated universal propositions. This fundamental and essential error in the mode of investigation is not the only one imputable to this science. There seem to be many others, among which the following in particular may be enumerated, viz. The representing of those *common or general qualities* under which the individuals of each species or genus is comprehended, and which characterises each species or genus and distinguishes it from others, not only as *ideas* but as *abstract existences.*—2. The representing all the conclusions of reason, and intuitive reasoning in particular, as deduced from the comparing of *ideas* only.—3. The representing of these assumed abstract general ideas, or logical universals, and the truths deduced from them, or more justly from those general qualities for which they are substituted, as truths *absolute, immutable, necessary,* and-*eternal*, having no dependence whatever either on created things or on the Creator of things.—4. The representing the discovery of these general qualities as the result of *pure intellection*—and 5. That it is on *these* that all science is founded, and of *these* that all science is constituted:—these are fundamental and fatal errors in all the systems of logic. That there are no such existences as *abstract general ideas,* and that it is not on the comparing of *ideas* so much as on the comparing of those *things* of which they are the signs that conclusions are formed and science established,

established, has already been attempted to be proved, and it is hoped not without success; and that there are no absolute, immutable, independent truths, necessary and eternal, of which we have any knowledge—whether of the kinds supposed above or of any other kind; as when it is asserted, *Ency, Brit.*, article *Metaphysics*, " that every proposition of which the contrary " is clearly and distinctly perceived to be impossible is a necessary truth, " as well as an eternal; that some truths are necessary and eternal, others " contingent and temporary. Of the first kind is the proposition, that " all the three angles of a plain triangle are equal to two right angles; " of the second, that the world exists.---The first depends not upon time, " will, or any thing else; and the Supreme Being himself could not make " it false: whereas he who created the world could annihilate it, and thus " reduce what is now a truth to a falsehood,"—will it is presumed be readily allowed, when it is considered that it is not possible to conceive what can make these truths necessary if it is neither the will of the Supreme Being nor the natures of things; and that if they actually were independent, immutable, necessary, and eternal, the Deity could not be the first and only cause of all things.

48. TRUTH, whether as perceived by means of sense or natural signs, or as expressed in propositions by means of words or artificial signs, may be defined to be THE AGREEMENT OR CONFORMITY OF THE REPRESENTATION WITH THE THINGS OR EVENTS REPRESENTED. If by the eternity or necessity of truth, or of truths, the eternity and necessity of the truths expressed by identical propositions only is meant, as that a man is a man, or that a man always was and will be a man; this is not only mere trifling, as such propositions, from the subject and predicate being identical or the same, only assert that a thing is what it is, and prove nothing; but it is also unfounded, for the truth thus expressed though a truth while that thing exists, is yet not absolute or eternal, and could not possibly be so, unless that thing were of itself independent, absolute, and eternal; as its duration must necessarily depend on the duration of that thing to which it refers. Those propositions which have been supposed expressive of abstract and eternal truths signify only that it is a truth that such and such relations subsist between certain things; as that all men are mortal, that the three angles of every plain triangle are equal to two right angles, that

milk of all kinds is apparently white to human beings, &c. or are expressive only of the truth of relations, or of certain mental inferences thence deduced; and, when these propositions are not identical as they often are, and these relations real and not nominal and fanciful only, the truths they affirm with regard to these relations, and to the inferences deduced from them, can be truths only as having a reference to those things of which these are the relations, and concerning which the inferences are made; and if created things and rational beings had not existed, these truths—though the non-existence of them has been maintained to be not only impossible, but inconceivable, even though all things were annihilated—could never have existed: as, in that case, these relations and those mental inferences from them on which they depend, and in the just representation of which they consist, could not have existed. While things remain the same, these truths must likewise remain the same; and if things were necessary and eternal, they would be so also; but the existence of truths without the existence of those things with regard to which, and to which only they are truths—or the existence of truths with respect to nothing or nonentity—is in itself impossible, and in supposition absurd. The doctrine then of ABSTRACT TRUTHS is necessarily unfounded and erroneous, as well as that of ABSTRACT IDEAS, it being as impossible for a truth to subsist of itself, or as a necessary, eternal, independent being, as it is for the mind to form an idea or mental representation by means of abstraction of the co-existence of qualities repugnant and destructive of each other, as that of an abstract idea of a triangle, or of what is neither oblique nor rectangle, equilateral, equicrural, or scalenon, &c.

49. We have no knowledge of any ABSOLUTE impossibility, or any ABSOLUTE necessity, or of any other impossibilities or necessities than those resulting from the natures of things, and therefore RELATIVE, or such as have a relation to created things. We cannot even form a conception of absolute necessity, or of absolute impossibility; and it is absurd to speak of the absolute natural impossibility or necessity, or of an absolute impossibility or necessity from the nature of the thing itself:—absolute and natural being repugnant and incompatible. The impossibility and necessity in every case we are acquainted with results from the nature of things, and our knowledge of them from our knowledge of that nature:—it is experience
that

that teaches us that a thing cannot be otherwise, as well as that it is so. Possibility and impossibility are not, as has been asserted, fixed natures independent of the Deity. Impossibility and necessity are not independent beings distinct from substance, but mere attributes or relations of things with respect to each other; or, as conceived by us and expressed in propositions as truths, mere inferences from facts, or from the natures of things, as discovered by observation and experience. It is in every case the IMPOSSIBILITY that imposes the NECESSITY; the NATURE OF THINGS that imposes the IMPOSSIBILITY; and the AUTHOR OF NATURE that imposes on created things THOSE NATURES from which these impossibilities result:— so that the Supreme Being is the original and real cause of the possibilities and impossibilities in nature, as well as of every thing else; and hence the existence of these supposed eternal, immutable, universal, and necessary truths, must depend on His will, as " he that created the world could an- " nihilate it, and thus reduce what is now a truth to a falsehood." Every proposition which is a necessary truth from the contrary being impossible, owes that necessity to the impossibility, and the impossibility to the nature of things; as propositions which affirm the impossibility of the existence and non-existence of the same thing at the same time, or the impossibility of any thing being formed of qualities repugnant, incompatible, and destructive of each other. All propositions which both affirm and deny the same attributes, or which affirm incompatible attributes of the same subject, must, as having a reference to created things, or to nature and the natures of things, necessarily be false, and those affirming the contrary necessarily true, since that which is asserted in the former of these is not only not conformable to, but is contrary to the nature of things, and therefore necessarily in the nature of things impossible, and consequently false; and since the latter proposition, or that expressive of the falsity of the former or of this impossibility in nature, must, from the falsity of the former, necessarily be true; and hence, in contradictory propositions, if the one is false, the other is necessarily true. The truth of this last proposition, however, or the impossibility on which it rests, is also founded merely on the nature of things, as not being an absolute impossibility, but an impossibility in nature only. It is said, indeed, that whatever implies a contradiction is *absolutely* impossible. But in what can this contradiction consist? surely in nothing but in the affirming and

denying

denying of the same attribute in the same subject; but a contradictory proposition, or such as does so, can have no meaning, the opposing affirmations necessarily ballancing and destroying each other; as when it is asserted that a power acts and acts not at the same time. It is not in the contradictions which the affirmations in the proposition imply that the impossibility consists, but in the impossibility of reconciling the attributes or qualities predicated of the things or subjects with the natures or the attributes or qualities of the things or subjects themselves; or of imposing on things attributes which are incompatible with their natures, which nature has denied them, and which therefore in the nature of things is impossible; as the attribute of non-existence to what actually exists, of the same body moving in opposite directions at the same time, &c.—that which is impossible of itself must be so of its own nature, and if it is of its own nature, it must be so *relatively* to that nature only, and not *absolutely*. If there actually are any such existences as abstract or absolute truths, they are not in nature, and we of course, who have no knowledge but what is derived from nature, are and necessarily must be entirely ignorant of them. But that there are actually none such, we have the strongest reasons for believing, since if such did exist as eternal, immutable and independent beings, the Deity, as was formerly observed, could not be the first and only cause of all things.

50. The great, and indeed almost the sole aim and object of all systems of Logic has been first, the classification of things, or rather, according to their notions, of ideas, by means of inductions more or less perfect, into genera and species. Secondly, the forming of propositions expressive of the generality of those qualities, real or supposed, which characterise each genus or species thus formed, or of the specific qualities which are general or common to all and each of the individuals composing each species, and of the generic qualities which are so to all and each of the species composing each genus, and which on that account they denominate logical universals or general propositions. And thirdly, from these general propositions, to draw conclusions with regard to particulars. It is manifest from this statement, that this mode of reasoning, and the systems of Logic established on it, is founded upon the two following principles, viz. First, that individuals possessing the qualities characteristic of any particular species, or of any

particular

particular genus, and at the same time those which distinguish them from all other species or genera, may justly be regarded as belonging to, and being included in that particular species or genus. And secondly, that from the *generality* of the generic and specific characters or qualities, it must necessarily follow, if the classification has been accurate and just, that whatever is affirmed or denied, or in the language of Logicians predicated of any genus, may with entire confidence and truth be predicated of all and each of the species of that genus; and that whatever is predicated of any species may be predicated of all and each of the individuals comprehended in that species.

51. It must also be sufficiently manifest that this mode of reasoning, and the system of logic founded on it, which consists merely in classification, and inferences thence deduced, cannot possibly possess any validity or utility, but what it must derive from the accuracy and justness of the classifications; and, if the principle and manner of investigation has been erroneous, or the induction partial and defective, whereby the classification has been formed, that very little reliance can in most cases with safety be placed in the conclusions deduced by its means. A knowledge, however, of the genera and species, and of the characteristics of each, into which all the things in nature have been arranged by their Creator, in as far as it can be acquired, by as comprehensive an induction of facts established on indubitable intuitive evidence, or actual direct experiment, as nature and humanity will admit of, and the affixing of appropriated names to each species and genus thus accurately ascertained, is an object of great importance, as it would not only confer a very great degree of validity on this mode of reasoning, in as far as it extends, and render its deductions in most cases conclusive; but also be of great utility in other respects, since on being informed that such a thing belongs to such a genus or species, we would, in fact, by that means be informed in the most concise manner, and in that which is most easily remembered, that the thing has been found on observation and actual experiment to be possessed of those attributes, or characters which mark or distinguish that particular genus or species; whence among other advantages we would be enabled to profit the more, and the easier of the discoveries of others: besides, the knowledge of certain attributes being general or common to many individuals

viduals is one great source of the association of our thoughts—that in any one thing which happens to be the immediate object of our thoughts that is common to it with others, naturally recalling to our own minds one or more of these others, and thereby their respective specific and other properties; while this kind of knowledge likewise affords in many cases, where positive proof is not to be obtained, presumptive proofs, with respect to the natures and relations of things, which if they do not amount to perfect certainty yet approach so near to it, as to carry along with them the very highest degree of probability.   The attainment of knowledge of this kind with accuracy and precision, is, however, attended with considerable difficulty, especially with respect to the extremes or limits of the different genera and species, from their seeming at these limits or near their respective terminations to intermingle together, and to pass from one kind of species or genus to another, almost insensibly or without exhibiting any characteristic differences that can easily be perceived: but, except at their extreme limits, they may in general readily be distinguished from each other; and in general those which are most comprehensive, or which contain the greatest number of species or of individuals, are the most distinguishable and the easiest ascertained, being those which form the great classes or divisions of nature.   These the ancients attempted to ascertain, and called them categories, or predicaments. The categories, according to Plato were five, viz. substance, identity, diversity, motion, and rest;—according to Aristotle they were ten in number, viz. substance, quantity, quality, relation, action, passion, where, when, situation, and clothing. Mr. Locke, with much better judgment, reduced the categories to three; or resolved all created things, or all nature into the three classes of substances, modes, and relations. Some have thought that these do not include time, space, and number; but this is a mistake. This enumeration of categories, appears to me, however, to be imperfect, in not including properties of things, as there are properties, I imagine, which are not comprehensible under any of these three classes or categories;—thus it is an essential property of a triangle, whatever the mode or kind of triangle, or kind of substance of which it is formed, and without relation or reference to any thing else, to have three sides and three angles, and no more; and that quality possessed by material substance of reacting, or of acting when acted upon, is neither

a suba substance, nor a mode of being, nor a relation, nor a cause, except only when an act, and when not an act, or in a latent or dormant state, it exists in the matter not as a power, but as a property only; a property in the matter of reacting, or of acting when acted upon.

52. Though the mode of reasoning mentioned above is that which has almost entirely occupied and engrossed the attention, study, and exertions of logicians, and is that on which they have founded their systems of logic; yet there are several different kinds of reasoning besides this, and all of them like this, founded on experience or experiment. All reasoning being consequential, all the different kinds of it must necessarily proceed upon the same principle, that of drawing just inferences or conclusions by necessary consequence, or some other connected relation from facts and phenomena; and the professed aim and object of all is the discovering of truth, knowledge, and utility. Reasoning may be addressed either to the understanding, or to the passions, or to the prejudices, &c. of mankind. It is that addressed to the understanding only, that comes within the province of logic; the others belong to rhetoric. As all the various kinds of reasoning proceed upon the same principle, they can differ from each other only in the differences of the kinds of evidence on which they are founded, and the manner and means according to which they are conducted. Among the various different kinds of reasoning, the following may be enumerated, viz.

1st. Reasoning founded on the evidence of consciousness, with respect to self existence, identity, &c. 2d. Reasoning founded on the common sense of mankind, with regard to the justness of their particular perceptions, — as explained in Essay I. of this — 3d. Reasoning founded on intuitive experimental evidence, or direct experimental appeals, without the aid of intermedia, to the discriminating and judging faculty of the mind through the medium of the senses --- it is reasoning resting on the above kinds of evidence only, that can justly be regarded as demonstrative, as it is these kinds of evidences only that impress entire conviction on the mind. 4th. Reasoning on intuitive evidence, which does not amount to demonstration as not resting on actual indubitable experiment, but on the comparing together, without the aid of intermedia, ideas, remembrances, thoughts, &c. 5th. Reasoning founded on the evidence of analo-

analogies, and similitudes real or supposed. 6th. Reasoning founded on the evidence of authorities or of human testimony. 7th. Reasoning founded on the evidence of facts, or propositions granted, or admitted to be true whether they are actually so or not. 8th. Reasoning founded on the evidence afforded by nature, with regard to that regular and undeviating mode of operation and succession of events so conspicuous in the works of nature which we denominate the laws or course of nature. 9th. Reasoning founded on the evidence of assumed first principles, axioms, postulates, or propositions, not resting on actual experiments, or on consciousnesses. 10th. Reasoning founded on the evidence of first principles, axioms, maxims, postulates, or propositions, resting on actual correct experiments or consciousnesses. 11th. Reasoning founded on the evidence of first principles, maxims, axioms, propositions, or of facts and statements, the contrary of which imply a contradiction, and which are evidently, as experimentally and rationally ascertained from the natures of things, impossible in nature. 12th. Reasoning founded on fanciful, false, or sophistical evidence. — &c.

53. It is manifest that the evidence of the kinds, Nos. 8th, 10th, & 11th. is in reality that of actual experiment or experience or consciousness—the knowledge of the course of nature being founded on experience, and these first principles, maxims, axioms, or propositions, being expressive only of the unvarying results of fundamental experiments and consciousnesses, it consequently follows that the reasonings and conclusions founded on them, if accurate and just, must amount to actual demonstration and be conclusive.

54. The different manners of reasoning are all included under the three following kinds, viz. First, INTUITIVE reasoning, or reasoning by means either of a direct appeal to consciousness, and the common sense of mankind according to the signification of that phrase proposed in Essay I. of this; or by means of a direct experimental appeal through the medium of the senses to the discriminating and judging faculty of the mind. Second, INDUCTIVE reasoning, or the inferring of generals from particulars; or that that quality, law, or mode of action, &c. which has been found on observation and experiment to hold in every particular case in which it has been sought for, and that without any exception, though the cases have been

numerous

numerous and various, is general or common to all cases of that kind whatever. This generality, however, is only an assumed generality, the induction on which it is founded being necessarily limited and partial, it being impossible for us, from the incompetency of our powers and opportunities, and the wondrous variety of things in nature, to obtain indubitable experimental proof with regard to each particular case; and hence the conclusions thus drawn or inferred, though in most cases admitting of the highest probability, do not amount altogether to certainty. This kind of reasoning is manifestly founded on the former—that of intuitive—generalization being only an inference by induction from observation and experiment; and this kind of reasoning or these conclusions are the more to be relied upon, the more general the inductions on which they are founded. And third, DEDUCTIVE reasoning, or reasoning by deducing necessary or unavoidable consequences, whether by means of intermedia or not, from phenomena, facts, or propositions, known or admitted, and from these forming conclusions or judgments. This kind of reasoning is evidently founded on either, or on both of the two former. All the other modes or manners of reasoning are comprehended under and are only different varieties or species of these; as reasoning analytically and synthetically, à priori and à posteriori, directly or apodictically, and apogogically or indirectly, reasoning by dilemma, &c. or as applied for different purposes, as for the tracing of causes from their effects and of effects from their causes, or for the investigation and discovery of causes or powers with their various modes or laws of action from known events or facts, and of facts and events from known causes or powers and their known modes or laws or action; as well for deducing inferences or conclusions from maxims, propositions, and arguments, &c. and the arguments used in these different kinds and manners of reasoning may be thrown into different forms, as either into that of syllogism, or into what may be called that of reasoning by the immediate consequence.

55. The word reason admits of different significations, as being employed to express other meanings besides that of the reason, or reasoning faculty of the mind. The original and real meaning of it as referred to things, and not as a faculty of the mind, seems to be relation:—and hence conformity to reason can mean only, with propriety, conformity or nature, or to the natural order and relations of things; and to act agreeably to reason, to act

agreeably to nature, or to the natures or relations of things; and, according to this meaning of the term, the reasoning power, or faculty of the mind, can, with propriety, mean only that power of the mind whereby it selects the proper objects or things, and brings them together, for the purpose of comparison and observation, and thence discovers their mutual relations. So that reasoning, or to reason concerning things, can signify merely to investigate and discover the natures or mutual relations of things, as those of agreement or disagreement, connection or repugnancy, proportion, cause, and effect, &c. and, in reality, the truths or facts discovered and ascertained by means of these investigations, or of reasoning, are nothing but relations, or the qualities of certain things relative to others, and the inferred existence from the relations or effects thus discovered of things before unknown to exist.   But the term reason is used not only as expressive of a power or faculty of the mind, and as expressive of the mutual relations of things, but also as expressive of a cause necessarily resulting from these relations; and hence the reason of a thing, or of the thing, according to this last meaning of the term, signifies that the thing, or effect, is the necessary result or consequence of the then circumstances, or of the mutual relations of the things producing it, the meaning of the word reason in such cases being generally synonimous with that of cause, and of the word thing, with that of effect; and in some cases nothing else seems to be meaned by the reason of a thing, besides the means, mode, or manner of its operation, or of that operation by which it has been effected; and by the knowledge of the reason of a thing, nothing besides the knowledge of the mode of operation whereby it has been produced.

56. Since then the applying of things to each other, and thereby comparing them together, whether ideas, remembrances, thoughts, or external existences, and thence deducing conclusions or judgments, is reasoning; and since the mind is passive, unless in as far as attention is concerned, and as it is excited to action by the will, or end or object proposed, in exerting itself in selecting and applying to each other the things best suited for the experiments, &c. and for discerning or perceiving those relations in them, in the discernment of which its judgments respecting them consist, the reasoning power, or that by means of which their relations are discovered, must be that power of the mind whereby it selects the objects most conducive to
the

the end proposed, or most proper for elucidating the subject of inquiry, and then applies them experimentally to each other, and presents them so applied at the same time to its own inspection. This power of selecting and bringing together, must depend much on the perceptions and remembrances of the natures and relations of things, and on association in as far as these remembrances depend on it, as well as on the perception or discernment of those that are most suited to the purpose among the things thus perceived or remembered by the mind. Since human knowledge respects the relations and natures of things only, and since reasoning is nothing but the comparing of things together, either *immediately or directly*, or by means of experimental applications and perceptions of things themselves, or *mediately and indirectly*, by means of remembrances and ideas, the result of experiments and perceptions with respect to things formerly made, whereby judgments are formed with respect to the relations of things, and thereby knowledge acquired, it must be manifest that the truth and certainty of our knowledge, in as far as truth and certainty is compatible with and attainable in a state of humanity, must necessarily depend on the certainty of the means by which it is acquired, or on the validity of the evidence or proof on which it rests ; and it must also be manifest, that the selecting and comparing of two things together, whether by actual experiment, or in thought only, intuitively, or without the intervention of any third thing, or thought, and thence deducing a conclusion or judgment with regard to the relations of these things, must be reasoning, and the result of it, the acquirement of knowledge. On the things employed, and on the manner of employing them, in making the comparison, does the evidence and proof of the knowledge thus acquired, relative to sentient beings having senses and faculties in a sound state, rest. When acquired by means of actual experiment, or immediate, direct, or intuitive perception, the evidence of the relation, fact, or truth, thereby discovered, rests on the evidence of the things themselves ; and if the method employed in applying and comparing them, or in making the comparison on which the judgment is founded, is unexceptionable, the proof of the fact or truth discovered is as satisfactory, full and perfect, as the nature of things admit of; since the same relations must, from the nature of things, always under the same circumstances, invariably subsist between the same things, and of course our

deduc-

deductions from them be as certain, necessary, and immutable, as the things
and their relations on which they are founded : and, from the conviction it
necessarily impresses on the mind of its certainty, and from its not being possible even to conceive any means of proof more direct, or more satisfactory, the
fact or truth may, with the utmost propriety, be said to be demonstrated, and
this method of reasoning to be demonstrative, or by means of demonstration.

57. When the comparisons on which the judgments are founded are
made by means of remembrances and ideas of things substituted for the
things themselves, then the proof, though it is also in this case intuitive, or
the result of immediate direct discernment, as it was of immediate perception in the former case, does not amount to demonstration, as the evidence
on which it rests is not sufficient for affording intire conviction to the mind
of its certainty; but if it refers to, and is supported by, written testimony
of the results of experiments actually made with the things or objects of
inquiry, of which experiments and results no doubt can be entertained, then
as the evidence in reality rests on actual experiments, and not on remembrances, ideas, or supposed qualities, or analogies, the proof adduced
amounts to demonstration, as affording such intire conviction of certainty
as to leave no grounds for doubt.

58. In reasoning, by comparing things internal or external together, we
acquire a knowledge of facts, or of certain of the relations of things ; which
facts or truths thus discovered and determined, lead us to other comparisons, and these again to other new truths, and so on in succession till we
arrive at the object of our inquiry.   The things thus compared in each simple act of reasoning are only two in number ; and the discernment or perception of their relation, real or supposed, in each stage of the progress, is
always immediate and direct, or intuitive, even when the judgments are
erroneous, from having been formed from comparisons and discernments of
imperfect and fallacious recollections or ideas, or from supposed analogies
among things which have no real existence in nature. It often happens,
however, that we cannot obtain direct intuitive evidence of the relations of
certain things, by the immediate means of the things themselves, whose
relations we wish to investigate and determine; and when this is the case,
we are under the necessity of having recourse to intermedia, or to a third
thing or object capable of being immediately and directly applied to and
                                                                    com-

compared with these things respectively, and by that means to determine their relations among themselves, an operation frequently necessary in each successive process of a long train of complicated reasoning. When relations are thus investigated and determined by means of intermedia, this kind of proof is not strictly intuitive; as the relations which are the objects of enquiry are not immediately discerned or perceived by means of the direct agency of the things themselves, of which they are the relations on the senses and mind, though the whole process of the reasoning may have been conducted and carried on by means of a connected series of intuitive proofs: if this connected series of intuitive proofs, however, has been by means of direct accurate experiments either made at the time, or formerly made and referred to by means of undoubted written testimony, so that each particular proof amounts to a demonstration, and the whole are so connected together that each succeeding demonstration depends on the immediately preceding, the reasoning has been strictly demonstrative throughout, and the result of the whole must necessarily be such as to terminate in entire conviction with respect to the certainty of the truths or relations thus investigated and determined, as resting on the stable and permanent basis of demonstration.

59. Demonstration then is founded either on consciousness or on experiment; and when on experiment, it consists either in a single experimental proof necessarily conveying conviction to the mind with respect to the truth of the judgment or conclusion it deduces from it, or in a connected series of such judgments, all whose premises are experiments, either made at the time, or formerly made and referred to on evidence not admitting of doubt. Demonstration is not peculiar to the mathematical sciences; every kind of reasoning, whatever the subject, which consists in just and rational deductions from consciousness, common sense in the meaning expressed in Essay I. and unexceptionable experiments conveying full conviction to the mind, or in a connected series of these, is strictly demonstrative, whatever the science it may be applied to or may concern; and there is no truth and certainty in any science, or in any mode of reasoning, but what is ultimately derived from experience or experiment, as experienced consciousnesses, sensations, perceptions, &c. and rational deductions from these. Rational certainty may no doubt be obtained by other means with respect to conclu-

sions

sions from premises, but the facts hence inferred may notwithstanding not be true; since their truth must rest on that of the premises; and if the premises are false, the conclusions, however justly deduced, must necessarily be so also, whether these premises are remembrances, ideas, or definitions, or propositions granted or pre-established on definitions. No principle can be worse founded than that adopted from the ideal system of philosophy, and inculcated in the treatises and lectures on Logic, viz. " that intuitive " reasoning can be employed in investigating the relations of ideas only; " that the knowledge acquired in this manner is what is properly called " science, and that, as the same relations must always invariably subsist " between the same ideas, our deductions in this way must constitute eter- " nal, necessary, and immutable truths;—thus, if it be true that the whole " is equal to all its parts, it must be so unchangeably, because the relation " of equality is attached to the ideas themselves, and must ever intervene " when the same ideas are compared."

60. And it seems rather strange to make the relation depend entirely on the *ideas*, and not at all on the *things themselves* by which these ideas are produced, on the signs, and not on the things signified by them; and not to limit the duration of the truths thus discovered by the duration of the things concerning whose relations they are truths, but on the unfounded supposition of ideas, or mental representations of things, being independent existences, necessary and eternal, to regard the truths respecting the relations of things, acquired through this medium of mental representation or ideas, as necessary, eternal, and immutable.

61. All just reasoning is founded on experience, or on experiments either made at present or formerly made, and referred to; and the most complicated reasonings are nothing in reality but connected serieses of judgments from connected serieses of experiments either presently made or formerly made and referred to. When the conclusions or judgments resulting from these experiments are expressed in language, they are propositions, and hence the inferences deduced from a connected series of experiments, with their consequent judgments so expressed, are said, and supposed to be inferences from the propositions, or judgments thus expressed, and not from the experiments on which the verity of these propositions rest: and when the experience or experiments on which these judgments are founded are

so far from being recent, though the judgments are remembered and referred to, that we are unconscious of having acquired them by that means, we are apt to regard them as innate, or as the result of pure and speculative intellectual intelligence not founded in or derived from any thing in nature; and hence it is, that reasoning has been defined to be, and has been supposed to consist in, the deducing of one proposition from another, or of unknown propositions from others that are known.

62. All propositions are founded on experience, even those said to be deduced merely from definitions, or from the definitions of their terms. For definitions themselves, if proper, adequate, and just, can be derived from nothing else, or can have no other foundation, the terms defined when simple having no meaning, or expressing no meaning but what they derive either from experienced consciousnesses, sensations, or perceptions, &c. and which meanings therefore cannot be defined, that is, rendered intelligible, otherwise than by means of exciting the sensations, &c. of which they are the name or description, by a direct appeal to the senses by means of the things capable of exciting and producing them, or by means of the things themselves which the terms signify or express; and when compound those expressing certain consciousnessess of the mind excepted, having no meanings but such as necessarily result from and depend upon the simple terms of which they are compounded, as being expressive only of their combinations. Even geometrical definitions, or the meaning of the terms expressive of the figures used in geometry, cannot be understood by those who have no previous knowledge of these figures, and can be rendered intelligible to them no otherwise than by a direct experimental appeal to the senses by exhibiting to them the figures themselves of which these terms are the names. The same is the case with respect to the postulates of geometry; since these facts, the truth of which they require to be admitted, could not possibly have been known before their reality and practicability had been experienced.

63. Those propositions which have been denominated geometrical axioms, and those which have been called first principles, self-evident, necessary, and eternal truths, maxims of common sense, and first truths, which were first treated of by Aristotle in his Analytics, and have been recently treated of by Father Buffier, Doctor Reid, &c. and which they represent as not admitting of proof, are all, as well as every other kind of propositions,

tions, nothing more than conclusions or judgments deduced from experience, observation, and induction, expressed in words, which are all founded on the nature of things, and are truths with respect to the natures and relations of things only, and which therefore possess no validity or evidence but what they derive from them.   Many however of the axioms or maxims so much celebrated as the fundamental principles of all science are nothing but identical propositions, and identical propositions are only nominal definitions from which no knowledge is to be derived, as no more can be known of the subject by their means than was known before, the terms of the proposition being either the same or synonimous ;—as the maxim, " animals are animals," or the axiom the nineteenth of *Euclid*, " a whole is " equal to all its parts," which amounts only to this, that a thing is equal to itself, the subject and predicate, or a whole and all its parts, being only different names for the same thing.   Axioms and postulates, and maxims or first truths, have been said to be assumed and assented to without proof, as not admitting of any.   This however, except with respect to such as are identical, is far from being the case ; they are propositions expressive of conclusions or judgments by induction founded in and derived from experience and observation of the natures and relations of things, and such as admit at any time of being experimentally and intuitively proved by an immediate direct appeal to the senses.   They do not indeed admit of and cannot require any other kind of proof than this, as this is the most obvious, concise, valid, and satisfactory of any, and that on which any degree of validity the others may possess must ultimately depend ; the truth of the proposition being intuitively perceived and self evident---that is evident from the things themselves subjected to experimental inspection for the purpose of perceiving the relation between them that is affirmed or denied in the proposition—no doubt can possibly be entertained by the mind respecting its certainty.   It is often necessary also in many cases to have recourse to a direct appeal to the senses for defining or explaining the meaning of the terms of these axioms, as well as those of other propositions, as often being the names of things which can be rendered intelligible no otherwise than by exciting the perceptions of the things of which they are the names by means of the things themselves.   Thus the axioms of Euclid, viz. axiom 1st, " things equal to the same thing are equal to one another ;" 2d, " if equals
" be

" be added to equals the whole will be equal;" 3d, " if equals be taken " from equals the remainders will be equal," &c. are all manifestly deductions from observation and experience; though by some strange and unaccountable fatality the contrary opinion has prevailed for two thousand years; for they all are either results of intuitive perception founded on experience, or are conclusions rationally deduced from these; and are such as admit at any time of being experimentally proved by a direct appeal to the senses: as by applying experimentally together, first one of two things to a third thing, and rendering the two things thus applied equal to each other if they were not so before, then by applying the other of the two things to the same third thing and rendering that thing also equal to it if it was not so before, and then applying the two things thus rendered each equal to the third thing to each other, when the truth of axiom first will be experimentally proved, on finding that the two things, each equal to a third, are equal to each other; and in the same manner may the others be proved. The proof of axiom ninth indeed, viz. " a whole is greater than its part," depends on the definitions or meanings of its terms, whole and part, and these can be rendered intelligible no otherwise than by the experimental exhibition and division of some whole into parts. Hence it appears, that the knowledge and belief of what have been called first truths, maxims of common sense, axioms, and first principles of science, are neither innate nor instinctive, or derived from the constitution of our natures, nor the effect of any law of human thought or judgment independent of the will and external nature, but are the effects merely of rational deductions from nature and experience. All philosophy and science is founded on experience and induction, and consists in these, and in conclusions necessarily resulting and justly deduced from them. The logical, metaphysical, and mathematical sciences, like all others, are founded on experience and induction, and have a reference, and are applicable merely to the natures and relations of created and dependent things, in place of being founded in and derived from sources purely intellectual, and being conversant only about abstract ideas, and abstract truths, independent, necessary, and eternal, according to the doctrines handed down to us from the Grecian philosophers; and they possess no validity, and cannot with safety be relied upon, but in as far as they rest upon and are derived from this basis of experience and induction.

64. In

64. In reasoning verbally, or by means of propositions, we substitute these maxims or axioms for the experiences they severally indicate or express, whereby these maxims become the basis or first principles of science; and when they are just inferences from actual unexceptionable experiments, no basis can be more secure or certain. If these maxims concern the relation of the agreements of the attributes of certain things among themselves as established in nature, and discovered by experience and observation, and are expressive of the generality of this relation as inferred from an induction of particular facts, they become what are properly called logical universals; and if the induction was complete or sufficiently comprehensive, and the experiments or facts on which it is founded perfectly correct, the attribute or attributes they predicate of the genus, may with the utmost certainty as a necessary truth, necessary in the nature of things, be predicated of each of the individuals composing that genus; since it is on individuals found actually to possess these attributes that the genus is formed, and since it is in these attributes being predicable of each individual that the generality of the proposition consists.

65. According to the doctrines promulgated by the late Professor Kant of Prussia, doctrines which have acquired so very high a degree of celebrity in several parts of the Continent, as to have been publicly taught in some Universities even during his own lifetime, PURE KNOWLEDGE, or what he calls knowledge à priori, is entirely independent of nature, experience, sense, and reason; and may be easily distinguished from knowledge derived from nature and experience by means of the senses, and rational deductions from these, or, what he is pleased to stile, EMPIRICAL KNOWLEDGE, by means of two criterions, each of which is pronounced to be of itself an infallible test for this purpose. These tests are NECESSITY, and STRICT UNIVERSALITY. Experience, it is asserted, teaches that a thing is so, but not that it cannot be otherwise, and therefore is *necessary*. Experience, it is also asserted, never affords a *strict universality*, but only a limited and assumed universality as being necessarily derived from a partial and imperfect induction of facts. And hence that *necessity* and *strict universality* are infallible criterions of *pure intelligence, or knowledge à priori*, not only as being inseparably connected with it, but also as being incompatible with empirical knowledge, or that derived from experience, &c. These are the fundamental

damental principles on which this system is supported ; and, with the intention of proving their justness, *reference* is first made to the mathematical science, all the propositions of which are represented as being the result of pure intellection only, and the truths they unfold as strictly universal, necessary, and eternal, as being altogether unconnected with, and independent of experience and created things ; and then to the proposition, " that " every change. must have a cause." That the definitions, the postulates, and the axioms of geometry, the basis on which it is erected, and on the validity of which the validity of all the propositions depends—those purely experimental excepted, as the fifth proposition of the first book of Euclid— are all founded on experience, and the natures of created things has, it is hoped, been already proved in a manner sufficiently satisfactory ; and that it is to created things, their modes, properties and relations, as to the ratios of things, and the ratios of the ratios of things, or what is commonly called proportion, that the mathematical sciences exclusively refer and are applicable, is a fact too manifest to require either proof or illustration. It is likewise evident that the proposition, " every change must have a cause," has no meaning but what it derives from that of its terms, and that when thus considered, it is mere tautology, as signifying only, that that which is caused is caused, or that that which is the effect of a cause, as every change must be, is the effect of a cause ; or, that that which is produced by a cause is produced by a cause—cause signifying that which produces change, and change that which is produced by cause ; and thus it appears, that this proposition, like many of the other pretended truths of pure intellection, abstract, independent, immutable, necessary, and eternal, is in reality only an identical proposition proving nothing, and from which nothing is to be learned that was not known before. Besides the universality of such propositions, like that of all others we are acquainted with, is in reality only an assumed universality derived from an induction of such particular facts only as have come under our observation ; it is merely a conclusion from experience, and rests allenarly on the multiplicity and constant uniformity of the result of that experience :—a knowledge of cause, or of change, or of the three angles of every triangle being equal to two right angles, &c. in human beings, antecedent to observation and experience, is not to be conceived, and is seemingly too absurd and ridiculous even to be

supposed.

supposed.　Neither are these propositions, nor the truths they express, independent and eternal, as they necessarily are derived from, refer to, and depend upon those things with regard to which they are truths ; nor are they necessary any otherwise than in the nature of things, since there could not possibly be change, &c. if things, or things capable of change, &c. existed not.

66. Reasoning à priori, as well as reasoning à posteriori, is founded on experience ; and, if properly conducted, may be equally useful, valid, and satisfactory. From the experience of what has hitherto uniformly happened, we reasonably expect that events of the same kinds will regularly continue to happen, that like causes will produce like effects, contrary causes contrary effects, &c. ; and from the observance of certain events always succeeding others, and that certain effects are invariably produced by means of the same modifications, directions, and combinations of the same efficient causes, we are necessarily induced to infer, that there is in the universe a regular course of nature, or settled order of causes and consequences, &c. agreeable to undeviating laws established by the Author of nature ; and from the knowledge acquired of these laws, or of the course of nature, from the observation of phenomena and experiments purposely made, and rational deductions from these, we are enabled to infer causes from effects, and effects from causes, &c. by a process of consequential reasoning without the intervention of any medium, with a great degree of certainty, when the causes, effects, &c. are of the same kinds, not only with respect to things that are present or past, but also with respect to things to come, and thereby to foresee and predict many future events and results, and, with some degree of probability, even when the causes, effects, &c. are not entirely the same or of the same nature, when there is evidently a great similitude between them in several respects :—thus it is that we are enabled to discover the times when certain events of great antiquity happened, as eclipses of the Sun and planets, &c. and to predict with certainty the periods at which future events of the same kind will take place for an indefinite time.　And thus it is that an ingenious mechanic will often know with precision, from the knowledge of the laws of nature he has acquired from experience, what will be the effects of a machine he has contrived, à priori, or before it is realized or put to work, even when it has no existence but in

his

his own imagination—that a chemist, after having analysed a particular substance, and accurately ascertained the natures of its component parts, and that mode of union whereby they formed that substance, can be at no loss to determine and describe à priori the means and manner whereby such a substance may be generated, and then to prove experimentally that it actually is generated of such materials by such means, &c. We cannot, indeed, in many cases be perfectly certain, if our observation or experience has been perfectly correct, or if the application of it is altogether perfect, or of course of the justness of the result of our reasonings, till we have reduced our theory to practice; but we are certain that if it is not so, it must be owing either to inaccuracy in our observations or experiments, or in the train of reasoning founded upon them. This mode of reasoning is no doubt à posteriori, in as far as it is founded on facts or experience; but it is à priori, in as far as it deduces results from these facts, or from experience previous to practice or to any direct experimental proof of them ; and this is all that can with propriety and justness be understood by reasoning à priori. Many discoveries have been made by experiment, and some of them casually, which could not have been made à priori, as no reasoning could naturally have led to them, or directed the enquiry ; as those of the polarity, and the attractive and repulsive powers of the magnet, the electric qualities of some bodies and the conducting of others, &c.

67. By the analytical or experimental method we are enabled to discover entities or existences, or powers and properties, actually existing in things with which we were unacquainted before; also the modes of action, or laws which regulate these powers, and by an induction of particulars to generalize them; and it is from our experimental knowledge alone of these laws of action of efficient causes, that we are enabled to determine the effects that necessarily must result from them, under particular circumstances, or to reason synthetically respecting them. By the synthetical we are enabled to deduce results of which we have no actual experience, and thereby not only to account for certain causes and effects, which under the then circumstances could not otherwise be accounted for; but also to foretel future events, and to produce or create what actually did not exist before, as the new machine of the mechanic, &c. The validity of synthetical reasoning must nevertheless, however just the deductions, depend

pend on the validity of the premises or data; that is on the justness and
accuracy of the observations and experience on which it is founded, or
from which the inferences are deduced; and hence hypotheses founded on
mere suppositions or phantoms of the imagination which have no real
existence in the nature of things merit no regard. Thus then are mankind furnished with a kind of prophetic spirit, foresight, or prescience; but
a kind founded on experience only. That of the Deity is absolute, antecedent to, and independent of, all experience. It is infinite; ours partial
and extremely limited. Divine knowledge differs from human, not only
in degree, but in kind. There is no human knowledge purely à priori, or
absolute. All our knowledge is merely relative to and depending on the
natures and relations of created things, the only things with which we have
any direct communication, and all the truths we are acquainted with
are nothing but inferences rationally deduced from these:—we cannot even
form a conception of absolute knowledge. All art is founded in nature,
or in the knowledge, imitation, and application, of what are called the
laws of nature, to the purposes and uses of mankind. All pure and speculative, as it has been called, as well as all practical wisdom, is founded in,
and derived from experience, or the results of many repeated experiments;
there is no priori road to science and wisdom, sense and sensible objects are
the foundation of all. It is in the book of nature, or in the nature of things,
we must look for instruction of every kind.

68. Though our reasoning often consists in deducing inferences from general propositions, or in deducing particular propositions from general,
as when it is said all men are mortal, therefore some men are mortal, there
is no occasion for expressing our reasoning even in these cases syllogistically
or for throwing the argument into the form of a syllogism, as it can serve
no good purpose whatever; for syllogism, the invention of which is claimed
by the mighty Stagirite as exclusively his own, is not a means or way of
discovering truths; but is only a particular verbose formal way of expressing them when discovered, as the truth must be known before the syllogism
can be formed; every syllogism assumes in the premises, or rather in the
major proposition, the thing to be proved; for the induction on which the
major or general proposition is founded is not perfect and to be relied
upon, if the particular or subject of the minor proposition is not included
in

in it; and if the subject of the minor is known to be included in it, the conclusion must also necessarily be known. It is not unusual to form syllogisms, by throwing in an identical proposition as the minor proposition, of the syllogism — as in stating the above reasoning syllogistically, when it is thus expressed, all men are mortal, some men are men, therefore some men are mortal — which is most egregious trifling, since there evidently can be no meaning or use in such a procedure. Indeed reasoning directly without the intervention of any medium by the immediate consequence, or from consequence to consequence to the last resort, in a connected train or series of propositions, in which either the predicate or consequent of the one becomes continually either the subject or antecedent of that immediately following, is in all respects preferable to the method of syllogism, which has, on that account, now fallen into almost general neglect and is seldom or ever used. This manner of reasoning, or reasoning closely and in train, is not only the most elegant, but is also the most perspicuous, familiar, satisfactory, impressive, and convincing; and it is applicable with equal propriety to all the different kinds of reasoning; as whether the reasoning is from maxims, the contrary of which necessarily involve, in the nature of things, a contradiction or impossibility — whether by unavoidable consequence from facts or propositions admitted, or from what is known or granted — whether from generals to particulars, or from causes to effects, or from particulars to generals, or from effects to causes — or whether the reasoning is strictly demonstrative — all the various kinds being ultimately founded on the same basis of experiment and comparing.

69. The UNDERSTANDING of the mind can properly mean only, I imagine, that faculty or rather those faculties whereby the mind conceives and perceives the relations or reasons of things internal or external; or the manner and means by which truth is or may be discovered, a thing is or may be made or done, or an end or object is or may be obtained; — the *understanding* of the signification of artificial signs being nothing more than the *remembrance* of the significations affixed to them by ourselves or others. Under the term understanding then, all the faculties or powers and properties of the mind seem to be comprehended, but those of the passions and affections, and the will or the determinations of the mind as excited and influenced by these.

70. When

70. When the mind experiences any strong sensation, the effect of immediate external violence, as of a blow or wound, the infliction of torture or punishment, or of some derangement of the animal œconomy, whereby inflammation and violent pain is produced, and especially when the action of the cause whereby the sensation is produced is sudden and unexpected, and the mind not prepared for receiving it, the mind is always much agitated by the shock or impetus producing the sensation, and this agitation of the mind produces corresponding agitations in the body, and appearances in the countenance expressive of the pain then experienced, or of the pleasure, if the sensation then produced is of a pleasant kind, as by a sudden and unexpected relief from torture and pain. --- The mind is entirely *passive* in these cases; and the agitation and consequent bodily motions are the effects merely of the shock or impulse.---But though this is the case, it is not to these sensations that the terms appetites, affections, and passions, are applicable, or to these agitations or motions, that the term emotion is applicable.—These sensations being those which are first experienced, and on the experience of which the knowledge of pleasure and pain, or of good and evil are founded, they may with much propriety be denominated the primary sensations to distinguish them from all others. --- The passions, affections, and appetites, are also sensations of the mind; but they differ in several respects from these, though they originate in them, or in that knowledge of pleasure and pain or of good and evil which is derived from them, and in that predilection for pleasure or good, and repugnance to pain or evil, which these sensations or this knowledge necessarily engenders in sentient, intelligent, and rational beings; it being essential to the nature of such beings, to endeavour their own well-being or happiness, and consequently to love and pursue what is good or beneficial for them, and to hate and avoid what is evil or injurious to them, and in this love or hatred as variously modified and directed do the passions, &c. consist. Since all the passions and affections then of the mind originate in the primary sensations or feelings of pleasure and pain, or a knowledge of good and of evil; and that predilection for, or attraction to the good, and repugnance to or repulsion from the evil, which that knowledge necessarily inspires and engenders in human beings, they must all necessarily arrange themselves into the two classes of love and hatred; and from these necessarily proceed those of desire and aversion,

every

every one naturally desiring what he loves and having an aversion to what he hates; and of these all the others, as hope, joy, gratitude, fear, sorrow, anger, &c. are necessary derivatives.---It is not in the primary sensations, and the feelings of pleasure and pain thence experienced, and the knowledge of good and evil thence acquired, that the passions and affections consist; but in the love and hatred, desires and aversions, and the consequent hopes and fears, joy and grief, gratitude and anger, &c. which those experiences and this knowledge engender in the human mind. --- In primary sensations the love or hatred is merely the effect without being the cause of sensation; but in the passions and affections, the love or hatred is not only the effect but also the cause of sensation. ---In primary sensations, it is the sensations themselves we either love or hate; and they excite no action or tendency to action in the mind, further than a desire or attempt, either to protract or to shorten their duration, as they are either agreeable or the contrary. — Whereas in the passions and affections we transfer in a great degree, by an act of the mind, the love or hatred from the sensations to those objects, agents, or circumstances, which are the real or supposed, voluntary or involuntary, causes of them --- and hence they differ from primary sensations in as far as they must always have an object real or imaginary, and are always attended with a retrospect or reference, real or fanciful, to causes or to qualities capable of acting on the mind, and of whose action or power of action the mind has a recal or fanciful experience or knowledge.---The affections differ from the passions, in being more durable and less violent---and they sometimes precede and sometimes succeed passions, certain affections under certain circumstances rising to passions, and certain passions under certain circumstances moderating into affections;---and emotions differ from both, as signifying those corporeal motions, gestures, and appearances of countenance, which are not the result of primary agitations and feelings of the mind, but of those agitations and feelings, which attend or constitute the passions and affections.--- The *passions and affections of the mind* may then be defined to be *either those sensations, or the sensations proceeding from them, which the perception or contemplation of objects, agents, or circumstances, real or imaginary, which are the known or supposed causes of good or evil, with respect to us, excite in our minds.---* The passions and affections are oftener produced by the thoughts or re-

P   membrances

membrances of real objects, or causes of enjoyment or of evil, or by thinking on the supposed imaginary agency of mere fancied ones, than by any real primary sensations of pleasure or pain, or by any good or evil, actually produced by the *direct* agency of those real objects or causes themselves, which so much occupy the thoughts and engage the fancy :—a mere sight of certain objects or causes, the effects of which have been often experienced and deeply felt, or even of any sign, indication, or representation of them, or other associated circumstance or thought which recals the remembrance of them and of the effects they produced is sufficient, without any other direct agency or their affecting the mind any otherwise, to generate in it those sensations denominated its passions and affections; and the casual recurrence of sensations any way resembling those the mind experienced from the direct operation of these objects or causes on it, are capable of producing these effects, sometimes in a still stronger degree.— When these remembrances often recur, or when these thoughts and remembrances become habitual from reiterated and long continued pains, or pleasures, from remorse, or conscious guilt, from jealousy, rage, revenge, or from the mind having been too long, too much and too eagerly engaged with them, or too intent on or desirous of any object, the passions or affections thus produced and fostered become so vivid and acute, so obstinate and durable, that it is not in the power of the mind, however great the pains it may endure, or however much it may will it, to divert its thoughts from these objects, or to divest itself of these passions and affections which are so distressing to it;—and which, from this cause, often degenerate in time into a state of settled melancholy or madness.—This is difficult even in cases of recent afflictions : thus Juliet, alluding to the banishment of her Romeo, says, "I would forget it fain ; but oh ! it presses "on my memory like damned guilty deeds on sinners minds:"—and in cases of long continuance and confirmed by habit, there is " no ministering " to the diseased mind, no plucking from the memory the rooted sorrow, no "razing out the written troubles of the brain, and with some sweet oblivious "antidote, cleansing the mind of that perilous stuff which weighs upon the " heart." When the passions and affections thus excited and produced, are of a pleasurable nature, or when of a mixed kind, and the mind is of opinion that the pleasurable prevail on the whole, the will accords and co-operates

                                                                with

with the other causes, in forming and maintaining them; and even when they are of a most melancholy and distressing nature, the will often acquiesces and concurs in supporting, fostering, and feeding them, when the mind is impressed with the opinion, that there is a duty or virtue in suffering in this manner; whether from religious motives, and with the view of expiating of sin by that means; or from moral motives, as a proof of affection for, and a sacrifice justly due to the memory of a beloved husband, &c.; or whether from despondency or despair, and the mind having no relish for any thing else, feels, on that account, even some degree of gratification in indulging in what is otherwise sorrow and affliction, and in indulging thus in silence and in secret, when it is supposed the disclosure of it could tend only to give unnecessary grief to others, or to expose the frailties or misfortunes of the sufferer, as is not unfrequently the case of many a love-lorn maid, " who does not tell her love, but lets concealment, like a worm in " the bud, feed on her damask cheek, and pines in thought, sitting, like " Patience on a monument, smiling at grief."

71. The mind, though intirely passive in the reception of these kinds of sensations, as well as of the primary, is yet, in place of being passive, highly active in producing them, as excited to action by its own feelings, remembrances, ideas, internal energies, opinions, or fancies, or by external agency; and of this action, sensations, passions, and affections, the most exquisite and poignant are often the result:—thus the mind, by means of remembrances, or of any representation, sign, or indication, or other associated circumstance, whereby the remembrance of objects, agents, and events, may be produced, or the ideas, images, or mental representations of objects and agents, real or fanciful, conjured up, will not only excite appetite, but even rouse the passions and affections at will, and with them the most vivid and acute sensations. To what a high pitch of rage, &c. will a tragedian, by these means, work himself up?—Who, " but in a fiction, in a dream of " passion, can force his soul so to his own conceit, that from her working, " all his visage warms; tears in his eyes, distraction in his aspect, a broken " voice, and his whole function suiting with forms to his conceit; and all " for nothing;—for Hecuba!—what is Hecuba to him, or he to Hecuba?"— Here remembrances, phantoms, and ideas of things seem to act the same part, and to produce the same effects on the mind, as things themselves.

In

In the passions of fear and aversion, in despondency, despair, sorrow, grief, and melancholy, the mind seems, either from the external action on it, or as prompted and excited by the will, to shrink and contract itself, as a means of avoiding or receding from danger or distress; and, on the contrary, in those of desire, hope, joy, anger, and rage, it seems to expand itself in all directions, and acts, as excited and prompted by those sensations and the will, so as either to obtain the objects of its desire, or to oppose, prevent, repel, or punish any violence or injury with which it may be threatened.

The state of the mind is affected and influenced by that of the body; thus the natural appetites, or the desire of gratifying them, &c. excite and produce passions and affections often of great intensity and permanency in the mind, as well as the state of the body, with respect to its appetites, by that of the mind, as affected and influenced in its action by the sight, feeling, or remembrance of those objects or agents whereby they may be appeased or remedied, or by the remembrance of the mental gratifications attending that circumstance, or the casual recurrence of pleasures, somewhat similar, or associated with them; and many even of the vital, and seeming vegetable functions of the body, are in many cases, in some respects, under mental controul. Since all pleasures and pains are merely mental sensations, it is manifest that the cravings and the gratifications of appetite cannot be carnal or corporeal, though commonly represented as such, and though the mind seems to be necessarily affected by the state of the body or instrument, so as to know when the body or instrument is in an apt condition for gratifying it in this manner. It is the mind that feels uneasiness from want of rest, of a proper supply of nourishment, or of salutary bodily discharges; and it is the mind that experiences enjoyment or gratification from the removing of these uneasinesses, and the agreeable sensations with which they are succeeded. *Appetites, then, are particular uneasy sensations of the mind, produced by the external agency of particular states of the body on it, as the uneasy sensations of hunger, thirst, lust, lassitude, and longings, &c. which are sometimes denominated carnal desires, because they generate desire and other passions and affections in the mind, and sometimes corporeal wants or cravings, as admitting of relief by means of appropriate applications and gratifications for altering the particular state of the body from which they proceed.*

What

What further regards the passions, affections, and appetites, in general, appertains more particularly to the science of morals.

72. That power, or faculty of the mind, whereby it generates, and produces action in itself, and thereby in the body, as it is excited by its desires and aversions, or passions, affections, and appetites, is denominated the WILL, and those actions, which are the effects of it, are denominated voluntary actions. Those desires and aversions, as has been already observed, are the results of primary sensations, or of experienced pleasures or pains, good or evil, and a perception of the objects, agents, or circumstances, by which they have been produced, together with a knowledge, thence rationally deduced, with respect to those objects, agents, means, or ends, that are capable of, or liable to produce in sentient beings, either the one or the other; and hence the mind, in willing or in voluntary action, has always some particular object or end in view, as a mean to the principal end happiness, or the attainment of enjoyment or good, and avoiding of pain or evil. Will, without an object or end in view, is not possible or conceivable; an end being implied in the very definition of the term will, or included in the only meaning it properly admits of. The will then, or determinations of the mind, must of course necessarily be influenced, first, in a certain degree, by the nature of the particular object or end; secondly, in a certain degree, by the nature of the sentient being, the same object often inciting different inclinations, or the same in different degrees, in beings of the same species or class; and thirdly, in a certain degree by the understanding, or by judgments rationally deduced from facts previously ascertained, with respect to the efficacy, practicability, and propriety of adopting of certain means, objects, or agents, in preference to others, as being in the then circumstances most conducive for the attainment of good, and avoiding of evil. The judgments of the mind, as influenced by motives, determine the will and voluntary actions; and if they were not influenced by motives, there could not be will or voluntary action, and laws with their sanctions, divine and human, could be of no avail.

73. But whatever influences the will may be subjected to, as considered philosophically, or when taken in a philosophical sense, there can be no doubt of its being free in the common or vulgar sense, or in the general acceptation of that term, or when the will is confounded with the being or

agent

agent of which it is the will, and the being and will supposed to signify the same thing, or rather the freedom of the will, and the freedom of the being to follow his will, to signify the same thing, the being or agent being free when under no artificial or legal restraint, or when free to follow his will or the natural propensities of his mind. Mankind in general, by the term liberty, mean nothing but freedom to follow their own several inclinations, or their will. They never trouble themselves with inquiring whether or not the will itself is free; that is to them a matter of indifference, so long as they are permitted to do what they incline. By the term *natural liberty*, when applied to the agent, nothing with propriety can be meant but freedom to follow the will; and by that of *civil or political liberty*, nothing but freedom to follow the will, when it is not prejudicial to others, or injurious to society.

74. There are, however, not only many bodily, but also many mental actions, that are not voluntary. Our thoughts are often not at our command, and do not obey the will; many of them will often, from associations among themselves, or from other associated circumstances capable of exciting sensations and thoughts in us, intrude themselves upon us, in direct opposition to our inclinations, frequently producing long trains of sensations which the mind would gladly dispense with, and put a stop to, if it could; and these intrusive thoughts will often induce us to say and do many improper things, and even to commit actions contrary to our will, and to our interest; so that it is not in the power of the will to controul and determine our thoughts and actions, or in our power to obey our will, in all cases, even when it would be attended with safety and advantage.

75. Those determinations of the will, which are the effects neither of meditation nor of instruction, and which are immediate and direct, and yet, at the same time, unerring in their consequences, are called instincts, and the actions thence proceeding, instinctive actions. These determinations, and the actions consequent of them, may, I imagine, be regarded as the effects of natural propensities, or of desires and aversions excited and produced in sentient beings by the direct agency of external objects on them; and hence *instinct* may be defined *desire or aversion acting in sentient beings, in consequence of the direct agency of external objects on them, and determining them to action in such a manner as infallibly to attain*
certain

certain ends or objects, either essential to the preservation of their existence or necessary to their well being, and that seemingly antecedent to experience, deliberation, reasoning, or instruction. Instinct seems in some respects akin to appetite; or to that timidity, or to that temerity, which respectively proceed from a very high state of bodily health, or from great bodily imbecility. Instinctive action seems in a great degree to be mechanical, and the sentient being in some cases seems to be attracted through the instrumentality of its senses by the proper objects; at least the external objects of sense seem, in some cases, to lead seemingly instinctively to those external objects of sense which are capable of satisfying or allaying the cravings of internal sensations or appetites; or those objects seem through the senses to attract the notice of the sentient being as peculiarly proper for that purpose, and thereby to induce the being to move towards them as if attracted by them, and to employ them in the proper manner, as indicated by their senses, for relieving and satisfying their desires; thus the new born infant is led seemingly instinctively, by the smell, to the nipple of the mother's breast from whence it sucks milk, the substance on which it probably was nourished before it was born, and with the smell of which it is familiar. There are other kinds of instincts, or apparent instincts, however, which cannot be accounted for in this manner; or, if not the effect of education, on any other known principle of action; as the regular manners according to which the different species of birds build their nests, each species invariably retaining the same form and mode, and a form which differs from that of all the other species.

It was my wish in the course of these Essays to have paid some tribute of respect to the memory of that learned, ingenious, and worthy man, who took the lead in opposing the ideal system, and that at a time when it was in the zenith of its reputation, and when it was deemed a kind of heresy in philosophy to express any doubt with respect to the validity of its tenets, the late Dr. Reid, but the principles as well as the manner according to which we have treated the same subjects, though our object has been the same, in as far as a refutation of that system is attempted, has differed so much from each other as not to have afforded any proper opportunity.

ESSAY III.

OF SUBSTANCE AND POWER.

———————

PART I.

1. ALL causes, except the First Cause, the Author of all things, are physical. Those relating to the mind which have been stiled *moral*, being as much so as those relating to inanimated substance which have been denominated *physical*. But as all natural powers or causes arrange themselves under two classes or genera, viz. those which have a reference to the mind and its operations only, and those which have not, it becomes necessary in language for the sake of perspicuity to distinguish these different classes from each other by means of appropriate names; and as it has been usual to denominate the former of these moral powers, and to appropriate the term physical exclusively to the latter, I shall in compliance with custom observe the same phraseology though not strictly proper.

2. According to the doctrine of Mr. Hume, as founded on and deduced from the ideal philosophy, power is a word either absolutely without meaning, or a mere substitution for the term antecedence—cause and effect, words which have no other meaning than that of a constant conjunction of events, whereof the one always invariably follows the other, while the phrase necessary connection means nothing but this conjunction; and this being the case, we have not and cannot possibly have any knowledge of power, of cause and effect, or of necessary connection, since there can be no knowledge of what actually has no existence. This is one of the most important of the doctrines which the ideal system unfolds, as being pregnant with consequences of the most momentous kind. Like the other

doctrines

doctrines of the ideal philosophy, it has had no influence on the unlearned; and it has had none even on philosophers except in speculation, since in their reasonings as well as their actions in the common occurrences of life they never seem to entertain any doubt with respect to there really being such things as power, causes, effects, and necessary connections; and evidently in all cases regulate their conduct accordingly. In speculation, however, its influence on the learned has been very great indeed, as it now seems to be agreed among them that there are no physical causes; and some of them even adopt Mr. Hume's doctrine in its utmost extent, and deny the existence of all cause, efficiency, and necessary connection whatever, being of opinion that we have no acquaintance of any other things than mere phenomena.

3. Since I have never in the course of these Essays entertained any doubt of there being such existences as powers, causes, even physical causes, effects, and necessary connections; but, on the contrary, have every where not only assumed their reality, or actual existence, as a fact not admitting of doubt, but have also founded the doctrines they contain on this fact, the far greatest part of them being established on deductions by just reasoning from effects to causes, and from causes to effects; since it would be absurd in the extreme to treat of power without entertaining this opinion; and since it is necessary to refute this doctrine of the ideal system as well as the others, from a refutation of that system being one of the objects of these Essays, it imports me much to establish if possible this fact beyond controversy; a fact, on the establishment of which the refutation of the ideal philosophy and the validity of the principles and doctrines I have advanced so much depends. To some perhaps any particular refutation of this doctrine may now seem unnecessary, from the fundamental principles of the ideal system, and the opinion of there being human knowledge purely intellectual, which does not appertain to the nature and being of the mind itself, the basis of this doctrine, having been already refuted; but as others may be of a contrary opinion, I shall proceed to examine and discuss the arguments of Mr. Hume in support of this doctrine with that particular attention the celebrity of the author and the great respectability of many of those who have adopted his opinions merits.

4. The first thing that particularly attracts the attention on perusing

Q Mr.

Mr. Hume's Enquiry concerning the Human Understanding, and especially that section of it, entituled, Of the Idea of Necessary Connection, is, that it is not of things and their qualities that he treats, or of that of which he denies the existence, but of impressions and ideas only, though he argues by constant reference to things, as if they actually existed: the next is the vague, indefinite, and various different significations he affixes to his terms, even those on the definitions or meanings of which he establishes his system :—thus, according to his doctrines, sensation, impression, and perception, all signify the same thing or are synonimous; perception and idea are also synonimous; and idea signifies besides either a faint impression, or a faint sensation, or a thought, or a meaning, or knowledge, &c. as best suits his arguments at the time. And the first observation that occurs in consequence of this is, that if these meanings, assumptions, or data, on which he founds his system are granted—as that impressions and sensations are the same, that ideas are faint sensations, and that perceptions and sensations are the same—the validity of the system itself must necessarily be admitted; for if sensations are perceptions, it follows as a necessary consequence that there can be no existences external to the mind, of which we can have any knowledge at least, or no existences in nature but impressions and ideas, that is stronger and fainter sensations, since in these alone, according to these assumptions, all perception necessarily consists. If these assumptions and principles, of sensations being perceptions, and consequently of nothing being perceivable but sensations, or what according to his doctrine is the same thing impressions and ideas, are admitted, the consequences Mr. Hume deduces from them are inevitable: allow the premises and there is no denying the conclusions. But, on the contrary, if these assumptions and principles are erroneous, as has been attempted to be proved in the preceding Essays, they must necessarily lead to erroneous conclusions, and thereby vitiate and invalidate every doctrine that is established on them.

5. The first argument Mr. Hume employs with the intention of proving the non-existence of power, cause and effect, and necessary connexion, is, that because the mind feels no sentiment or *inward* impression, from the impulse of one billiard ball being attended with motion in the second, or from this succession of objects, there is not in any single particular in-

instance of cause and effect any thing which can suggest the idea of power or necessary connexion. The second argument is, that if there was power or energy in any cause, that power or energy would be discoverable by the mind, we could foresee the effects, even without experience, and might at first pronounce with certainty concerning it, by the mere dint of thought and reasoning, but since we cannot do this, there cannot be power or energy in any cause. The third, that there can be no power or energy because there is no part of matter that does ever, by its sensible qualities, discover any power or energy. The fourth, that though we are every moment conscious of power in our own minds, while we feel that by a single command of our will we can move the organs of our body, or direct the faculties of our minds, and their operations, and hence acquire the idea of power or energy, and are certain that we ourselves and all other intelligent beings are possessed of power: yet there really is no such thing as power, we really have no idea of it, and we really possess it not; because this certainty of our possessing power, of moving our limbs, &c. are facts, which, like all other natural operations, can be known only by experience, and can never be foreseen from the apparent energy or power in the cause which connects it with the effect, and because we are not conscious of the means by which it is effected, or because we are ignorant of the means by which the soul acts on the body. The fifth, that because we are ignorant of the manner in which the soul raises up a new idea, therefore the soul can possess no power to raise up a new idea, &c. The sixth, that the soul cannot possess power, because the power it possesses is limited, and we cannot assign the reason for its being so limited. These are the sum, scope, and amount of the results of Mr. Hume's reasonings on this subject expressed nearly in his own words; and he adds, that it is only from having observed that one particular species of events has always in all instances been conjoined with another, that we call the one object cause, and the other effect; and from having observed several instances of this nature, we feel these objects or events to be connected in our imagination, and from this conclude that the objects or events thus conjoined are also connected.

6. In examining these several arguments, and this inference from the natural conjunction of events with which they are succeeded, I shall not

observe

observe the exact order in which they are stated by Mr. Hume; but with the intention of rendering my reasons with respect to them more concise, methodical, and perspicuous than they otherwise would be, I shall refer the examination of the first of them, till such time as I have examined some of the others; and shall begin with the second, viz. That there cannot be power or energy in any cause; because if there was, that power or energy would be discoverable by the mind, we could foresee the effect even without experience, and might at first pronounce with certainty concerning it by the mere dint of thought and reasoning, which we cannot do. If by the power or energy of the cause, the degree of force, or the effect it is capable of producing---which is always precisely as the degree of power in the cause, the effect and the degree of power by which it is produced being the reciprocal measures and values of each other---is to be understood, as is presumable must be the case, the purport of the proposition may be thus expressed, viz. That because the mind cannot by mere dint of thought and reasoning, antecedent to experience, foresee the precise degree of force or energy in any power or cause, and thereby the effect it is capable of producing, that cause or power cannot possess any force or energy, or be capable of producing those events ascribed to its operation, and as not possessing these cannot be cause or power: or, in other words, that if there was power or cause, the precise degree of energy or force in the cause and the effect it is capable of producing would be discovered by the mind, by mere dint of thought and reasoning antecedent to experience, or antecedent to the discovery of the effect, by the discovery of which alone the cause can be discovered, and the degree of its energy be ascertained. A proposition perfectly inadmissible, as denying the existence of cause because the mind cannot perceive what is unperceivable as not coming within the cognizance of sense; as denying capability in causes of producing those events they are from experience known to produce; and as being founded on a supposition palpably impossible in the nature of things:— it being altogether impossible for the human mind to form just conclusions, and determine as to consequences or effects, by mere dint of thought and reasoning without experience, facts, or any data, from which these conclusions may be deduced and on which these determinations may be established.

7. The third argument.—" That there cannot be power or cause, because
" there

"there is no part of matter that does ever by its sensible qualities discover any "power or energy, and that there is therefore no reason to think that matter can "produce any thing that we can call an effect"—is evidently unfounded; as being in direct opposition to fact, or to the real nature of things as ascertained by reasoning founded on experience; for the characteristic and essential quality of matter, solidity, consists merely in power, a power of resisting; and all the other sensible qualities of bodies, that is, the qualities whereby they become sensible, become so merely by acting on the mind through the organs of sense; and could not be sensible qualities if this was not the case, or if they did not discover power or energy, or were not powers and causes of themselves. Besides these incessant operations of substance on substance, and of material body on material body, in changing of each other's states which fall within our observation, and the power we ourselves possess of making one material body, as one billiard ball operate on another, and thereby produce change in its state at pleasure, are facts which establish the powers of nature, and the ability of matter to act upon matter, on too stable a basis to admit of being shaken or overturned; at the same time that the arguments adduced to prove the contrary, from being so directly repugnant to the testimony and dictates of consciousness, sense, and reason, and to what experience and observation are almost incessantly teaching us, can answer no other pur-pose, when properly canvassed, than to satisfy us of their having no foun-dation in reality or nature.

8. The fifth and sixth arguments, viz. That the soul can possess no power to raise up a new idea, because we are ignorant of the manner by which the soul raises up an idea, and that the soul cannot possess power, because the power it possesses is limited and we cannot assign the reason for its being so limited—are so palpably unfounded as not to require re-futation: it being sufficiently manifest, that our ignorance of the manner in which any cause operates, and our being incapable of assigning the reason why a power may be limited in any particular way, can afford no proof of the nonexistence of power, even in cases where its existence is not acknowledged and admitted as it expressly is in these arguments. With re-spect to the fourth argument—"That there is really no such thing as power, "and we really have no idea of it and possess it not, though we are every "moment conscious of power in our own minds, and *feel* that by a single

"com-

" command of our will we can move the organs of our body, or direct the
" faculties of our minds in their operations, and hence acquire the idea of
" power or energy, and are certain that we ourselves and all other intelli-
" gent beings are possessed of power, because this certainty of our possessing
" power of moving our limbs, &c. and of having an idea of power, are
" facts, which, like all other natural operations, can be known only by experi-
" ence, and can never be foreseen from the apparent energy or power in the
" cause which connects it with the effect; and because we are not conscious
" of the manner by which it is effected, and are ignorant of the means
" by which the soul acts on the body,"—it is to be observed, in the first
place, that it is obvious this argument refutes, invalidates, and nullifies
itself, involving, in common with the fifth and sixth, the palpable contradiction and absurdity of affirming and denying the same attribute of the
same subject ; and it is equally obvious that our ignorance with regard to
the manner and means whereby power operates cannot be admitted as a
sufficient reason for concluding that there actually is no such thing as
power, or for denying the existence of that, the existence of which is, by
the argument itself, admitted as a fact.   And in the next place it is not
only inconceivable, but also absurd, to suppose that human reason can
deduce conclusions independent of experience and observation, or that the
human mind is possessed of any other source, data, or materials, than
those furnished by experience from which its reasoning faculty can form
conclusions; or that it is possible for the mind to make discoveries of any
kind antecedent to all experience by mere dint of thought and reasoning.
Mr. Hume's reasoning in this case is founded on and proceeds from the
principles of that erroneous and deceitful logic which has descended to us
from the Grecian philosophers, and which inculcates that all science and
true knowledge is the result merely of pure intellection, and the purport and
intent of which is to produce a persuasion that no knowledge with respect
to power, causation, necessary connexion, or indeed to any thing else,
can possibly be acquired by means of rational deductions from facts and
phenomena furnished by experience.   I shall scrutinize these reasonings
more in detail in the succeeding sections.

   9. Having discussed all the others, I now proceed to the examination
of the argument first stated by Mr. Hume, viz. " That because the mind
                                                                " feels

" feels no sentiment, or *inward* impression, from the impulse of one billiard-
" ball on another, or from this succession of objects, there is not in any
" single particular instance of cause and effect any thing which can suggest
" the IDEA of power or necessary connection." Since it is obviously not
on the mind that the billiard-balls act in producing these changes in each
other's states, but on each other only, it must be sufficiently manifest that
the mind can, on account of their mutual action, experience no sentiment
or *inward* impression, further than is necessary for producing in it the
perception of this mutual action in the balls, and the effects of it, or the
changes in their respective states in consequence of it; but this circumstance surely cannot afford any just reason for inferring, that there is not
in any particular instance of cause and effect any thing which can suggest
the idea, which in this case can with propriety be understood to mean only
the knowledge, of power, or necessary connection, or furnish even a probable presumption, and far less any proof of these changes being effects
without a cause, or that there are no such existences as power, cause, and
necessary connection; nor can these conclusions justly be inferred from its
being effects only that we perceive in this case, as well as in others, or
from our not perceiving in this case and others, what is to us necessarily
imperceptible, as not being objects of human perception, the power, the
cause, and the necessary connection by which the balls produce these
changes in each other. The reasoning of Mr. Hume, in this case, is
evidently founded on the ideal philosophy, and is deduced from the hypothesis, that of that of which there is no impression or sensation, there can
be no IDEA, and that that which is not representable in IDEA, not only
cannot be KNOWN, but also cannot possibly EXIST, and of course that power,
cause, and necessary connection, as not being representable in idea, cannot
possibly exist. Having in the preceding Essays attempted, and it is hoped
not altogether without success, to prove and expose the unsoundness and
deceitfulness of that philosophy which denies existence to every thing but
sensations under the names of impressions and ideas, and, by that means,
as well as others, to prove the actual existence of things cognizable to sense,
and of which we have perception, and the reality of human knowledge
with regard to them, it now remains only for the intire refutation of the
ideal philosophy, to prove the actual existence of things not cognizable

to

to sense, or of which we have no perception, and which, therefore, are unrepresentable in idea; or to prove that we actually have KNOWLEDGE of things, and of the relations and connections of things, of which we have no IDEA, and to point out the manner and means whereby this knowledge is acquired. In attempting this, I shall treat at the same time of the inference drawn by Mr. Hume from the above arguments, and that regular succession of events which takes place in nature, of there being no necessary connection between these events, &c. as above stated, with the intention of refuting that inference at the same time as these subjects are naturally connected together.

10. Mr. Hume's theory of perception, as formerly taken notice of, when treating of that subject, is* that what is called perception, is merely the effect of a natural instinct, or of an instinctive faculty of the mind, whereby it is deceived into a belief that its own sensations, or impressions and ideas, are things external to it, and that when it is conscious of the former, it perceives the latter; and it seems to be an object of his philosophy, not only to substitute *ideas* for realities, but also to substitute *instincts* for rational deductions, and thus to establish it as a principle, that little or no knowledge is to be acquired by means of rational inference from facts and phenomena discovered by experience, and thence to impress a conviction, that what is not perceivable by the mind, according to his theory of perception, that is that what is neither cognizable by sense, nor representable in idea, not only cannot possibly exist, but also that, if it did exist, it would be altogether impossible for us to acquire any knowledge of its existence or nature.

11. The opinion so prevalent among philosophers, even previous to the writings of Bishop Berkeley and Mr. Hume, of there being no such actual existences as power, cause, and necessary connection, seems to have been derived from, and to depend upon the supposition and persuasion, that if any such did really exist, they must necessarily exist as separate, distinct, and independent beings, subsisting of themselves, and, as such, not only be palpable to sense, and representable in idea, even the tie or vinculum which connects the cause with the effect, but also be capable of

---

* See Hume's Essays, vol. iii. pp. 330, 331.

acting

acting immediately and directly either on the mind, or on the external organs of sense, and through their agency on the mind, and that we would be capable of forming a conception, at least, if not a perception, of the manner and means by which they act; and from none of these being the case, no such separate distinct existences, or the manner and means by which they act, being cognizable by sense, or falling within the range of human perception, it being effects only in every case that we perceive, and we being at the same time altogether incapable, for any thing that has hitherto appeared to the contrary, of forming even a probable conjecture with respect to the manner and means by which they would act, did they actually exist. To the prevalence of this opinion, prior to their publication, has the favourable reception which the reasonings and doctrines of Mr. Hume on this subject have experienced, in some degree been owing, and in some degree to the indefinite and indistinct conceptions, and the crude and vague notions entertained in general with respect to the nature of power and necessary connection, and especially to that kind of power with which we are most conversant, to which we give the name of mechanical, never having been so much as suspected to be a primary quality of matter, or a power essential to matter, as matter, though its existence as such cannot with more justice or truth be denied, than that of solidity, or any of the other powers of matter, whereby sensations, &c. are produced; and though the existence of these, notwithstanding they are equally with it impalpable to sense, and unrepresentable in idea, as separate distinct existences, has been admitted by all, except those who adopt the opinion of there being nothing in nature but impressions and ideas.

12. Were these opinions and doctrines well founded, human knowledge would be very limited indeed. Were we acquainted only with our own sensations, or with these, and things cognizable by sense as separate independent existences only, and were incapable of becoming acquainted with any thing else, by means of reason, or of rational inferences from facts and phenomena, our knowledge would not only be very circumscribed, but the little knowledge then possessed would also be of very little value. This, however, is happily far from being the case. By means of rational deductions from facts and phenomena, not only is perception, or the knowledge of such external things as are cognizable by sense, or representable in idea,

R

acquired,

acquired, in the manner described in Essay I. but by the same means can a knowledge of existences, and of several of their properties, which are not cognizable by sense, or representable in idea, also be acquired, and that existence established by facts and arguments that must place it beyond controversy.

13. For, though a knowledge of power, cause, and necessary connection, cannot be acquired, or their existence proved directly and immediately, even in the case of animal action, from consciousness, sentiment, or *inward* impression, or from sensations, or impressions and ideas, from power, cause, and necessary connection, neither being objects of consciousness, nor of perception, as not being cognizable to sense, and representable in idea, as separate distinct independent beings, and as being altogether incapable of acting on the mind immediately and directly, or of acting immediately and directly on the external organs of sense, and through their agency on the mind, and thereby of producing in it consciousnesses, *inward* impressions, sensations, or ideas; yet a knowledge of them can be acquired, and their existence proved, by means of rational investigations and deductions, from experience, from experienced consciousnesses, sensations, phenomena, and facts; or from their action, as manifested by their sensible effects in those changes of state which take place in nature, in the operations of substance on substance, and of material body on material body; and in the consciousnesses, sensations, &c. they produce in the mind, not indeed immediately and directly of themselves, but through the instrumentality of material bodies operating on material bodies, and on the external organs of sense, whether as permanent and essential, or as unessential, temporary, and superinduced qualities of the material bodies, by the instrumentality of which they act. The knowledge of power, causation, and necessary connection, then, cannot be, and is not directly and immediately acquired by means of consciousness, sentiment, *inward* impression, sensations, or phenomena, or by these alone, but is rationally deduced from them, and without the exercise of reason never could have been acquired. For though we are conscious of action in ourselves, we are not conscious of the power by which it is produced, from its not being an object of consciousness, and acquire the knowledge of its existence only by means of rational deductions from the experienced consciousnesses of its action, and the perception

of

of the effects thence resulting; it is merely from these, and from finding on experiment, that we can at will generate action in ourselves, of which we are conscious, that we rationally infer, and experimentally prove, that we are possessed of a power whereby we can direct the faculties of our minds and the limbs of our bodies in their operations, and by their agency produce effects or changes of state in other things, beings, or existences; and it is not from mere appearances, or from casual experience and observation only, but also from experiments made for the express purpose of ascertaining the fact, that it is rationally inferred, and the justness of the inference is intuitively, or experimentally and demonstratively proved, that there actually are such existences in nature as power, cause, and necessary connection.

14. Thus, it is not so much from the casual and frequent observance of the action of one billiard-ball on another, that we infer that there is a necessary connection between them, whereby this action is produced, and that the motion of the second is the effect of the action of the first on it, or, in other words, that the first is the cause of the motion in the second, as from finding, on making the experiment, that one billiard-ball may at any time be made to generate motion in another at rest; and it is not so much from casual observation, as from finding on experiment, that motion may be either generated or destroyed at pleasure, in the water-wheel of a mill, and consequently in the mill itself, by either applying the water to the wheel, or by diverting it to some other course, that we both infer and prove that it is the water, by means of its gravity, that is the cause of the motion and action in the water-wheel, and that the action of the water-wheel is the cause of the action of the mill, &c. Thus, also, when we perceive a stone, or other material body to descend towards the earth, in place of either remaining stationary, or of moving in any other direction, we rationally conclude that it must necessarily be determined to motion in that particular direction; since if not determined to motion, it must necessarily remain stationary, as it would be contradictory and absurd to suppose that it would or could move without any necessary determination to motion; or, though urged or determined to motion, if that determination was equal in all directions. When we perceive that the body not only moves by the shortest direction towards the centre of the earth, but also is capable either

of

of moving certain obstacles which were stationary out of its way, or, if they are not moveable by it, of impressing and altering their figures, and if they are sentient beings of thereby producing in them sensations of pain, &c. we rationally ascribe power or force not only to that by which the body is necessarily determined to motion in that particular direction, from its being capable of determining it thus, but also to the body itself from its being capable of removing obstacles, and of producing pain in sentient beings, &c. and this necessarily, since it is to capability of producing change of state or a tendency to change of state that the terms cause, power, and force, are exclusively appropriated:—to the former of these powers referred to above, that by which the body is urged towards the center of the earth, the name of gravity has been given; and it is to the latter of these, or that whereby one material body acts upon another, that the name of mechanic power has been appropriated.

15. To the power, or to that which is capable of producing change of state, we give the name of cause, and to the change of state produced the name of effect, while that in which the change is produced, is named the substance or thing effected, and sometimes affected. When it was discovered from natural phenomena that all material bodies are necessarily determined to approach each other, and by means of rational deductions from these phenomena, that this determination is mutual, and according to certain determinate forces for each particular case, and that these forces are in all cases *cæteris paribus* directly as the densities, or quantities of matter in the bodies, it was rationally concluded, that this mutual determination must necessarily be in consequence of the operation of some power, and this power was denominated the power of gravity, and the mutual determination of material bodies for each other the attraction of gravitation. The particular degree of force whereby any particular body is thus attracted to the earth, is in vulgar language called the weight of that body; and the relative forces of attraction in bodies to the earth, and the relative quantities of matter in them, is usually ascertained by ascertaining their relative weights by means of balancing. When we have perceived that a piece of iron will seemingly of itself, and even in direct opposition to its gravity, move to a magnet, and any small body to an excited electric, we rationally conclude, not only that it must be by means of some power that this change is effected, but also that this force or power cannot be that of

gravity,

gravity, since it is superior to that of gravity, as it acts in opposition to it in these cases, and with superior efficacy, and since to suppose the contrary would be absurd, as being contradictory to the premises on which the conclusion is founded, or to the facts or phenomena from which it is deduced. And when we have perceived that the effect produced by one elastic body impinging against another is *ceteris paribus* double of that produced by one non elastic body impinging on another, we rationally conclude that this effect must necessarily be owing to some power or cause, though that power or cause is not cognizable to sense nor representable in idea, more than the gravitating, magnetic or electric powers, and that that power must necessarily be the elastic, as the effect produced in this case could not without absurdity be ascribed to any other power, since no other power, but that by which the bodies restore their forms after having been compressed by the impact, enters into this case more than entered into the former when the impinging bodies were non-elastic; and in this manner in other cases also is the existence of power, though neither cognizable by sense, nor representable in idea, rationally and justly inferred and clearly and conclusively proved.

16. It has on these principles, or by means of rational deduction from facts and phenomena, also been concluded, that every mechanical effect, and there can be no doubt but it holds with regard to every natural effect whatever, is necessarily determined by a certain precise degree of force or power: it being found by experiment and calculation that no other degree of it, operating under the same circumstances, can possibly produce any particular effect, but that particular degree of it by which that particular effect actually is produced; and that the same degree of power never operates under the same circumstances, without producing precisely the same effect: and this having been accurately ascertained in many cases, may by induction be regarded as a general law and established principle, and hence that there is no change or degree of change, which takes place in nature, but what is the necessary result of a precise determinate degree of power or force, or is the necessary effect of an adequate cause, as necessarily determined by the laws of nature, or those qualities of things whereby that successive train of causes and consequences, or that connected chain of events, which regularly succeed each other, forming what is called the course of nature, is produced and regulated; each particular

kind

kind and degree of power, or each cause producing invariably under the same circumstances the same changes or effects, however different the times in which the events may take place, or the intervals by which they may succeed each other.

17. It is from the observance of that necessary dependence which actually takes place in nature of one event on another, and of the necessary dependence of changes or effects on powers or causes, that the mind rationally infers and experimentally and logically proves, first, in the way of analysis, the necessary connections and relations of effects to causes, in deducing from known effects their proper proximate causes, by ascertaining in each particular case the precise degree of power, or force or energy in the object by which the effect or change of state in any other object is produced, and thereby the adequate and real cause of that change; and, then, regarding the cause thus found as the effect of some preceding cause, the mind proceeds in the investigation in the same manner till that cause is also discovered, and thus ascends in the enquiry from cause to cause, till they necessarily terminate in a first cause. When inverting the order of investigation, the mind, from known powers or causes, and their known modes of operation thus rationally and experimentally ascertained, acting under given circumstances, rationally deduces and experimentally ascertains and proves those effects these powers or causes always will and always must under these circumstances necessarily produce; and thus in the way of synthesis proves what had before been proved in the manner of analysis, the actual existence of powers or causes, and the necessary mutual connection and dependence of causes and effects, or of one event on another, and thereby that that regular succession of events which forms the course of nature is not an effect without a cause, and that that constant conjunction which is observed to take place in nature between certain objects and certain events among themselves is not merely fortuitous, but the necessary consequence of this necessary connection : and that in each case on experiments, reasonings and principles, so cogent, clear and conclusive, as must necessarily, it is presumed, impress full conviction on every rational and unprejudiced mind.   For, however ingenious, subtile and acute the reasonings of Mr. Hume may be, whereby he attempts to prove that that regular succession, or what he calls conjunction of events which takes

place

place in nature, is not the effect of any necessary connection among them, these reasonings cannot justly be regarded as being well founded, conclusive and satisfactory, since it is surely unphilosophical, and even absurd to regard that which is regular, steady and determinate, as merely fortuitous, or as an effect without a cause, and since it follows as necessary consequences, that, if this regular succession of events is not an effect without a cause, it must necessarily depend on the nature of things as established by the will of the Deity, and if on the nature of things, that it must be impossible for it to be otherwise than as it actually is while the nature of things continues the same; and this being the case, it follows that it must also necessarily be the effect of a connection among the things, objects or events themselves, and that this connection must be a necessary connection, since that must be necessary in the nature of things, the contrary of which is in the nature of things impossible.

18. It is also equally unphilosophical and unfounded to suppose the conclusions rationally deduced from this regular succession of events in nature, and the knowledge thence acquired with regard to power, causation, and necessary connection, to have no other origin than in the *inward* impressions and feelings of the human mind: thus inverting the natural order of things in making external existences depend on mental impressions, and not mental impressions on external objects. And nothing surely can be worse founded than that doctrine so much insisted on, and on which so much stress is laid, of its being merely from one species of event being in all instances followed by another, that we call the one object cause, the other effect, &c. since there are many particular events that constantly follow each other, of which the one is not even by the vulgar supposed to be the cause, and the other the effect, or the preceding the cause, and the immediately succeeding the effect; for no one ever supposed that darkness was the cause of light, or light the cause of darkness, or that day was the cause of night, and night of day, though they not only constantly succeed each other, but that immediately and according to a regular order; though all are convinced that this constant conjunction in regular succession is not fortuitous, but a necessary connection as being effects necessarily resulting from some cause or causes; which causes the vulgar imagine to be the rising and setting of the sun, according to stated times in a regular order,

and

and the learned know to be the action of the sun's light on the earth, and the motion of the earth round its axis. This mode of reasoning is applicable to the regular changes and successions of the seasons of the year, to the succession of years themselves, to that of the phases of the moon, the regular flowings and ebbings of the sea, and innumerable other events of a similar nature. Power then does not depend upon or consist in the constant conjunction and regular succession of changes of state in the same object, but on that which causes these changes in it; and though the one state of the object itself has not power to cause the other, yet there is such a thing as power, and such powers as cause these changes in it.

19. Were there no such existences as powers, were there no causes and effects, and no necessary connections between the objects and events in nature; or were the laws or modes of their operation entirely unknown to us, no useful purpose could ever be accomplished or end attained by human beings either in the moral or physical world. Without their aid and this knowledge, it would be impossible for them to conceive or construct even the simplest machine proper for producing any required effect, and to obtain by that means any proposed end; since these powers are the only means that can be employed for obtaining these effects, and since the proper adaptation of them for obtaining the end proposed must necessarily be regulated by a knowledge of their particular forces and modes of operation; and that this is actually the case, there is ample proof both analytical and synthetical from that exact correspondence which is found to subsist between theory and practice in these cases, the performance of the machine being conformable in most cases to the conception entertained of it before it was constructed, and the end proposed to be obtained by it being obtained by its means when constructed. In any machine, as a water-mill for grinding of grain, for instance, the engineer or millwright who conceives and executes it, does it on the supposition that the gravity of the water is the power which is to give motion and effect to the whole by generating motion in the water wheel, which he supposes will generate it in that part of the mill it immediately communicates with, and that part in the next, and thus in succession, till the effect required is produced; and this he finds in practice, or in making the experiment, to be actually the case:—nor is it possible for any rational being to doubt of the truth of these reasonings, or

these

these facts who is not blinded by metaphysical prejudices, or bewildered in the obscure labyrinth of those metaphysical subtilties, paradoxes, delusions and errors, in which the received doctrines of ideas, abstractions, and reasonings purely intellectual, are involved.

20. There is no species of knowledge of so much import to mankind as that of power, cause and effect, and necessary connection; since upon it the most valuable part of our reasonings, those regarding the adaption of means to ends, and thereby the production of the events and objects required, as well as the arts and all the sciences (the mathematical and a few others perhaps excepted), and also the prudent and proper regulation of conduct in life in a very great degree necessarily depends. It is upon these facts, reasonings, and principles that the moralist, the politician, and the metaphysical as well as the natural philosopher must necessarily proceed in their investigations, if they are to be attended with success, or with discoveries of use and importance; and even the researches of the mathematician can be productive of no substantial advantages, unless the physical facts, powers, and principles to which their calculations are applied, are first by this means, and on these principles accurately investigated and ascertained, so as to be established on sure and satisfactory evidence. The sciences of metaphysics, morality, and jurisprudence, have nearly as much dependence on this kind of knowledge, and consequently on the physical facts from which it is deduced, as mechanics, hydrostatics, chemistry, and the other sciences commonly regarded as more strictly physical. It is also by means of this knowledge alone that we are enabled to foresee future events, and thereby to prepare either for being benefited by them, or for avoiding any inconveniencies or evils with which they might otherwise be attended. By its means we are enabled to acquire dominion not only over the inferior animals of the creation, but also in some degree over the elements themselves, and even over the powers of nature so as to render them in many cases subservient to our will, and conducive to our purposes; and thereby, in a certain degree, to controul events and govern futurity.

21. Since these doctrines which deny the existence of powers and causes, and their operation in nature, have never been adopted by any but in speculation, none ever having trusted to these principles in regulating their conduct in the occurrences of life, it must have required no common degree of

s   acuteness

acuteness and ingenuity, of eloquence and command of language, to have given to such a distorted semblance of nature, to such a perversion of reason, as that of the ideal philosophy and the doctrines deduced from it, such a degree of plausibility as to have impressed conviction with respect to its validity on many deservedly eminent for knowledge and abilities. Nor has this acuteness and ingenuity wanted its reward, the authors having been regarded by many not merely as philosophers but as sages, not merely as prodigies of genius but as benefactors of the human race who by their profound researches and sublime discoveries have divested science of vulgar prejudice and error.

Having now concluded all that appears to me necessary for the refutation of these arguments and conclusions of Mr. Hume, and for the establishing of the existence, efficacy, and operation of things even incognoscible by sense, of power, causation, and necessary connection, I shall now, as before, proceed in my investigations, treating of these as things the reality of which is admitted; though, for the removing of any remaining doubts or scruples which others may entertain with respect to the principles above developed, and for their complete elucidation and establishment, this subject will be occasionally resumed, and these principles further confirmed in the subsequent parts of this Essay.

PART II.

1. No created thing can exist absolutely, since all must necessarily depend on their Creator. Most or all of them may perhaps also depend on each other in a subordinate degree, though we are ignorant of the means. But, though any particular thing may thus depend upon other things for its existence, entity, or being what it is, and not any other thing or nothing, yet if it is distinguishable from other things, is capable of affecting and being affected, and of being modified in various respects without altering its being or essential qualities, or those of whatever formed, or on whatever depending, which constitute it or make it what it is, though some of its relations to other things may thereby be altered, it may be regarded in as far as existing absolutely, and may with strict propriety be denominated a SUBSTANCE.

2. All

2. All entities, or all existing things, are not, however, included under the term substance; for properties, modes, and relations, as different degrees of motion, differences of figure, &c. and differences in the modes of action thence resulting, though not powers or substances of themselves, are things or entities relatively to such other things or entities as may be, or are capable of being differently affected by the action of the same powers, under circumstances otherwise similar, from differences in these; and these entities, or differences in properties, modes, &c. being by these means manifest to sense, soon become objects of mental perception and contemplation, and thereby known to us, not in idea only, but as really and actually existing in the nature of things.

3. There cannot be modification, without something to modify, all modifications having necessarily a reference to something modified, or capable of modification. There cannot possibly be any modifications of privations; and hence rest, which may be the privation of action or of motion, is incapable of modification; darkness, or a total privation of light, is the same; and this holds of the total privation of every other thing capable of modification. Different degrees of motion are modifications of a modification, or a modification modified, since motion itself is only a modification of some thing or substance.

4. Except in the case of modifying a modification, it is necessary for the something capable of modification, to be of a limited extension, and to be distinguishable from other things, &c. that is to be a substance. Mere modes, or manners of being, as number, extension, motion, &c. admit of being modified simply, or in one way, and in degree only; but substances properly so called, or distinct beings, admit of being modified in more ways than in one, and differing from each other otherwise than in degree, as not only in number, but also in size, figure, and motion, &c. and each of these in different degrees. Perhaps any particular or single power can be modified simply, or in degree only, unless that the direction in which it acts, and the extent of surface on which it acts, may be varied, if these can be regarded as modifications of it; this, at least, seems to be the case with mechanic power or impulse.

5. ACTION is the exercise of power, in the causing of change of state, or a tendency to change of state. Changing of state, in consequence of being

acted

acted upon, in place of being action, is passion in the substance, whose state is thereby changing. It is only from changes, that we infer powers, and learn their several modes of action, or what we call their particular natures. We perceive and attend to their respective different modes of action, and finding from observation and experience, that the same power, when the circumstances are directly similar under which it acts, invariably acts in the same way, and produces the same change, we thence conclude that it is necessarily constrained to act in that particular manner, and therefore call these modes of its action, the laws of its action, and the nature of the power. Of power, or powers, we can otherwise have no perception, conception, or knowledge, from powers being, though substantial, immaterial with respect to us, or not material relatively to the human standard, and therefore not capable of affecting our senses, or of being cognizable to sense, otherwise than through the medium and instrumentality of matter; nothing being capable of *immediately* affecting our senses, but what is material, or at least of affecting them in such a manner, as to be perceptible to us. It is from the changes of state, or effects produced, that we infer an adequate cause; and it is to this cause that we give the name of power. Hence POWER OR FORCE may be defined *that by which change of state, or a tendency to change of state, is produced.* Judging from the changes or effects only, we give to power different names, ascribing those effects that seem to us of different or opposite natures to different or opposite powers or causes. It is from the measures of the effects, that we infer the degrees of power in the cause, and that we conclude that certain degrees of power will always, under certain circumstances, produce certain effects, and hence deduce the mode of action of the power, or those modes of action, we call laws, which, by constituting its nature, seem to regulate it. It is common, indeed, to regard the inert material instrument by means of which the power acts, and from which, in some cases, it necessarily results, and in others, whether adventitious or not, seems to inhere, as the power, and to denominate it such, as the descending load of a clock or pile-engine, the main spring of a watch, a piece of steel rendered magnetical, &c.; and this appropriation of the term is useful in mechanics, and in some other cases.

6. There cannot be changes of state, without motion, but there may be power and action, as in the cases of a compressed elastic body, and of

pressure

pressure from gravity, &c. Hence rest, relative to motion, may not be a cessation of action, though it must of motion, as a body, though it moves not, may not be at rest relative to action; and since powers cannot only subsist, but also act, when at rest relative to motion, it would seem that neither their subsisting nor acting depended essentially on motion in them; and perhaps they never either act or move, but in the case of powers of different natures opposing or attracting each other, and when the action is reciprocal; and though action seems more essential to them than motion, yet certain kinds, as the mechanical, are capable of subsisting without either of them, since it is under particular circumstances only that they either act or move.

7. Powers, though not in act, are still powers; that being a power which is capable of action. Causes are always powers, but powers are causes only when in act; and it is only when they are in action, that they are relations, or at least that they have any immediate reference to the thing acted on. But they may be merely relative in another respect, or in as far as they are powers with regard to some particular things, and not to others, as the magnetic to iron only. There is no such thing in nature, nor among created beings, as a power of spontaneous and arbitrary action, or of acting in different ways under the same circumstances, but all is necessary and determined, each power or cause being only the effect of a precedent power or cause, and all originating in the Supreme Power, or First Cause.

8. Powers, except such as result from combination, organization, or mechanism, in place of being the effect or result of modification, are by their mutual actions the cause of it, and the necessary and only cause of it, since nothing else is capable of effecting change of state. There may be various powers in nature, of which we have no knowledge, subsisting as much by themselves, or as distinct substances, as any we are acquainted with, for we can know those only that directly or indirectly affect our senses. That which affects our senses must necessarily be either the action of some power, though perhaps acting through the instrumentality of matter, or the privation of the action of some power which we have recently experienced. What affects them not is to us as nothing.

9. Substances, relatively to animated beings, consist of powers or sensible qualities only, for destroy these, and with them the substances themselves

themselves vanish. And they are with respect to such beings, precisely what their respective sensible powers or qualities make them to be; for these cannot be altered, without a corresponding alteration, relatively to such sentient beings, in the substances they respectively form also taking place. Relatively to each other, inanimated substances are what their respective powers of acting upon, or of mutually affecting each other, make them; for if they possessed no powers, and were therefore incapable of mutual action, they would necessarily be to each other as nothing; and if they possess powers, they must necessarily act upon or affect each other agreeably to those powers of acting upon and affecting each other they respectively possess. Substance then, as a relative existence, and we have no knowledge of any others among created things, must necessarily consist of powers, since it is impossible for it to exist thus otherwise, that being something to that thing only it is capable of affecting, and of being affected by, and nothing to every thing besides. The terms then something and nothing, substantial and unsubstantial, material and immaterial, are merely relative, as being expressive only either of powers or properties, or of the privation or the negation of powers or properties, which powers and properties are mere relations, as being powers and properties only as having a reference to something else as a standard, and being either the one or the other, that is either powers or properties, or the privation or negation of these, according to the nature and qualities of that thing to which they are referred as a standard; that which is something with respect to one thing, being as nothing with respect to another, as the magnetic power to iron, and to nothing besides.

10. Power, or that which acts, must necessarily be something to that at least which it acts upon; and to act, it must necessarily be extended; and if of a limited extension, it must necessarily possess modes, as figure, &c. and form a proper subject or substratum for these. But as these are the distinguishing characteristics of substance, as well as of power, it must be evident that not only a combination of powers, but even a single power may form substance; and since nothing further is required to form substances, than powers and combinations of powers, it must follow as a necessary consequence, that the substances so formed, cannot possibly have occasion for any support or substratum, or for any other powers or
substances

substances to subsist or inhere in; nor when formed of combined powers for any other cement or bond of union, than that of their mutual attractions, or of those chemical affinities whereby mutual attractions take place between them.

11. It is the sensible powers or qualities that with respect to sentient beings constitute the essence, that is the particular substance itself, or that which makes it, relatively to those beings, what it is and no other thing; but as a substance may vary in qualities or become different from what it was relatively to any sentient being merely from alterations in the sentient faculties of that being, without there being alteration in the substance itself, its real essence or absolute existence must be perfectly independent of this relation; and as these powers in substances, whereby those sensations are excited in our minds which we mentally transfer to the substances themselves, and then denominate the sensible qualities of these substances, are, as all other powers, only inferred from effects as not being manifest to sense, we must be entirely ignorant of the real natures, and therefore of the real essences of things, or of that by which the sensible essences or qualities are produced:—it may however be proper to observe here, that what is said above with regard to the sensible essences is applicable and refers only to those qualities of substances Mr. Locke denominates secondary, and also that under the term qualities I often include both powers and properties.

12. It must be evident that properties, as duration, extension or magnitude, limitation or figure, mobility, divisibility, number, arrangement or situation, proportion, ratio, or relations of every kind, &c. or combinations of them if such were possible, cannot by any means possibly form substance, when it is considered that not one of them can possibly exist by itself, or as a separate and distinct entity, but that all necessarily require some power or powers, or combinations of these, as a support, substratum or substance to exist in, and of which they are the properties:—those of duration, and extension or space, and time, may perhaps at first view seem to form exceptions, but when maturely considered that will be found not to be the case.

13. Substances have usually been divided into material and immaterial, and of each of these many varieties exist, so as to admit of an indefinite number

number of subdivisions. These substances or combinations of powers which are *solid* relatively to the human body as a standard, and consequently to each other, constitute MATTER, or are those denominated material whatever their other powers or properties may be. Those which are not *solid* relatively to this standard constitute the other order of substances, and are those denominated IMMATERIAL. Solidity consists in effectual resistance from obstruction to free mutual penetration, and thereby to the occupation of the same portion of space by more than one being of the kind at one time. Hence those substances which effectually resist from obstruction mutual free penetration, and thereby individually occupy a particular portion of space to the effectual exclusion of all others, are solid relatively to each other; and if they are also solid relatively to the human body they are those that are denominated material. None of those qualities of matter Mr. Locke calls primary, and on which he supposes those he calls secondary and all others to depend, are, or consist of powers, but that of solidity alone; all the others being merely modes or properties.

14. As solidity then, or what is the same thing solid magnitude, since solidity implies magnitude, evidently consists in nothing but a power of preventing both contraction and expansion in itself, and the intrusion of any other solid or similar magnitude into the space it occupies; and as we have no experience, knowledge, or even conception, of any single power capable of producing effects repugnant and subversive of each other, or such as those of both attracting and repelling, or contracting and expanding, or of acting of itself in directly opposite directions at the same time and with equal force, we must, I am inclined to suppose, necessarily conclude that solidity, or the formation of matter, is not the effect of one power—but rather of powers of directly opposite natures, acting on each other with equal intensities:—the one being essentially attractive, and the other essentially repulsive, but each kind attractive of the other.

15. If MATTER is created at all, and is not necessary and eternal, it necessarily must be created of what is IMMATERIAL, that is not material relatively to the same standard, and therefore such must be the nature of its elements or constituent powers or principles; but though immaterial they must be possessed of finite extension, as otherwise they could not by their union possible constitute finite magnitude. Every power however

must

must necessarily be possessed of this property, since without it, it could not be capable of action, and if incapable of action could not be a power; and that they actually possess it we know from their effects. Though one kind of these powers is supposed essentially attractive, and the other essentially repulsive, they are not supposed to be so in an indefinite degree, as of the repulsive repelling and the attractive attracting even to annihilation, for that would involve the absurdity of each being annihilable, under certain circumstances, by that on which its very essence, being, or existence depends; or of attraction destroying attraction, and repulsion repulsion. This besides would not be consonant to nature and reason, since from these we learn that all created things must necessarily be finite; and that none are annihilable, except modifications, combinations, and organizations, with their effects, by any power but that by which they were created.

16. These powers of opposite natures do not destroy each other on combining together, as equal and opposite motions in unelastic bodies do upon impact, for such powers are not annihilable, by that or any other natural means; but in place of it constitute matter, and continue to act on each other, since on the continuance of that action must the maintenance of their union, or the continuance or duration of that matter they form necessarily depend; and, other circumstances being the same, so long as these powers continue to combine in equal quantities with equal force or intensity, so long will they continue to add to the mass or volume equal magnitudes of equal densities in equal times; and, if there are differences in the degrees of intensity, the greater or less the intensity the greater or less the density of the matter thereby formed. By density, I do not here mean gravity or weight, for that seems to depend on other principles, but only the degree of condensation of the powers contained in a certain space. But whatever the degree of intensity or density in this case, the attracting and repelling constituting powers must always necessarily be in equilibrio, the repulsive equalling the attractive, and *vice versa*, so as perfectly to saturate and neutralize each other—for saturation and neutralization can properly mean nothing else but the effect of opposite powers counterbalancing each other and thereby becoming latent and insensible, except in as far as new powers essentially different from the constituent may result from their union—and by thus exerting the whole of their force on each

T   other

other in maintaining this equilibrium become not only solid, but also inert, with respect at least to other substances in the same state; and so as to be even incapable of acting chemically on other bodies, except under certain circumstances:—and thus may matter, or that which is solid and inert, be formed merely of active immaterial powers; or may active immaterial powers be formed into that which is solid and inert.

17. Solidity, as has already been observed, is merely relative; that being solid to one thing which is pervious to another; and though matter, or neutralized powers, is solid with regard to us, from our bodies being formed of the same, yet it might not be so to rational beings otherwise constituted, and what was solid to them from being formed of the same materials with themselves might not be so to us.

18. We have no knowledge of any thing but what is ultimately acquired by means of sensation; and nothing but either matter or what is solid with respect to our bodies, whether gravitating or not, or what acts through matter as a medium, seems capable of affecting our senses and thereby of becoming known to us. What affects them not, either directly as matter, or indirectly through matter as a medium, is, and necessarily must be, to us, as nothing.—That which is immaterial, but which affects our senses through the medium of matter, and thereby becomes known to us, whether it is a property of matter, or a power depending on and resulting from matter, or a power existing absolute and independent of it, and using it only as an instrument, cannot be to us an occult power or property: since we have the testimony of our senses as to its operation and efficacy from its sensible effects, and therefore intuitive and rational evidence of its existence. Thus, even in the cases of having observed the traces of human footsteps on the sands of the coast of an uninhabited island, and of having observed a regularly formed and commodious house in a desert, we are enabled by rational inference, with certainty, to assign the causes of these effects; since no doubt can be rationally entertained of these impressions having been made by feet of human beings, who had at some period visited the island though now uninhabited, there being no other rational or even probable way of accounting for them; and since no doubt can be rationally entertained of the well formed commodious house having been the result of human ingenuity and human workmanship; as it might easily have been
pro-

produced by that means, and could not possibly, agreeable to the nature of things, have been produced by any other:—and since no doubt can therefore be rationally entertained of these productions or phenomena being effects, or of their having had causes---though these causes, or those who produced the effects, never came under the cognizance of the senses of those who draw this inference from those effects, and therefore are as much unknown to them, and as much occult to them, in as far as occultness depends on that circumstance of the cause never having come under the cognizance of sense, as immaterial powers, of whose effects we are sensible, but which come not within the cognizance of sense—and if thus, by a process of just reasoning from effects to their adequate causes, the existence not only of material, but even of immaterial causes posessing intelligence which never came within the cognizance of sense can be discovered and proved, there surely can be no doubt but by the same process the existence of other immaterial powers which are not intelligent, and which never came within the cognizance of sense, may also be rationally and justly inferred from their sensible effects; and thereby that existence decidedly and decisively proved.

19. That only is occult whose existence is occult; and of which the qualities hypothetically attributed to it are not rationally and truely inferable from phenomena:—as the Monades of Leibnitz; the Vortices of Des Cartes; the Phlogiston of Becker and Stahl; the Oxygen, Hydrogen, Azot, &c. of Lavoisier; and the causes hitherto assigned for attractions and repulsions, as of gravity, &c. which are all merely hypothetical, their existence being supposed but not proved; and, perhaps, doubts may even be entertained as to those hypothetical qualities assigned them being justly deducible from the phenomena. But however that may be, no doubts can be rationally entertained with respect to the existence of immaterial powers, or to the genesis of matter from what is immaterial; since it is manifest from their sensible effects, and from numerous other phenomena in nature, that such powers actually do exist; and since it is also manifest, that if matter has been created at all, and is not necessary and eternal—as supposed by the ancients, Spinosa, and other atheistical authors, who represent it as being impossible even for Infinite Power to create or to annihilate it---it necessarily must have been cre   ou of

what

what is immaterial, since it would be absurd in the extreme to suppose any thing to have been created out of itself, or that matter could be created out of what was material. And from the known nature and qualities of gravitating matter, and the reasons assigned above, it seems highly probable that it may have been generated originally of such immaterial elementary powers as those supposed above, which, by forming new combinations among themselves, as influenced by different circumstances, now produce all that wondrous diversity and variety in the natures, or in the powers or qualities of the several substances they form.—

20. I do not, however, give this genesis of gravitating matter, which is not warranted by experiment, or does not rest on intuitive evidence, as an established fact; but merely as what appears to me as a rational deduction from these known powers or qualities of gravitating material substances, of their effectually resisting, and with equal force, any further expansion or contraction in themselves—powers on which their solidity manifestly necessarily depends since it consists in them and could not possibly exist without them—and which, though it affords not what may perhaps be called physical certainty, may yet perhaps, when corroborated by other reasons which will be afterwards adduced, have some pretensions to be regarded as a probable conjecture at least:—and should it be proved in the sequel, by experiments both analytical and synthetical, that any other kind of matter, or matter not possessing gravity, can be thus resolved into, and be again generated of powers of opposite natures, which are palpable to sense, and are known to exist separately, this analogy, for it cannot be called induction, as no general inference can be drawn from one particular case only, will no doubt give such additional validity to this conjecture, of gravitating matter being also formed of powers, as to make it amount almost if not entirely to a rational certainty.

21. The mechanical philosophers, and Mr. Locke, seem to think that all powers depend upon matter, and are merely results of different modifications of it—that this something inert is not formed of powers of opposite and balancing natures, but that all powers are formed of this something inert; and that mechanic action is the only manner in which matter is capable of operating, and momentum the only power it possesses, which, from the various modifications induced by it in matter, may be so diversified

as

as to produce all that wondrous variety of powers, or rather according to them modes of impulse, which take place in nature.

22. Changing of state may be either merely the changing of modifications, the substances otherwise remaining the same, and this is all that ever is effected by mechanic action; or it may be changing of the substances themselves, so that they shall be essentially different from what they were, and this is effected principally if not entirely by means of the affinities and elective attractions of the original elementary powers or constituent principles of matter. In the first of these mechanical, and in the last chemical, action consists; and as there are two kinds of action, so there are two kinds of powers in nature by which matter is peculiarly affected—chemical and mechanical—the first kind constituting it, and the last resulting from it, and therefore incapable of subsisting of itself, or of forming substance.

Mechanic power or force is that which causes change of modification in substances or bodies, and consists in that resistance to change of state in its modifications of motion, rest, direction, and form or figure, which is innate and essential to matter as matter. It is perhaps the only power that matter as matter possesses, except that of solidity on which this power partly depends, and is really as well as solidity a *vis insita* dependent on the matter itself, as being common to matter however modified, and as having otherwise evidently no existence; it, as well as solidity, being new powers resulting from the combination and neutralization of the original or elementary powers of which the matter is formed, but differing essentially from these powers; and which, though not elementary powers, are really essential or primary powers of matter. The modes and degrees of action of this power are as numerous and various as the various different modifications of matter, with their various different centres of magnitude, density, gyration, &c. and in the investigation and determination of these does the science of mechanics consist.

23. About the middle of the last century the great and important discoveries of Sir Isaac Newton had brought the mechanical philosophy into such high favour and repute that it alone was deemed sufficient to account for all the various phenomena of nature. The valuable chemical discoveries of latter times have however proved its insufficiency in that respect, and that to account for many of the phenomena in a just and satisfactory manner recourse must be had to other principles than those afforded by that philosophy

losophy alone. But though this is the case, and though mechanical power consists merely in the action and reaction resulting from motion and rest, and differences in the modes of motion as to degree and direction, in matter, yet the variety and importance of its operations and effects are such as when attentively considered to appear truly surprising. For all the powers in nature, chemical perhaps excepted, of which we have any knowledge in or through inanimated things, admit of having the extent, direction, and degree, of their action modified by the material medium, body, or instrument, by means of which they act on other material bodies; and these differences in the modes of action of the efficient power are effected by the agency of mechanic power, or that whereby matter resists change of its state; which power also acts differently under different circumstances, or with differences in extent, degree, and direction, according to differences in the sizes, figures, &c. into which the matter or material instruments are formed. No powers, elementary or chemical excepted, are capable, whether material or not, of affecting matter otherwise than by generating or destroying motion, or a tendency to motion in it; and as these effects can in these cases be produced only by means either of mechanic power, or of attractions and repulsions, the actions of these powers in producing these effects, that of the mechanical excepted, may all be resolved into those of attraction and repulsion.

24. These effects are, *ceteris paribus*, the same, whatever the nature of the efficient power; as whether attractive or repulsive, or whether the motion is generated and continued by gravity, the wind, by steam, or by gunpowder, &c. and the motion thus generated in the material instruments or machines, may be so varied in its action, in consequence of the various modifications of the matter constituting the instruments or machines, as to be capable of producing a wonderful variety of effects; of raising loads, grinding grain, spinning yarn, weaving cloth, measuring time, playing tunes, &c. and the capabilities of performing these, are called the powers of the machines. Thus the *efficient* power by which the machines are wrought, whether attractive or repulsive, is capable of appearing in innumerable different characters, of acting innumerable different parts, and of producing innumerable different effects; so that the same power may thus, Proteus-like, assume innumerable different appearances. But whatever the character it supports, the part it acts, and the effects it produces, they

must

must all necessarily depend on the *mechanic* powers or machines employed, or on the nature of the material organ or instrument by which the action it generates and supports is modified and directed, at the same time that the material organ or instrument itself is so far passive as to act only in consequence of being acted upon by it; and thus also may matter be made to modify matter, one material instrument or machine serving as the means of forming another and different material instrument or machine. When the velocities generated in these cases do not accelerate, either the efficient power must have discontinued its action, or the reaction or force of the resistance must have become such as to be equivalent to that of the efficient power, and thereby such as not only to prevent any further acceleration, but to require the continued and incessant agency of the efficient power to support and maintain the then velocity or degree of action.

By chemical action, I mean that attraction whereby the constituent powers or elements of bodies unite, and adhere when united. And not that attraction whereby the integrant parts of bodies unite and adhere, as these parts may in some cases be separated from each other by means merely mechanical, and as no other alterations in their properties take place, either from their aggregation or separation, than what may result from differences of modification only.

25. By elective attraction, I mean that species of chemical action whereby either certain constituent or elementary powers of matter, or certain bodies or combinations of these, unite, under certain circumstances, with certain other bodies, or combinations of these, to the rejection and exclusion of others, even though they were united with them before, and therefore with a seeming preference or election; these effects, however, like all others, are regulated by fixed and established laws, these combinations or elections differing as the differences of temperature, &c. but being always the same, under the same circumstances. There seems to be no other kind of chemical repulsion but this resisting and rejecting of combination, under particular circumstances, if it may be so called, since in every case it appears to be only a necessary result or effect of elective attraction: neutralized combinations of powers, or what is the same thing, material bodies, seem in no case to be of their own natures repulsive of each other, but the reverse; and that the different elementary powers of which

they

they are formed, are not so, is proved by their unions in forming them; and in the cases of affinity or elective attractions mentioned above, this rejection is evidently the effect of the stronger attraction between the combining elements, or bodies themselves, than between them and the elements and bodies they reject; while the seeming repulsion which takes place in the case of two bodies only, as of oil and water, resisting or rejecting chemical combination, must proceed from the elements or constituent powers of each of these bodies having a stronger attraction among themselves, or for each other, than for those of the other body, under the then circumstances. There are indeed, in nature, elementary and material substances, essentially repulsive, or of which the parts of each mutually repel each other; but these different substances are nevertheless attractive of each other, and of gravitating matter, or matter essentially attractive, also. And any separations and dissipations, or seeming dissolutions they produce in the parts of gravitating matter, are not chemical or elementary, but integral; and though in many cases they have great influence on the modes of corpuscular arrangement, chrystalization, &c. of substances, yet even in these cases they do not prevent attraction and aggregation, but only modify its action; at the same time that those separations and dissipations of the integrant parts of gravitating substances, which are sometimes produced by their means, are never a consequence of any reciprocal repulsion between them and the gravitating matter, or of any diminution of that mutual attraction which is known to subsist between them and gravitating matter in other cases, but always solely of that mutual repulsion which takes place between the parts of the substance itself by which that effect is produced. It is for these reasons that I have taken no notice of repulsion in my definition of chemical action.

26. The different attractions which take place between different gravitating substances seem never to change to repulsions, though they may sometimes appear to do so, from the greater affinity of certain substances to others, than to those with which they are combined, from a change of temperature, or other circumstance, whereby they reject those they are combined with, to combine with the others, unless these attractions are electrical or magnetical; and, in these cases, attraction is never changed into repulsion, and *vice versa*, without the electricity of one of the attracting bodies being
changed,

changed, if the attraction is electrical; or the magnetism of one of the poles at least of one of the attracting bodies, being changed, if the attraction is magnetical.

27. Since the elective attractions, which, as sensible and palpable effects of which all the phenomena of chemistry afford instances, are known to take place between material bodies; and since the chemical changes of state, or of combinations thereby produced, like all other changes of state, must necessarily be the effects of some power or powers; and as neither our experience and observation, nor the manner in which these effects take place, give us any reason to suppose that these changes are produced by any extraneous and foreign powers, we must necessarily conclude that they are the effects of powers which are innate and essential to the bodies themselves; and as we also have experimental and incontrovertible proof that the compounds formed by the chemical combinations of material bodies differ essentially in their qualities from those of the bodies of which they are compounded, those of the constituting bodies being annulled by the process, as in the formation of neutral salts, &c. we must likewise necessarily conclude that these powers must be of contrary natures, since no others could possibly produce that effect, or counteract each other in such a manner, as from exerting their whole energy on each other, and in equilibrio, intirely to obliterate or annul their former qualities, or relations to other things; or, in the language of chemistry, perfectly to saturate and neutralize each other. But, if all compound bodies are formed of powers of contrary natures, or if all that wondrous variety of chemical changes and combinations which we observe to take place in nature are the effects of the reciprocal action of such powers, we may, I imagine, from such an induction, with reason and intire confidence conclude, that all material bodies whatever are formed of powers, and of such powers; and thus, then, the chemical, and those I have denominated the constituting, or elementary powers of matter, will be the same. This deduction and conclusion must appear the more logical and just, that it has already been shown, that a compound, or body formed of such powers, must necessarily be SOLID, relatively to other compounds or bodies of the same kind, and that it must also necessarily be so far INERT, as to be incapable of changing its state of *modification* of itself; and that I can now add, that it must also be incapable of having its *nature*

U

changed

changed otherwise, than by the reciprocal action between its elementary powers and other elementary powers, or between its elementary powers and the elementary powers of some other material compound or substance, whereby a new material compound or compounds, differing essentially in their qualities from those of their proximate principles, or of the substances of which they are generated, may be produced : indeed, the elective attractions alone appear to me to afford a proof of the existence of such elementary constituting powers, as satisfactory, clear, and convincing, as can be desired, or reasonably required.

28. The constituent or elementary powers of gravitating matter, at least, seem never to exist in an uncombined or separate state, one combination of them never being dissolved but in consequence of a new one instantaneously taking place, that is of a change of affinities ; and hence, for this reason alone, though there were no others, these powers must necessarily be insensible and unknown to us in such a state. That mechanic power must also necessarily be the same, must be evident, when it is considered that it can have no separate or independent existence, as being innate, or merely a necessary result from the combination and neutralization of the original, elementary, or chemical powers of which the matter is formed.

29. By chemical elective attractions bodies or compounds are destroyed, and new ones are generated, but the component powers are not destroyed, probably not essentially altered by the process, only differently compounded, whereby they constitute bodies of a different nature from what they did before ; for in all the operations of nature and art nothing seems to be created, and nothing seems to be annihilated besides modifications, and the qualities thence resulting ; an equal quantity of elementary powers seems to exist both before and after each operation, and the quantity and quality of these remaining the same, nothing can possibly take place in these operations, besides changes in the modifications, and in the combinations of these powers. By these it also appears, that the elements, or constituent powers of which bodies are formed, are not so much neutralized by their union in constituting them, but that they are still, under the proper circumstances, capable of acting on each other chemically, and thereby of producing changes and new combinations and modifications.

30. It

30. It is this chemical action among the elementary powers that is the foundation of all generation and corruption, of growth and decay, of fermentation, dissolution, and regeneration; or of all that beautiful and wondrous variety of substances and the *essential* changes to which they are liable which exist and take place in nature.

PART III.

1. At the commencement of this Essay the causes and powers of nature were divided, in compliance with custom, into physical and moral, though not with strict propriety, since all created things are necessarily physical; and in the course of the Essay it has been shown that there are two kinds of physical powers by which inanimated material bodies are particularly and principally affected, viz. chemical and mechanical. But these are not the only physical powers by which gravitating matter is affected. There are several others known to us, as the corpuscular, the gravitating, the elastic, the electric, and the magnetic powers; some of which have only been lately discovered, and it is not improbable but there may be many others with which we are unacquainted. None of these powers, except the chemical or elementary, seem to affect matter any otherwise than in its mixtures and modifications, and in the qualities thence resulting.

2. Though all powers to be powers must necessarily be efficient, or be capable of producing effects, yet, perhaps, it may not be improper on some accounts, to distinguish and divide physical powers into the two classes or kinds of efficient and mechanical; meaning by the former, the powers of attraction and repulsion, or powers that are either attractive or repulsive, as the elementary and the corpuscular powers, those of gravity, elasticity, electricity, &c. or those by means of which material substances are generated and destroyed, animals and vegetables grow and decay, and machines are wrought from motion generated and continued in them by their agency: and by the latter, or mechanic power, the power of material bodies to effect changes of modifications in each other by their reciprocal operation, as urged and compelled to action by the agency of any of the efficient powers. Or they may be divided into original and derivative;

those

those called above efficient being deemed original; and the mechanical, as resulting from and depending upon the combination of the chemical or elementary powers of which the matter is constituted and the different forms into which the matter is fashioned, being justly regarded as derivative.

3. The mechanical power naturally divides itself into two kinds, which I denominate the material, and the instrumental or organical powers. By the material, I mean not the material cause of Aristotle, which differed in gravitating material bodies according to differences in the forms and modes of arrangement of their particles and which had a reference merely to the differences in the effects thence resulting, but that innate essential power, or primary quality of matter, which has no respect to such differences, and is common to matter in general or to all material bodies, or to matter as matter, however modified or however its particles may be formed or arranged, and which has commonly, but in my opinion improperly, been called the vis inertiæ of matter, and which is to be treated of in the immediately succeeding Essay. By the instrumental or organic power of matter, I mean that power which results from and depends upon modifications of material substances, as to form and organization, whereby they are fashioned into instruments, machines, and engines, whether the material substances thus organized are gravitating or not, or are material or immaterial to the human standard, or are both in part; and whatever the nature of the efficient or original power, by which the action may be generated and continued in them. These instruments and machines are altogether incapable of generating, or of continuing action of themselves; and for that purpose, besides the material always require the operation of an original or efficient power. The instrumental or organical powers are as numerous and various as the various different instruments, machines, and engines, and the various different powers they severally possess. Some regard animals as machines, and attempt to deduce all the animal powers, mental and corporeal, from the operations of the animal machines. Those machines which are inanimated possess not intelligence, and their operation has no dependance on it, but it requires a considerable degree of it to contrive and execute them: to contrive and execute the meanest vegetable or animal is far beyond the reach of human abilities. There cannot be action in inanimated substances, without either the operation of two powers,

                                                                            or

or the reciprocal action of two agents, whether these powers are original or mechanical, or whether the action is in consequence of powers attracting or repelling each other, or in consequence of resistance to change of modification in the agents.

4. Power and force are not always the same or synonimous; and there may be action without reaction, or without that action being reciprocal, but not in inanimated substances; for there may not only be power where no force is exerted, as in the case of power not in act; but there also may be power in act, and effects or changes produced by its agency without its exerting any force in the production of these changes, and without the action being reciprocal or the power being affected by that which it effects: as in the case of a person who voluntarily moves out of the way of a fragment of a rock rolling with impetuosity down the side of a mountain, &c. Hence the very great difference in the mode of action of the moral powers or causes from the mode of action of the physical, or of those powers or causes which influence the will, and thereby determine the mind to action, from those whereby unintelligent substances act on each other, or from the action of matter upon matter; and hence the impropriety of attempting to account for the one kind of action by those laws which regulate the other: in moral action there are no mutual attractions and repulsions, no reciprocity of action; except, perhaps, in certain cases of mind acting upon mind through the instrumentality of the senses, as in particular infectious passions and affections, in sympathies and antipathies.

5. Those powers or causes which influence the will and determine the mind to action are usually denominated final causes, or motives. The mind in certain cases however is excited to action, by means of other powers and causes besides final causes or motives, as by the agency of external objects producing involuntary sensation and thereby involuntary action in it; but this action is more properly physical than moral. The motive, final cause, or power, which influences the will, and thereby induces a sentient, intelligent, and rational being or agent to act in any determinate manner, must necessarily be the benefit expected to be derived from that action, as the attainment of an end or object desired; whether that end or object desired is material or immaterial, a mental gratification or a material means whereby that gratification may be obtained; and both the desire

and

and the consequent action often depends more on the intelligence, or knowledge of the benefit, gratification, or other advantage that may be rationally expected to result from the action, than on the immediate direct operation of the object desired either on the senses, or on the fancy, for in many cases the object desired may at the time have no existence in nature or among created things: this was the case with all machines before they were conceived and executed, and with many other discoveries in the arts and sciences, which, in the language of Aristotle, existed before *potentially*, or as possibilities, but not *actually*, or in reality; and which, therefore, as having no *actual* existence could not possibly be capable of acting, or of producing any effect whatever. It is therefore the knowledge, real or supposed, or in other words the opinion entertained of the benefit, the gratification, or the profit, that would result from the attainment of these objects, and of the probability of attaining them, and by their means the gratification or end desired, and not the objects themselves that are the final causes or motives which induce the mind to act with the intention of obtaining them; it is merely this opinion that renders them the objects of desire; for even wealth and power, as conducive to happiness, could not induce desire or action in sentient beings capable of being benefited by them, if these beings had no knowledge of the benefit to be derived from them, or, though they had such knowledge, if they had no knowledge of the means by which they might be acquired, and therefore regarded the acquirement of them as impossible. These objects are desired only as means or subordinate ends; it is happiness, or the benefit expected to result from the attainment of them, that is the ultimate end or object of desire, and it is the opinion entertained of this benefit as conducive to happiness that is the power, motive, or final cause, which induces the mind to action, and which determines that action, while this opinion is itself in every case determined by, or is a necessary consequence of, the previous circumstances; as of the state both of the body and mind of the being as to health, &c. the degree of knowledge possessed by that being, the then situation of that being relative to other beings and objects, and the manner in which that being is affected by them, &c.

ESSAY

ESSAY IV.

OF MECHANIC POWER AND ACTION.

1. IT has already been observed in Part II. Article 21st, of Essay III., that there are two different kinds of powers in nature by which material substances are peculiarly affected---chemical and mechanical---the first effecting changes in the substances themselves whereby they become essentially different from what they were; the other producing in them changes of modification only, the substances otherwise remaining the same; in Article 5th, of Part II. of that Essay, that action is the exercise of power in causing change of state, or a tendency to change of state;---and in Article 21st of Part II. of that Essay, mechanic power has been defined to be *that which causes change of modifications only in bodies*, and has been represented to consist in that resistance to change of state in its modifications of rest, motion, direction, or form, which is inherent in and essential to every substance that is necessarily, from being formed of balanced or saturated and neutralized powers, dense and impenetrable, relatively to every other substance of the same kind, and altogether incapable of changing its present state, whether of rest, motion, direction, or form of itself.---And hence mechanic action may be defined *causing change of state, or a tendency to change of state, as to rest, motion, direction, or form, by means of mechanic power or force.*

2. Mechanic power or force then, according to this definition, consists neither in motion, nor in rest, nor in direction; but in resistance to change of state as to these. And mechanic action not in changing of state, but in mechanically causing or urging to change of state. Hence neither a state of motion, nor a state of rest relative to motion, in an inert body exempted
from

from external influence, is either action, or the effect of action or power, since in place of changing of state, or of causing change of state, it is continuance in the same state.

3. The doctrines of the *inertia*, a term I believe first used by Kepler, and of the *vis inertiæ* as it has been called, of matter, have hitherto, however, been embarrassed with such difficulties, and involved in such obscurity, as to have created doubts in many with respect to their validity. Not a few, perhaps the greater part of mankind, are still of opinion that action in matter consists in motion only; and that motion in it is the effect of an intrinsic motive power. Others again are as much convinced that matter is retained in its present state, whether of motion, rest, or direction, by powers either intrinsic or extrinsic to it; and that all its action, or resistance to change, is derived from these powers: and that this resistance to change of state is therefore necessarily in every case *ceteris paribus* directly as the force by which these powers retain it in its present state. While there are others who regard a state of motion in it only as requiring the agency of an extrinsic power to maintain, continue, and support it, and who are of opinion that this motive power communicates motion from one material body to another on their coming into contact, as from one in motion to one at rest, or moving with less velocity, by its abandoning that in motion or moving with the greater velocity in whole or in part, and entering into that at rest or moving with less velocity; and on this hypothesis they have endeavoured to account for mechanic action.

4. It has also been objected by those who regard motion as action, and an effect of power, that the *inactivity* of matter, the cause assigned by Sir Isaac Newton for the continuance of bodies in their state of rest, or of uniform motion in a right line, till made to change it by external force impressed, is not only insufficient for the purpose, especially in the case of motion, but that it is also an assumption without proof, inferred indeed from the phenomena, but not supported by reasons sufficiently cogent to warrant its adoption, or if adopted to afford conviction to the mind of its being adequate to the production of the effects attributed to it—that it is not possible for inactivity or passiveness to be cause or power, or for passion to be action —and, it may be added, that this way of accounting for continuance of motion in matter, as assuming in the premises what ought to have been
                                                                        proved

proved—that motion is not the effect of any power either intrinsic or extrinsic—is a mere *petitio principii* which, by cutting in place of untying the Gordian knot, gets rid without resolving it of that question so long disputed, " What is the cause of continuance of motion ?"

5. With a view of obviating these difficulties, and removing every doubt and objection with respect to the *inertia* of matter, an attribute which has been denied it by Leibnitz and others, it may be observed—

6. First, That Sir Isaac Newton's Law of Nature, with respect to the continuance of bodies in the same state, whether of rest or of uniform motion in a right line till made to change it by external force impressed, whatever its cause may be, must necessarily be admitted, since our experience furnishes us with the most ample testimony and convincing proof of its invariable agreement with phenomena.

7. Secondly, That it is a misconception of the doctrine and meaning of Newton, to imagine that by the inertness or inactivity of matter he means, in cases where no mechanic action or changes take place at least, a cause or power: since, on the contrary, in place of attributing continuance in its present state, when not acted on externally, to the agency of power, he imputes it entirely to its not being changed by the agency of power. As this way of reasoning, however, affords only presumption or probability, or at most only a negative or indirect proof not conveying full conviction to the mind that it cannot possibly be the effect of power, I shall now attempt a direct and positive proof that it neither is nor can possibly be the effect of any power or powers either intrinsic or extrinsic to it. Thus, it may be observed—

8. Thirdly, That a state of rest relative to motion in matter may be the effect of intrinsic, constituent, or elementary powers of contrary natures balancing, or saturating and neutralizing each other, and thereby becoming latent and insensible and altogether incapable of effecting any change of state in the matter or substance they form, is sufficiently manifest; and it must also be equally evident that a state of rest in matter cannot possibly be the effect of any intrinsic power or powers not constituent, and which are not thus balanced and restrained, and which are capable of effecting change of state in it, since the action of such power or powers on it would necessarily have a contrary effect, and change its state from rest to that of

x   motion;

motion; and that though the same state directly opposing itself does in certain cases destroy itself from the mutual and equal resistance to change of state in the opposing bodies, yet that this is applicable to a state of motion only, that of rest never opposing itself:—and hence, therefore, since the state of rest in matter or in any other substance that is inert from being formed of balanced and neutralized powers cannot possibly be owing in any case to the bodies being retained in that state by the action of any intrinsic power or powers not constituent and balanced, that hypothesis which makes the state of rest in matter to depend on the agency of such a power or powers must necessarily be unfounded.

9. Fourthly, That though force or power is required to cause changing of state as to motion and rest, it does not thence follow as a necessary consequence, as sometimes assumed in argument, that motion or changing of place, in bodies moving freely, also requires force or a motive power to support and continue it; nay, the contrary must necessarily be the case, since motion in a body cannot possibly require the agency of any power for its support or continuance, but on the hypothesis of its being opposed by some power acting in an opposite direction to that of its motion, and capable of destroying it:—an hypothesis not only unsupported by facts, and therefore by rational inferences, but also contrary to the data, as then the body would not move freely; and since no such action can possibly take place in this case, no motion can be destroyed, and no motion being destroyed, no force can possibly be required for its support, so that it must therefore necessarily continue, and continue uniform, as in fact it is found to do. This hypothesis of the continued agency of an intrinsic power in the direction of the motion being necessary for the support and continuance of the motion necessarily implies, as already observed, that if it was not for the continued agency of this motive power, the velocity would diminish, and the motion be destroyed; but by what means, and by what cause, has not so much as been assigned, besides being proved, and is in fact unassignable, as motion cannot possibly be the effect of two intrinsic powers acting in direct opposition to each other; since it necessarily must be, if the effect of power, the effect of a power or powers acting in one direction only: For, if these contrary powers were equal and balanced, they could have no effect whatever on the state of the body, whether of motion or rest; and if

they

they did not balance, their action on it would necessarily be equivalent to that of one power only, acting in one direction only, with a force equal to that of the difference between their respective energies. To say that the motion itself is capable of itself, and actually does oppose and gradually destroy itself, though in one direction and in one body only, and therefore necessarily requires the continued agency of an intrinsic power to maintain it, would be assuming an hypothesis palpably impossible and absurd, inconsistent with experience and the nature of things, and therefore equally inadmissible with that which it is brought to support.

10. Fifthly, That since it is incontestibly proved by experiment that mechanic power, or resistance to change of state, serves equally for the generation and for the destruction of motion, it must necessarily follow that in mechanic pressure or impulse a state of rest relative to motion must be as much a state of action as a state of motion; and from this it follows that a body from acting mechanically, and having thereby lost or gained of motion or of rest, loses nothing by that means of its mechanic power, since it must still be capable of resisting any equal change in its state with equal force and effect. These conclusions are confirmed by the action in these cases being always found on experiment to be reciprocal and equal, which it could not possibly be if each state did not resist equal changes with equal force; and this being the case, it must be evident that bodies at rest, in place of being devoid of all power and mechanic action, possess it equally, other circumstances being the same, with those in motion : and hence the invalidity of that doctrine which ascribes all mechanic power to motion only.

11. Sixthly, That hypothesis which attributes continuance in the present state, whether of rest, motion, or direction in material bodies, to their being forcibly retained in it by the agency of intrinsic or extrinsic powers of different natures, and to this forcible retention, or to the same agency their resistance to change of state and mechanic action, besides being irreconcilable with experience and the nature of things, and involving many difficulties as to the modes and means of action of these powers, is in itself absurd, since if these contrary powers balanced they could have no effect whatever in these respects, and if they did not they could act only as one power and in one way; and since on this hypothesis matter or bodies when

in a state of rest relative to motion must necessarily have a natural propensity to a state of motion, as requiring to be actively and forcibly retained in their present state of rest, at the same time that the very same matter or bodies, when in a state of motion, must necessarily have a natural propensity to a state of rest as then requiring to be forcibly retained in their present state of motion; attributes which are opposite, repugnant, and destructive of each other, and therefore such as cannot possibly exist together in the same body or substance. The same reasoning is applicable to retaining in any particular degree of velocity, and in any particular direction. In a word, on this supposition, it must be the nature of matter or bodies to be eternally changing their state, so as never to be for any two instants of time in the same state, unless forcibly retained by some foreign power. But, as we have no experience or knowledge of such retaining powers, and no reason from phenomena for inferring their existence, or that propensity to change in matter which would make it requisite, this hypothesis also must necessarily be rejected.

12. Seventhly, That that doctrine which attributes continuance in motion only, and not of rest, to an adherent extrinsic power acting on matter is also not admissible must be sufficiently evident when it is considered, that, according to it, no action could possibly take place between one body in motion and another at rest on their coming into contact, and thereby changing their respective states as to motion and rest in whole or in part, since the effect takes place without their agency, nothing but contiguity in the bodies being required from the motive power passing by this hypothesis of itself from the body in motion to that at rest, on some unassigned, and indeed unassignable principle, since there is no evidence of the existence of such a power, and since no such effect actually takes place in nature as that of motion being communicated from one body to another, or of there being a mechanical generation of motion in the one body, and of rest in the other, otherwise than by means of mutual resistance and action taking place between the bodies, and of the body at rest acting with equal power and energy with that in motion. When it is considered, that when equal non-elastic bodies move against each other with equal velocities, their state of motion is destroyed upon the impact and that of rest takes place, and that the action in this case continues no longer than the
changing

changing of state, both disappearing and vanishing at the same time, which clearly shews their changing of state arises from their resistance to changing of state merely, and not from any inherent intrinsic, or adherent extrinsic powers, essentially active, urging them to motion; for, if so, these powers would not be destroyed by the impact, or along with the changing of state, but would still continue to act by urging the bodies to motion in opposition to each other. Besides this hypothesis of the continuance of motion in matter being produced by the equably continued action of an extrinsic power on it is necessarily involved in this dilemma, that the motion of a body moving freely must necessarily be either uniform, or equably accelerated according to the times of action; that if uniform, it cannot possibly be the effect of the equably continued action of any power on the body, and that if not uniform, it is contrary to phenomena and fact, and therefore cannot be admitted, as being, on that account, no way applicable to the present case. Hence then, the hypothesis of the agency of a motive power in this case must necessarily be rejected; the existence of such power being unknown, and there being no reason for inferring it or its agency from the phenomena. Had the velocity accelerated in place of being uniform, then indeed the existence and agency of some power, though that power should be imperceptible to us, might with certainty be rationally inferred; but in that event it would not have been agreeable to fact, or to what actually happens according to the common course of nature, nor in any respect applicable to the present case, as in place of being continuance in the same state, it would be a continued changing of state:—So that if not uniform, it cannot be agreeable to phenomena, and if uniform, it cannot be the effect of the continued action of any power. And

13. Eighthly, That if action, or if motion, was essential to matter, or neutralized combinations of powers, each particular particle of it must necessarily possess a power or tendency to act or to move either in some one particular direction, or in all directions at once. But a tendency in each particle to act or to move in all directions at once, could have no other effect than necessarily to produce a state of rest relatively to motion in it, from these powers effectually counteracting and balancing each other; and if determined in its action or motion with respect to any one particular direction, that determination must necessarily be owing to something external to it attracting

tracting or repelling it in that particular direction, since nothing in itself can determine to any one direction more than to any other. Hence it is manifest, that the particles not only of material, but also of all other substances, cannot as individuals unconnected with others be possessed of any power, action, or motion, or tendency to generate motion, either in all or in any particular direction; and therefore must necessarily, when not effectually acted on or urged by some external power, remain in a state of rest relative to motion and tendency to motion; and, if urged and moved by any external power, that it must be incapable of itself of stopping the motion thus produced in it, when that power forbears to act on it, from being incapable of acting of itself on itself in any one direction in preference to any other, and therefore in any direction whatever. But, though this must necessarily be the case with each particle of any substance taken individually, without any relation to any other particle of that or of any other substance, yet this may not be, and perhaps never is the case with particles taken collectively, as they may in this case, notwithstanding, be endowed with powers whereby certain particular kinds may attract, and other kinds repel each other, and thus by their mutual actions move each other in determined directions when within the spheres of each others action :—and thus those that are attractive of each other within certain particular spheres of action will combine and cohere together forming particular aggregates of different sizes, forms, and densities, according to the particular circumstances which influence and regulate the powers and their spheres of action, and the numbers and forms of the particles contained within these spheres respectively; while those that are mutually repulsive within certain spheres of action, will recede from each other, not only while within these spheres, or while this action lasts, but even afterwards, as being incapable of themselves of destroying the motion generated in them by it, if that motion is not stopt sooner by external agency; nor would this effect cease till they come within the spheres of action of particles of other natures, with which from reciprocal attraction they combine, forming according to circumstances aggregates of different sizes, &c. And, thus, as PARTICLES are formed by chemical combinations of elements, (Essay III. Part II. article 16th), so are particular SUBSTANCES OR BODIES by the aggregation and cohesion of particles, as determined by their respective spheres of action and other circumstances.

These

These aggregates of bodies must necessarily contain pores, or not be uniformly dense throughout, as the particles or atoms of which they are composed are, unless these particles are of any of the forms called the five platonic bodies, and unless applied to each other in such a manner as to produce that effect; and such as were the qualities of the individual particle, such must necessarily be the qualities of the individual substance or body produced by the simple aggregation and cohesion of these individual particles, without any alteration in their essential qualities having taken place; that is, each body taken as an individual, having no relation to any other, cannot be possessed of any motion, or tendency to motion, but as an individual having relation to other individuals, it may possess powers not only tending to, but capable of producing motion in itself and in others. Thus then it is evident that every inanimated body is and necessarily must be incapable of itself of acting on itself under any circumstances, and therefore of CHANGING ITS STATE, whether of REST, MOTION, or DIRECTION, &c. or of either ACTING or MOVING, if in a state of rest, if intirely exempted from all external influence and agency.

14. But it by no means follows from this, that matter is perfectly passive, and incapable of action; or because a material body is incapable of acting on itself so as to change its state of modification, that it is also incapable of acting on other such bodies so as to effect changes in their respective states of modification, and still less that passiveness is the cause of power and action in it; that being impossible, since passiveness is the negation of power, and no thing or entity can possibly result from, or be the effect of its own negation; and hence the impropriety of the expressions *vis inertiæ*, and passive powers, which being contradictions in terms necessarily implying impossibilities and absurdities, never should be used.

15. By inertness in bodies, or the *inertia* of matter, I wish it to be understood that I mean only inability in the body or substance to change its state of itself, and not that it is perfectly passive, or incapable of acting under the proper circumstances, on other bodies or substances, though incapable of acting on itself, and that material bodies from being constituted of balanced and neutralized elementary powers, and being thereby solid and dense relatively to each other, are so far inert as to be incapable of acting on, or affecting each other, any otherwise than mechanically, or

by

by means of mutual resistance, and the pressure and impulse thence necessarily resulting, and therefore in such a manner as to cause in each other
changes of modifications only, except when under particular circumstances,
and the influence of some extrinsic foreign power, as that of gravity, &c.
or powers not in a balanced and neutralized state, whereby they may be
rendered capable of acting on each other CHEMICALLY in a manner to be
treated of in detail in the subsequent essays.

16. There cannot possibly among created things be change of state
without power or force, since it is merely from changing of state that the
existence of these is inferred, and since it is to that which produces them
that these terms are exclusively applied, they not being objects of sense,
and therefore not otherwise cognizable than from the effects they produce.
We attribute the change to some power in act, or force exerted, not only
from having learned from experience and reason, that every effect or change
necessarily requires an adequate cause for its production, but also from
being informed by our own feelings and senses, that we cannot produce
change in our state, or in that of other things, by means of a change in
our own state, without generating that effect or exertion in ourselves, to
which we give the name of force or power, and that no change is effected
in the sensible parts of our bodies, by external agency, without exciting
the sensation, and exhibiting the appearances of force impressed.   But if
power or force is required to produce change of state in bodies, it necessarily must be, because bodies resist change of state with power or force.
And it is in fact this power or force whereby bodies mutually and equally
resist changes of modification, or of state as to rest, motion or direction,
that is the cause, and the only cause of all mechanic action.   And it is
only to this active resistance, to change of state in matter, and not to any
passive power in it, if such were possible, that the term mechanic force or
power can with propriety be applied.

17. Solid bodies in different states of modification as to rest, motion, or
direction, must necessarily, upon contact, from being mutually impervious,
change their states.   Thus, in the case of two unelastic bodies moving with
equal velocities in opposite directions, meeting, action must necessarily take
place, and change of state be produced, as it is perfectly impossible they
can in that case, from being mutually impervious, persevere in their state of
motion.

motion. And as this change of state cannot justly be imputed to passiveness in the bodies, since passiveness cannot possibly be the cause of action and become power, either internal energy or external agency must necessarily be required to produce it, though continuation in the same state can require neither. And since an inert body cannot change its state of itself, or by means of internal energy, it therefore necessarily must be changed, if changed at all, by external agency; that is by the action of some other solid inert body upon it, since there is no reason for inferring the existence and agency of any other power in this case, but the reverse, and hence it is that mechanic action has always necessarily a reference and relation to two bodies, each of which is both agent and patient at the same time; agent, in as far as it is the means of change of state in the other, and patient, in as far as its own state is changed by the action of the other upon it.

18. On the same principle it is also evident that a moving unelastic body must necessarily be opposed, and have its state changed, or motion intirely destroyed, by the action of any magnitude in its way, that is impervious to it, and that is absolutely fixed and immoveable, since in this case it could neither penetrate it, nor move it out of its way. Also that any magnitude at rest in the way of the moving body, that is impervious to it, and that is either incapable of itself, or if capable, does not exert its power of moving out of its way, must also necessarily obstruct and oppose the moving body; and that if it does not stop and destroy the motion intirely, it can be owing only to motion in the same direction being generated in itself—that that body must necessarily continue to resist and retard the motion of the striking body, till such time as it has acquired by the collision a motion of its own equal to, or exceeding that of the striking body after it; and that the moving or striking body can in no case after the collision, move with a velocity exceeding that which the obstructing body has acquired by it, since it can be owing to the motion generated in that body alone, that the striking body is permitted to move at all after the impact.

19. In the same manner, and on the same principle, the inert moving body, as being incapable of itself of altering the direction, or degree of its motion, must necessarily impinge upon the body at rest in its way; and it must also, on the collision, necessarily act upon the body at rest, from its opposing and resisting any diminution of its state of motion, with a

force equal to that whereby the obstructing body opposes and resists an equal change in its own state of rest; which force must necessarily continue to act on the obstructing body so long as that body continues to oppose the motion, or till such time as the moving body has generated in the obstructing body a degree of velocity in the same direction equal at least to that remaining in itself after the impact.

20. That this action of the one body on the other is a necessary effect of that power or force whereby they mutually resist change of state must be sufficiently manifest when it is considered, 1st. that in these cases no other power comes into action, and no other adequate cause can be assigned;—2dly, that change of state cannot possibly be produced in any body but by means of power or force, or that unknown adequate cause rationally inferred from the effect to which we give these names, as otherwise it would be an effect without a cause;—3dly, that bodies actually do resist change of state with power or force, from power or force as we know from our own feelings and exertions being required to effect it, which could not possibly be the case if they did not;—4thly, that this power or force is adequate to the effects produced, from its always being in precise conformity to them, the effects being *ceteris paribus* the measure of the degree of force, as the degree of force or resistance is *ceteris paribus* of the quantity of matter producing these effects—and 5thly, that it has been already proved, sections 8th, 9th, 10th, 11th, 12th, 13th, that mechanic action cannot possibly be the effect of any other power or cause either intrinsic or extrinsic to matter or substance; and this being the case, that it must necessarily either be the effect of this cause, or an effect without a cause, but this last being impossible in the nature of things, that it must of consequence necessarily be an effect of this cause.

21. That this innate energy or force whereby bodies resist change of state in themselves and thereby induce it in others, or whereby mechanic action is produced, is essential to matter as matter, or is a consequence depending on and resulting from matter, must be manifest when it is considered that if matter was not the cause, and the only cause of it, it could not possibly, other circumstances being the same, always vary in degree as the quantity of matter varies and always in direct and exact conformity to it, as on experiment it is indeviatingly found to do; and that this force is on

this

this account the measure and the only measure, gravity or weight excepted, of the quantity of matter in any magnitude or body, as the quantity of matter is of the degree of force; and hence it is that the quantity of matter in any magnitude and the density of that magnitude signify the same thing, both being measured and ascertained by the same means and the same standards, and the quantity of both being by these standards the same in the same mass or magnitude. That this innate active force cannot be attributed to magnitude, is equally manifest, since it is the same in different magnitudes having densities inversely as their magnitudes, and it is also manifest that it cannot possibly depend on or result from the qualities either of solidity, or of inertia, even were it possible for inactivity to be active, as in that event this active force could never possibly vary in degree in any case, but would necessarily be the same in all, since these are essential qualities common to matter as matter in every state, subsisting equally in the smallest particle as in the largest mass, and which do not admit of any change or variation without the annihilation of matter.

22. This power or force whereby mechanic action is produced must necessarily vary in degree according to the particular circumstances of each particular case. For, since it is a consequence resulting from and depending on change of state as to modifications of rest, motion, and direction, in matter or substance, it must necessarily in every case, other circumstances being the same, be directly as the change of state induced, and must therefore necessarily vary in degree, as these changes vary in degree; so that the greater or less the change or deviation from the present state, the greater or less *ceteris paribus* the force, and that precisely in the same degree. And as this force or power of resistance is essential to each particular atom of matter, each resisting equal changes with equal force, it must also necessarily *ceteris paribus* vary in degree as the number of atoms vary in the aggregates or bodies in which the changes are induced; so that the greater or less the number of atoms, the greater or less *ceteris paribus* the force, and that precisely in the same degree. And hence this power in every case necessarily must be in a ratio compounded of the quantity of matter and the change of state induced :—that is, in general, in a ratio compounded of the quantity of matter, and the velocity generated or destroyed; or in other *words* as the quantity of motion generated or destroyed,

stroyed, or in elastic bodies as the quantity of motion destroyed in one direction and generated in another by the reflection of the bodies on impact.

23. But if this is the case, it necessarily follows that an atom or indefinitely small particle of matter, can resist an indefinitely small velocity with an indefinitely small force only; twice that velocity with twice that force, thrice with thrice, &c. and that two atoms will *ceteris paribus* resist that velocity with twice the force that one does, three with thrice, &c. and as an indefinitely small force is required to generate or destroy an indefinitely small velocity in an atom of matter, and twice that force to generate or destroy that velocity in two atoms, it also necessarily follows, that that degree of force, which is required for generating or destroying an indefinitely small velocity in one atom of matter, could not possibly generate or destroy any greater velocity in a single atom, or any motion or velocity at all in a larger mass; and hence the insufficiency of that doctrine which inculcates that any mass however great may be moved by any force however small, provided the velocity generated in the mass is also indefinitely small. It also follows as a necessary consequence from what is advanced above, that mechanic power could not possibly, in the nature of things, be less than it actually is; for an atom of matter could not possibly resist, or be acted upon by a force less than an indefinitely small one, since none such can exist, or be acted on by no force at all; and also that it could not possibly be greater than it actually is, for if an atom of matter resisted the generation or destruction of an indefinitely small velocity in it, with more than an indefinitely small force, the resistance could neither be as the mass, nor as the velocity, nor in a ratio compounded of both, nor in any other determinate ratio whatever; and consequently the force necessary for generating or destroying motion in matter could not, in any case, be as the quantity of motion generated or destroyed, or change of state induced, since it fails in this fundamental case of which all the others are merely aggregates or amounts.

24. From the preceding reasoning being established on an analysis and induction of facts of the most unexceptionable and general kind — as being agreeable to universal experience—and from that exact conformity of the results with the theory which in every possible case takes place on
                                                                                            the

the synthetic application of the principles to practice, it may it is presumed, with entire confidence be concluded that Sir Isaac Newton's three laws, with respect to rest, motion and mechanic action in matter, are not only consonant to the natures of things, but also necessarily result from them; and that this action as being founded in the nature of things, could not possibly be greater or less, or different from what it actually is, unless it had been the will of the Deity to have formed things with natures entirely different from those they at present possess.

25. Though mechanic power or force is in every case of mechanic action precisely as the differences in the states of the acting bodies relatively to each other, as to rest, motion, or direction, and the differences in their respective quantities of matter, previous to the impulse or action; and also as the changes of state in the respective bodies induced by it; yet as the changes of state induced are only in some cases as the quantities of motion generated in the one body and destroyed in the other by their mutual action, and there is no loss of motion on the whole, the term moment, momentum, or quantity of motion, is not altogether proper for expressing mechanic power or force, or the particular degrees of it in particular cases, and in particular bodies, more especially when there is no motion in these cases, as in that of a poised balance, or the resistance to motion in a body at rest, I shall however in compliance with custom, which has now in a great degree sanctioned its use, employ it occasionally.

26. Though the density of a material body is discovered and ascertained by its weight or gravity, as well as by the mechanic power it manifests under particular circumstances, it does not thence follow that mechanic power and the power of gravity are the same; or because the moment or mechanic power is in most cases as the weight multiplied into the velocity that it is so in every case. For though the weight is always in exact conformity to the quantity of matter, and the moment or mechanic power is also always as the quantity of matter the velocity being the same, yet these powers are essentially different and perfectly independent of each other, as is manifest from that of gravity acting in one direction only, while mechanic power acts equally in all, and in conformity with and in opposition to that of gravity as much as in any other, a body moving freely by means

of

of gravity resisting any increase of velocity in the direction in which it is urged and moved by gravity equally with any other equal change in its state in any other direction; and hence it is evident that the mechanic power of a body has no dependence whatever on its gravity, and that other circumstances being the same, its mechanic power would be the same though it possessed not gravity; that there are substances possessing mechanic power which are devoid of gravity will appear in the subsequent Essays.

27. That the moment or mechanic power is not in every case as the weight multiplied into the velocity must be manifest when it is considered, that it cannot be so in the case of a body moving slowly upwards in direct opposition to its gravity, and in that of a body resting on the surface of a fluid or smooth horizontal plane and moving slowly along it, in that of the loads of a well-poised fly moving slowly, &c. though there should be no resistance to the motion from friction on the medium, since in these cases the gravity does not conspire with the motion of the body, but on the contrary either directly opposes it or opposes it by producing friction, &c. since the velocities with which the bodies move in these cases are by the supposition or state of the case less than that which gravity would in the first instant generate in them if they were permitted to descend freely, and since it necessarily follows from this that the moment thus generated in each particular body cannot possibly be equal in power and intensity to that of the weight or pressure of the body from gravity when at rest. This circumstance never having been attended to, no standard has ever been thought of for determining the moments in these cases. The determination by accurate experiment of that degree of velocity in bodies which exactly balances their gravity, would afford a sufficient standard for that purpose, for if that was ascertained, the moments in such cases, as in that of a vessel sailing slowly, &c. might then be easily determined by deducting from the weight of the particular bodies as much as their respective velocities fall short of that standard velocity which is equal to gravity. This standard may I imagine be easily discovered by those who are possessed of the very useful instrument so ingeniously contrived for experiments of this kind by Mr. Attwood. When the velocity of gravitating bodies equals or exceeds

that

that standard velocity which equals gravity, the mechanic power or moment is in every case whatever the direction of the motion as the velocity multiplied by the weight.

28. From the above it is manifest that the force of percussion in place of being in every case infinitely greater than that of pressure, as supposed and inculcated by many, is in fact in numerous cases considerably less : the impulse of a body moving very slowly being much less than that of its pressure from gravity when at rest. Pressure is in every case the effect of the joint operation of a tendency in one material substance or body, from being acted upon by some power, to generate motion in another body, and of a resistance or conteraction in that other body to that tendency or action. When the counteraction is not sufficient for preventing motion in the counteracting body the motion is regarded as impulse, percussion, propulsion, &c.; but when it is, and the action is of long continuance, even though the effect of percussion, it is called pressure, as in the case of a jet of water acting against a stone wall by means of the continued and incessant impulses of its particles on it. It is in consequence of resistance to change of state that mechanic impulse acts, but pressure urges to action, not from any resistance to change of state, but on the contrary from a propensity to it in the power producing the pressure through the instrumentality of the material substance or body, as in the case of an elastic substance forcibly retained in a state of compression, the elastic power in that case constantly urging to change of state. The very great difference in certain cases between the effects of percussion and of pressure when the forces are on the whole equal in both cases will be accounted for in a subsequent article by the case of a ball of lead resting on soft clay when treating of the cavities formed in soft yielding substances by means of percussion.

29. But though it is allowed by all that mechanic power or force is in a ratio compounded of the weight or quantity of matter and the velocity, yet differences of opinion prevail with respect to the measure by which it may be determined and ascertained according to these, some being of opinion that the degree of mechanic force is as the weight multiplied simply into the velocity, while others are of opinion that it is as the weight multiplied into the square of the velocity. This difference of opinion has divided the philosophical world into two parties, and produced a controversy which

has

has subsisted for more than a century, and which at first was in some cases conducted with a degree of intemperance incompatible with calm investigation, and with an asperity of expression and remark but ill suited to the dignity of philosophy. Leibnitz was the first who in a paper in the Leipsic Acts for the year 1686 expressly asserted that the force of a body in motion is as the square of the velocity. Some are inclined to think that he was led to adopt this opinion from its having been demonstrated by Huygens that on the collision of two bodies that are perfectly elastic the sum of the products of each body multiplied by the square of its velocity is the same after the impact as before it. This however holds only with regard to perfectly elastic bodies, or to one perfectly elastic and another perfectly hard, and does not hold with respect to soft unelastic bodies; and the force in perfectly elastic bodies is the same after the impact as before it, when the sum of the products of each body is multiplied by the simple velocity as well as when multiplied by the square of the velocity, except in the case of the impinging body being of less mass than that of the body it impinges on; and even then it is so if estimated in one and the same direction, or in that of the striking body before the impact, any motion after it in a contrary direction being deducted from it as negative.

30. As this opinion of the force being as the square of the velocity has been adopted and warmly contended for by many of the most celebrated of the philosophers of the Continent of Europe, as Leibnitz, Huygens, the two Bernoulis, Poleni, Wolfius, S. Grevesende, Camus, Muschenbrock, &c. and never has been refuted by arguments so satisfactory and decisive as to remove all doubt with respect to its invalidity in every case; and as it is a matter of much importance in mechanical science that the ratio whereby the force in each case may be accurately ascertained should be determined, I shall here subjoin such arguments as have been or may be used, in as far as I am acquainted with them, for and against this doctrine, adding such observations of my own as I imagine may in any respect tend to elucidate the subject and terminate the dispute by determining in a satisfactory and decisive manner the ratio according to which the mechanic force in every case ought to be estimated.

31. The principal arguments that have been advanced in support of the doctrine of the force being as the square of the velocity are deduced from
experiments,

experiments; and are, that of Huygens excepted, mentioned already, which will be afterwards considered, the two following, viz. 1st, That the force must necessarily be as the square of the velocity, since the force must be measured by the effect produced, and cannot be measured by any other means, and since the effect produced, or that which necessarily is the measure of the force, is as the square of the velocity, as is incontestibly proved by the cavities made in soft yielding substances, as clay or tallow, &c. the cavities formed by the same body falling upon the same substance with different velocities, being in every case precisely as the squares of the velocities by which they are respectively formed. 2dly, That the degree of force is to be measured by the effect produced by it, without any regard being had to the time in which it is produced, since if a point runs through a determinate space, and presses with a certain given force or intensity of pressure, it will perform the same action whether it move fast or slow. S. Gravesende, Phys. El. Math. § 723—728.

32. To these may be added, 1st, That if the force is simply as the velocity, then the alterations which take place in the forms of yielding bodies upon impact must necessarily be effects without a cause; since, agreeable to that doctrine, and to that of percussion as at present understood and inculcated, there is no loss of motion or mechanic force by that means, or on account of the production of these alterations in the forms of the percussive bodies, the quantity of motion being precisely the same before and after the impact, none of it having been employed for that purpose; whereas, on the principle of the force being as the square of the velocity, the production of these alterations by the impact is not an effect without a cause, but may be rationally accounted for: Thus, if one non-elastic body moving with a velocity equal to 4 feet in a second of time, strikes another equal non-elastic body at rest, the moment or quantity of motion in the bodies before the impact, as estimated by multiplying each into the square of its respective velocity, will be 16; and after it, as estimated in the same manner, 8 only; so that the one half of the force or moment goes on this principle to produce this effect: and it will afterwards appear that this degree of force is that precisely which is required for its production; and hence it is manifest this is not, as thus estimated, an effect without an adequate cause:—When bodies are elastic, the elastic power restores what is lost by this means. Secondly,

z   That

That if the force was not as the square of the velocity, the gain of force in the case of the collision of elastic bodies encreasing in size in geometrical progression, and the apparent gain and loss of force in the resolution and composition of motion, cannot rationally be accounted for, and that gain or loss, if real, would, if the force is as the simple velocity, be effects either without adequate causes, or with such causes as have not hitherto been assigned.   But, according to the principle of the force being as the square of the velocity, no such effects actually take place, there being really no gain or loss of force in these cases; as must be manifest when it is considered that the square of the diagonal of every rectangle, representing the force they either compose or are resolved into, is always equal to the sum of the squares of the two sides representing the forces thus composed or resolved, so that the forces or moments necessarily are the same after being composed or resolved as they were before, when estimated according to the square of the velocity; and, as there is no gain or loss of force when thus estimated, the absurdities are avoided of supposing effects without causes, or with such as cannot be assigned and thereby the effects accounted for.

33. The principal arguments that have been advanced in support of the principle of the force being *ceteris paribus* simply as the velocities, are also deduced from experiments, and are the two following, viz. 1st, That the principle of the force being *ceteris paribus* in the duplicate ratio of the velocities cannot possibly be admitted, since it fails in the fundamental cases which are the most obvious, and most simple, and therefore the least liable to misconception and error; as in the cases of the balance, and of these simple engines called the mechanic powers, in which it is manifest that the forces are *ceteris paribus* as the simple velocities: thus, if a body of four pound weight is placed at the distance of six inches from the centre of motion of a balance, and one of two pound weight at the distance of twelve inches, these bodies will be found to be in equilibrio, which could not be the case if the forces were as the weights or masses, multiplied into the squares of their respective velocities, for then the forces, in place of being equal, and thereby balancing, would be respectively 4 and 8:—and so of other cases.   2dly, That though the effects produced, or cavities formed, or spaces described, are *ceteris paribus* as the squares of the velocities in cases when these effects are not produced instantaneously, but in time, it is

not

not because the forces whereby they are produced are as the squares of the velocities, but because these effects are necessarily proportional to these forces, and to the times of their action in producing them conjointly:—a double velocity acting for a double time necessarily producing four times the effect, a triple for a triple time nine times the effect, &c. and hence the necessity of taking the times, as well as the velocities, into the account in estimating the forces whereby the effects are produced in these cases.

34. The first of these arguments being unanswerable, the maintainers of the Leibnitzian, or new principle, were under the necessity of narrowing its influence by abandoning it in as far as the cases included in that argument extended, and restricting it to cases of accelerated and retarded motions, and of percussion exclusively. This gave occasion to their dividing mechanical science into two parts—Statics and Dynamics—and mechanical forces into two kinds, calling the one the *vis mortua*, and the other the *vis viva*, and sometimes the *vis motrix*, meaning by the first that force which proceeds from pressure from gravity, &c. and that force which proceeds from the resistance of bodies at rest relative to motion to any change in their state ; and by the other, or *vis viva vel motrix*, that force whereby bodies in motion resist any change in their direction, or any diminution in their velocity; which last kind, they say, as depending on and resulting from the agency of a living active or motive power, is *ceteris paribus* as the squares of the velocities ; though the first, as being an effect of passion merely, or of a dead or passive power, is *ceteris paribus* simply as the velocities.

35. That there is no reason for inferring, and no proof of the existence of passive powers, or of any such power as this *vis mortua*, has already been shewn, sections 14th and 15th, and that this hypothesis can avail them nothing, has been proved by their opponents by the very simple experiment of generating a vibratory motion in a well poised balance having brachiæ of different lengths loaded with weights at their extremities which are inversely as their lengths, and by shewing that the living or motive force, as they call it, thus generated, soon terminates from the resistances from friction and the medium, and from the equal action of the bodies on each other in rest and in equilibrio, which could not possibly be the case if the forces were as the squares of the velocities. It likewise might, with

strict

strict justice and propriety have been objected to the above doctrine, that it cannot, even in cases of percussion, possibly be true, since it is directly opposed by experience and matter of fact, the reaction of a body at rest on impact being found on experiment invariably to equal the action of the impinging body on it, which could not possibly be the case, if that doctrine was true, or if the moving body acted with a force equal to the *square* of the velocity, while that at rest resisted or reacted with a force *simply* as the velocity.

36. So far have the maintainers of the old principle been decidedly successful in repelling and refuting some of the arguments of their opponents, and in accounting in a just and satisfactory manner for certain of the phenomena; but they do not appear to me to have been equally successful in refuting the other arguments adduced by them, and in the reasonings whereby they attempt to account for the cavities produced in soft yielding substances being *ceteris paribus* as the squares of the velocities whereby they are produced, or for those alterations which take place in the forms of yielding bodies on impact, &c.; for, with the intention of accounting for these on their own principle, they have actually abandoned that principle with regard to all cases of uniformly accelerated and retarded motions, and of course with regard to those of percussion also since there are no bodies perfectly hard and unyielding, and in these cases have in reality, though not nominally, conceded to their opponents all they contended for, when they argue for the necessity of taking the times, as well as the velocities into the account, in estimating the forces in these cases, and on this principle for the forces being in these cases as the velocities multiplied by the times. For this is only a different way of expressing the same thing, the velocities multiplied by the times being in these cases in fact the same with the squares of the velocities; the velocities being as the times, and each as the square roots of the spaces passed through during the generation or destruction of the velocities in the bodies by which the spaces are described; so that whichever of these modes of expression are adopted, there cannot possibly be any difference of opinion with respect to the degrees of force in these cases, since when estimated by either the one or the other, the results are precisely the same, and the forces as the squares of the velocities.

37. This doctrine, however, which makes the forces, in cases of uniform

acceleration

acceleration and retardation, the product of the velocities and times, or in other words, as the squares of the velocities, because the spaces described in cases of accelerated and retarded motions are as the squares of the velocities, or, what is the same, as the product of the velocities and times, though now universally adopted, I must confess appears to me altogether unfounded and erroneous. The subsequent considerations have induced me to adopt this opinion. In cases of uniformly accelerated and retarded motions, the generating and destroying forces, as acting uniformly, or producing equal effects or equal increments and decrements of velocity in equal times, must necessarily be *ceteris paribus* simply as the times; and these forces being as the times, those generated or destroyed by them, as well as the increments or decrements of velocity on which they depend, must also necessarily be simply as the times in which they are generated or destroyed, and not as the squares of the times, or as the squares of the velocities, or what is the same thing, in a ratio compounded of the velocities and times. And that this is actually the case, is manifest from, and proved by that uniform acceleration of velocity which takes place in a body falling freely by means of its gravity, as must be evident from the following table, or statement.

TABLE

TABLE shewing the VELOCITIES, &c. generated in Cases of uniform Acceleration.

Times or Seconds.	Forces acting in each successive Second.	The Velocities generated in each successive Second.	Spaces passed over.	Mean of the Velocities with which they are described.
1st	1	1	1 in one second	1 in one second
2d	1	3	4 in two	2 in two
3d	1	5	9 in three	3 in three
4th	1	7	16 in four	4 in four
5th	1	9	25 in five	5 in five
6th	1	11	36 in six	6 in six
7th	1	13	49 in seven	7 in seven
8th	1	15	64 in eight.	8 in eight.
8	8	64	64	8

Hence, times $= 8$; forces $= 8$; $\sqrt{64}$, or square root of the velocities or spaces described $= 8$; and the *mean* of these velocities, or the equable velocity with which they would be described in the same time, also $= 8$.— So that the mean velocities generated in each successive second of time, are simply as the forces by which they are generated; or the forces are even in this case as the simple velocities. And as the times equal the velocities, as may be seen by comparing the first and last columns of the table, it is manifest, that taking the times into the account, as well as the velocities, or multiplying the velocities by the times, must be equivalent to squaring the velocities.

38. Though the velocities during each successive second of time are as stated in the table, 1, 3, 5, 7, &c. yet the mean velocity in each of these successive seconds, or the mean velocities acquired by the end of each second,

second, come to be respectively, 1 by the end of the first second, 2 by that of the next second, 3 by that of the third second, and so successively, 4, 5, 6, 7, 8, &c.; and hence it follows, that the mean velocities generated by the end of each particular second of time, are precisely equal to the forces by which they are severally generated; the mean velocity generated by the force 1, in the first second, being 1; that in two seconds, being 2, the forces equal $1 + 1, = 2$, by which it is generated; that in three seconds being 3, equal the forces $1 + 1 + 1, = 3$, by which it is generated; and so in the others; and hence it is manifest, that the mean velocities give precisely the sum or amount of the forces by which they are generated, and that the last acquired velocities would describe double the spaces in the same times, as being precisely double the mean velocities for those several times; and hence also it is manifest that the forces are precisely as the simple velocities, in cases of uniformly accelerated velocities. And if so in uniformly accelerated velocities, they necessarily must be so in uniformly retarded velocities also.

39. When there is an acceleration of velocity from the continued action of the same force on the same body with equal degrees of intensity in equal times, it necessarily follows that that acceleration can be owing to no other cause than the inertia or inability of the body to change its state, by destroying the velocities thus successively generated in it by the successive actions of the force on it, since no other cause comes into action, and since it would necessarily move with an equable velocity, from the equable action of the force on it, were it not for this cause; and hence it is manifest that it is in consequence of this cause, that the spaces described are as the squares of the forces, in place of being precisely as the forces, as they would be if there were no acceleration from this cause. Were there no acceleration of velocity, the forces, or equal impulses, would carry the body in eight seconds through eight equal spaces only; but if, from the above cause, the velocity of the body accelerates uniformly, as stated above, they would carry it through 64, or 8 multiplied by 8, of these spaces; so that the spaces described in this case, being as the square of the forces, is not owing to the forces being as the square of the velocity, but to the acceleration of velocity from the above-mentioned cause, the mean velocities being precisely as the forces;

and

and if all the eight impulses, or the whole of the force was applied to the body at once, it would in the same time of eight seconds, though there would be no acceleration of velocity in that case move through precisely the same extent, as in the former case, or pass over 64 of these spaces; and, though in this case, where there is no acceleration of velocity, the spaces described are as the square of the forces, or the square of the times, and also as the square of the velocity, or as the velocity multiplied into the times, yet it is manifest that the force, or moment, is not as the square of the velocity, or as the velocity multiplied into the times; and that though the SPACES passed over are always in a ratio compounded of the velocities and times, and therefore, in certain cases, as in those given above, are in the duplicate ratio of the velocities, or of the times, it by no means follows as a necessary consequence, that the FORCES by which these velocities are generated, or that the MOMENTS resulting from them, are as the square of the velocities.

40. From the above it is also manifest, that in uniformly accelerated velocities, the velocities generated are precisely as the times in which they are generated, and consequently precisely as the generating forces, which are also necessarily as the times, from the power acting uniformly, or with equal intensity and efficacy in equal times. But if the generating forces and the velocities generated by them are *simply* as the times, the moments, or generated forces, which necessarily depend upon the generating, must necessarily, *ceteris paribus*, be so also, effects being ever necessarily as their adequate causes; so that it is absolutely impossible, in the nature of things, for the forces generated, in place of being *simply* as the times, to be as the times multiplied into the velocities, or in other words, as the squares of the velocities. The same reasoning is applicable to uniformly retarded motions, the retarding powers being, *ceteris paribus*, precisely as the times, though not depending on them, and their effects the destruction of motion, consequently is the same. Though the generating and retarding forces are as the times, and the velocities and forces generated or destroyed, are also as the times, it is not from any influence that time of itself has on these, but merely from the action of the generating and destroying powers being uniform; for the velocities and forces generated or destroyed would be the same,

same, whatever differences there might be in the times in which they are generated or destroyed, provided the forces by which they are generated or destroyed, are the same, or of equal power and efficacy.

41. In practical mechanics, when there is some obstruction to be over-come or work to be done by means of a machine, as in the grinding of grain by a mill, velocity can accelerate only either *ceteris paribus* by a gradual increase of the intensity of the efficient power, or by a gradual decrease of resistance, as of that of the machine from a state of rest to that of motion, or when the acceleration is the result of the joint operation of both these causes; and in cases of this kind the quantities or motion generated, effects produced, or work performed, or the spaces supposed to be described representing them, when the acceleration is uniform, being as the squares of the velocities is not, as stated by that eminent mechanical philosopher and very able engineer the late truly ingenious Mr. Smeaton whose opinion on this subject is now generally adopted, owing to the forces being as the squares of the velocities in these cases, but to the great superiority of the force applied over the resistances opposed to it, and to the gradual diminution of that part of the resistance which arises from the inertia of the machine to the motion gradually generated in it: for this acceleration and these effects continue no longer than till the machine by gradually accelerating acquires its maximum of velocity, from the resistance becoming so great from the great quantity of work done as to prevent all further acceleration; when, of consequence, the velocity necessarily becomes equable. And, though the effect produced or quantity of work done is much greater after the velocity has become uniform than before—it being precisely double for the same time from the initial velocity in this last case being precisely the last acquired velocity in the former case of acceleration, and from the operation of the efficient power being therefore in this last case at its maximum — it is presumed that even the supporters of the unrestricted Leibnitzian principle will not, in contradiction to constant experimental proof, maintain that the forces are in this last case as the squares of the velocities; it being manifest that in this case there is no acceleration, and that the quantities of motion generated or effects produced are not, as in those of uniform acceleration, as the *squares* of the velocities generated, though the forces generating them are *simply* as the velocities, but are

in

in every case of this kind, as well as the forces, merely as the *simple* velocities.

42. The above reasoning is applicable to cases of penetration, or to the different depths to which the same body moving with different velocities would penetrate a soft yielding substance till by the gradual diminution of its velocity it acquires a state of rest, since these are only cases of retardation; and from that reasoning it also necessarily follows that the forces in these cases cannot be as the velocities multiplied into the times or in the duplicate ratio of the velocities, though the cavities formed in the soft yielding substances are so. It is not the times in these cases that influence and determine the spaces the body descends through or the depths of the cavities it makes before its motion is destroyed; but on the contrary it is the spaces or depths penetrated that influence and determine the times in every case of this kind, and both spaces and times are *ceteris paribus* necessarily determined, by the degrees of resistance the body experiences on penetrating the substance, the times and spaces described being *ceteris paribus* the shorter the greater the resistance, and *vice versa*, and the only inference that can be rationally and justly deduced from the cavities or spaces described in these cases being *ceteris paribus* in a certain ratio of the times of action is, that the resistances in these cases must necessarily be uniform, or equal for equal times and spaces, to produce that effect.

43. In penetration, as in every other case of mechanic action, there are two different effects produced, and these by means of two different efficient powers or agents, viz. the cavities made in the soft yielding substance, by the falling of the body or bullet, and the gradual destruction of the motion in the bullet by the resistance of the substance in which the cavity is formed.

44. The resistances to penetration must necessarily be as the effects they respectively produce; that is as the velocities they *ceteris paribus* respectively destroy, a double velocity requiring *ceteris paribus* a double resistance to destroy it, a triple, a triple, &c. But if this is the case, and that it is the case cannot be doubted, the reason of the cavities formed in these cases being in the duplicate ratio of the velocities by which they are formed, cannot possibly be because the forces by which they are formed are in the duplicate ratio of the velocities since they are known from other circumstances

stances to be in the simple ratio of the velocities : but, this being the case, necessarily must be because the resistances in these cases are in the subduplicate ratio of the velocities.

45. That substances are penetrable on different principles, and according to different laws from those in which they are moved, must be sufficiently manifest from the following well known facts: viz. 1st. That a relatively small body moving with much velocity experiences much less resistance in penetrating a large penetrable mass than in moving it, or than in generating motion in the whole of it; and that the greater *ceteris paribus* the velocity, the more the mass resists motion and the less penetration; so that if the velocity is doubled the impinging body will on that account not only overcome the cohesion of the opposing particles with twice the facility it otherwise would have done if moving with half that velocity, but also on account of this facility of penetration, independent of the increased resistance to motion in the mass from the increased velocity, generate but one half of the motion in the mass in general that it otherwise would have done, and the less *ceteris paribus* the quantity of motion generated the less the quantity of force employed in generating it, and the smaller *ceteris paribus* the quantity of the percussive force that is employed in generating it the greater must the remaining quantity of it employed in penetration necessarily be, and the greater the quantity employed in that manner the greater must be the effect produced by it. If the substance was perfectly pervious and resisted not penetration at all, it could not be moved by any force thus applied; and if the power of cohesion of the particles of the mass exceeded the motive power of the body from the smallness of the velocity with which it moves, the moving body might generate a small degree of motion in the mass but never could penetrate it: also a power acting for any time however long on a penetrable substance with a force not equal to that of the cohesion of its particles could never penetrate it, though the aggregate of all the particular pressures or forces exerted upon it in the particular instants of that time might be prodigiously great, as being nevertheless exceeded by those of the power of cohesion during the same time, the force of cohesion exceeding that of the acting body for each particular instant of time, as in the case of a ball of lead resting on soft clay without being capable of penetrating it,

however

however long it may continue to act upon it by means of its gravity, and however great the aggregate of the forces during that time. And on the same principle, if the soft resisting substances are fixed and stationary, the greater the velocity the less will the parts of it that are not in immediate contiguity to that on which the impression is directly made, though near it, be affected by the motion. It is also manifest that when the power of gravity in the bullet resting on the resisting substance does not exceed that of the cohesion of the particles of that substance, and therefore is in that state incapable of penetrating it, that any augmentations in the times of action cannot have any influence in augmenting the degree of intensity with which the bullet acts and of consequence in producing penetration. 2ndly. Since the same body, as was ascertained by an experiment which Dr. Henry Pemberton in his Preface to his View of Newton's Philosophy informs us was made by Sir Isaac Newton, an account of which is inserted in the Philosophical Transactions of London, moving with a certain velocity penetrates through four times as many pieces of thin stretched silk placed at some considerable distance from each other, as it does when moving with half that velocity; it is evident that the body's producing four times the effect with a double velocity is not in this case in consequence of its generating a proportional velocity in the particles of the opposing substance which come into immediate contact with it, and of those particles acting on other particles with a suitable force, the pieces of silk being in this case too far distant from each other for acting on one another in that manner with effect; and though they were nearer could not from deficiency of mass. It is also evident from it, that the resistances in these cases do not depend nearly so much on the mass or moment of the resisting substance, as on its tenacity or resistance to penetration, since the mass of opposing silk in this case may be so small as to be altogether insignificant; besides, mercury though extremely dense is, as possessing but little tenacity, penetrable with great facility provided the velocity is not very great. And hence the effect or degree of penetration produced by increasing the velocity, and thereby the force producing it, must *ceteris paribus* necessarily be much greater than in the direct ratio of the increase of velocity; and that not because the force is in the duplicate ratio of the velocities, but because the power of penetration is thus increased,

while

while that of resistance remains the same; for the resisting power depending almost entirely on the tenacity or cohesion of the resisting substance necessarily remains constant though that of penetration vary. Penetration therefore must necessarily be owing almost entirely to the superiority of the moving or penetrating over the cohesive or resisting power; and hence must always *ceteris paribus* be determined by the excess of the former over the latter, so that when there is no such excess either from these opposite powers exactly balancing, or from the resisting being superior to the moving power, there can be no penetration; and if any particular part or portion of the moving power is required, as there necessarily must be in every case, to balance the cohesive power of the penetrable substance, as the one half of it for instance, the penetration must necessarily be effected by the other half of it only, or this excess; and consequently if the motive power is doubled, by doubling the velocity, the excess or penetrating power in place of being double will be three times greater than what it was before, and will require a proportional degree of increase of resistance to destroy it.

46. The increase of velocity, however, whereby the power of penetration is promoted is limited, and *ceteris paribus*, after exceeding that degree, is productive of the contrary effect, especially when the penetrating body is not of a wedge form, from the resistance from the mass or opposing particles being then greater than that from the tenacity, as in the case of a lead bullet when fired from a gun into water, which, in place of penetrating it, becomes flattened, and rebounds from the reaction. It is moreover evident, that when a body, as a bullet of lead or iron, penetrates to a certain depth in a soft yielding substance, as clay or tallow, it does not move a quantity of it before it equal in mass either to itself or to the cavity it forms in the substance, from the soft substance being little or nothing more compressed at the further extremity, than at the sides of the cavity; the soft substance, like a fluid, yielding in all directions, and with different velocities. These facts prove, in the most satisfactory manner, that penetration differs essentially in its mode and degree of action from propulsion in the direction of the moving power; and from them it may with intire confidence and justice be concluded that the effects, cavities, or impressions formed in the yielding substances are not in the duplicate ratio of the velocities because the forces in the percussive bodies are so, but because the

resistances in the opposing substances are in these cases in the subduplicate ratio of the velocities; and hence there is no necessity for having recourse to an hypothesis necessarily absurd—that without assigning any reason why or how they possibly can be so regards effects as not being directly as their adequate causes, or as the degrees of force by which they are respectively produced, but in the duplicate ratio of these—to account for the phenomena in these cases in a rational and satisfactory manner, these facts proving that the cavities produced in these cases are as the squares of the velocities, not because the forces whereby they are produced are so, but because the resistances to penetration are in these cases *ceteris paribus* inversely as the squares of the velocities; and hence also it is manifest that that doctrine which—attending to one only of the effects produced in cases of penetration the cavity formed, without adverting to the other the quantity of moment or force destroyed in the penetrating body, or to these other circumstances and the reasons formerly adduced why they cannot possibly be so—estimates the percussive forces in these cases merely according to the cavities produced, and therefore in a ratio compounded of the velocities and times, must certainly be erroneous and delusive.

47. It has never hitherto been ascertained with precision, by reasonings necessarily precluding doubt, what would be the laws and modes of action in the collisions of bodies perfectly hard, if any such there were in nature, or according to what ratio of the velocities the forces in these cases would be. The present opinion seems to be that these bodies would in all cases of percussion, with the exception only of not having their forms altered or compressed by the impact, exhibit the same phenomena and be regulated by the same laws that soft non-elastic bodies are regulated by in these cases. When the laws of percussion were first investigated, and in a certain degree determined by Doctor Wallis and Sir Christopher Wren, no doubt was entertained of the force being in these cases *ceteris paribus* as the velocities destroyed in the one body and generated in the other by the impact; and from the moment or quantity of motion estimated in one and the same direction, according to the simple velocities being the same after the stroke as before it, and from no alterations on this account taking place in the state of the common centre of gravity of the bodies by their mutual action, it was concluded that the forces were in these cases simply as the

velo-

velocities generated in the one body and destroyed in the other. The alterations or impressions made in the forms of the bodies by the impacts were but little attended to, either from being regarded as effects too trifling for having any sensible influence on the results, or as effects for which no adequate cause could be assigned from the moments of the bodies being no way diminished by their production, as being the same after the impact as before it.

48. Matters continued in this state till the justly celebrated Huygens discovered and demonstrated that bodies perfectly elastic, or that one body perfectly elastic and another perfectly hard, on collision preserves the same quantity of motion after the impact they possessed before it, when estimated by multiplying each body into the square of its respective velocity. A discovery which gave rise, as already observed, to that new and general principle so long and so warmly contended for, and which has never yet been abandoned, of the forces being in all cases of mechanic action as the squares of the velocities. The doctrine, however, of the forces being as the squares of the velocities in cases of percussion, as well as in others, was for long rejected, by the maintainers of the old principle, and they never, till difficulted how otherwise to account for the impressions or changes which take place in the forms of yielding bodies on impact, had recourse to the doctrine of the forces being in these cases, and in others of accelerated and retarded motions, as the squares of the velocities; or what is the same thing of their being necessarily in a ratio compounded of the velocities and of the times. From this concession proceeded that accommodating doctrine, now adopted, which, in part rejects and in part retains both the old and the new principles, and to account for these and other phenomena, makes mechanic power and action in certain cases, as those of mechanic statics, simply as the velocities; and in others, as those of equably accelerated and retarded motions, as the squares of the velocities.

49. The adoption of the opinion that perfectly hard bodies would on collision exhibit the same phenomena, and be regulated by the same laws that soft non-elastic bodies exhibit and are regulated by must undoubtedly have proceeded from the very little attention which has been bestowed on suppositious cases such as these which admit not of direct experimental proof there being perhaps no bodies in nature perfectly hard, since it is sufficiently

manifest

manifest on the slightest consideration that the effects produced on the collisions of such bodies must necessarily be instantaneous and not in time, from their not admitting of any changes in their forms, and thereby of any gradations, or accelerations or retardations in the velocities generated or destroyed; and consequently that the phenomena cannot be the same as in cases of soft non-elastic bodies; and that the forces, as having no dependance on time, must necessarily, even according to the preceding doctrine, be simply as the velocities. On this principle the modes and laws of action of such bodies, if such there were, for particular cases may easily be deduced. For it follows as a necessary consequence from the incompressibility of the bodies, and the effects being consequently instantaneous--- 1st, That two such equal bodies moving with equal velocities, or two bodies moving with velocities inversely as their masses, in opposite directions, on meeting would neither rebound, nor alter each others forms, but would instantly destroy all motion in each other. 2dly, That a body in motion directly impinging against another equal body at rest, would instantly generate a velocity in that at rest equal to its own, and thereby lose the whole of its own. 3dly, That a body in motion impinging directly upon a quiescent body of half its mass would on the impact instantly generate a velocity in the quiescent body equal to its own, and thereby lose half its own velocity. 4thly, That a body in motion impinging directly upon a quiescent body of double its mass, would by the impact instantly generate a velocity in the quiescent body equal to half its own, and thereby lose the whole of its own velocity. The other cases being easily deducible from the same principle require not to be particularly specified or stated, and from these it is manifest how very different the modes of action, and the laws which regulate them in the different cases of the percussions of perfectly hard bodies would be, if such there were, from those of bodies which are soft and non-elastic. It also appears that there is in these cases no loss of motion on the whole by the impact, as estimated simply by the velocities, whether the non-elastic bodies are perfectly hard or not, except in cases of motions opposing motions, or of motions acting in opposite directions.

50. The effects produced in cases of percussion, and the forces whereby they are produced, having a necessary dependence on the states of the bodies as to motion and rest relatively to each other before the impact, no

doubt

doubt has on that account ever been entertained with regard to these forces being merely as the quantities of motion generated and destroyed by the impact in the bodies respectively; or as the quantities of motion destroyed in the impinging bodies, and generated in the quiescent, or in those moving with a less degree of velocity than those which follow them in the same direction—more especially as it has been deemed impossible for a striking body to act with equal force and effect when it expends but a part of its quantity of motion, as when it expends the whole of it on the collision —and hence it has been usual to estimate the percussive forces in these cases by the quantities of motion generated in the one body and destroyed in the other, without regard to any other circumstance. This being the case, no attempts have been made to ascertain with precision the degrees of force required for and expended in the productions of those impressions which take place in the forms of bodies not perfectly hard on collision for each particular case of percussion; and this indeed would be a proposition of exceeding difficult solution were it not rationally deducible from the differences between the effects which actually take place on the collision of non-elastic and on the collision of the elastic bodies. But, from these, it may rationally and justly be inferred, that the degree of force necessary for altering the forms of the bodies in these cases is precisely equal to that which is required for altering the differences of their relative states of motion and rest, or the differences of their relative velocities, since it is well ascertained and is admitted by all, that the effects produced on the collisions of elastic bodies are—or at least that they would be so, if the bodies were perfectly elastic—*ceteris paribus* precisely double of what they are on the collision of bodies non-elastic, and that the increase of effect in the cases of elastic bodies is owing entirely to a new power, the elastic, coming into action in these cases, and since it follows as a necessary consequence of this that the degree of force whereby the bodies have been impressed and their forms altered must precisely equal that whereby the alterations in the differences in their respective states of motion and rest relatively to what they were before the collision have been induced; since the impressive power or force by which the forms of the bodies are altered must necessarily equal the restituent or elastic power by which they are restored again, and by which one half of the effect in these cases is evidently produced, and since the effects in these cases are manifestly double of what they are in those which are produced in similar cases, when the bodies are non-elastic; and hence that in each particular case of percussion—when the bodies are not perfectly hard, when one of them is not fixed and stationary, and when they do not move in opposition to each other—precisely the same degree of force is required for, and expended in the production of these impressions or changes in the forms of the bodies, that is required for, and expended in altering the states of the bodies as to motion and rest relatively to each other, that is precisely one half of the percussive force.

51. For these facts prove incontestibly that the resistances to changes in the forms of the bodies in cases of percussion, are precisely equal to the resistances to changes in their states as to motion and rest in each particular case of percussion, with the exceptions above mentioned, when the bodies are compressible; and hence it is manifest, that if the forms were unalterable from the bodies being perfectly hard, the whole of the percussive force would necessarily act in altering the states of the bodies as to motion and rest relatively to each other; and, from there being no repulsion in these cases as in those of the collisions of elastic bodies, that the effects above described, in investigating and determining the laws of percussion with respect to bodies perfectly hard, if such there were, would necessarily be produced.

The percussive force, and the action then on the collision of soft non-elastic bodies, though half the motion only is destroyed in the striking body on the impact, is *ceteris paribus* necessarily equal to what it would be if the bodies were perfectly hard, and the whole of the motion in the striking body was destroyed on the collision. For the mechanic force or resistance to change of state is the same in this case as it would be in the other, from each body resisting change in its form, as much as change in its state as to motion or rest; and therefore, though the resistance to change as to motion and rest is in this case *ceteris paribus* but one half of what it would be in the other, yet the resistances on the whole would necessarily be in both cases equal. Besides, if the masses and the differences of the states of the bodies as to motion and rest relatively to each other are respectively equal in both cases, the bodies on collision, whether perfectly hard or not, must necessarily impinge and act on each other with equal force and effect,

effect, since the percussive forces, if the masses are equal, must necessarily be as the differences in the states of the bodies as to motion or rest relatively to each other, and since the effects produced, however different in kind, and however different the times of the action in which they are produced, must necessarily be proportional to their adequate causes, or to the percussive forces by which they are respectively produced.

52. It is merely the differences in the states of the bodies as to rest, motion, or direction relatively to each other that produces the resistance or action between them on coming into contact, since there is no action between them even on contact when their states are the same; and since the action commences and increases, and diminishes and terminates, precisely with these differences in the states of the bodies, the degrees of action must necessarily be determined by the degrees of difference, and the difference being the same, the resistance force or action whereby that difference is destroyed, or the states of the bodies changed so as to prevent their further action on each other, must also necessarily be the same, whatever the manner in which the force is exerted for effecting that purpose, whether by altering the states only, or by altering both states and forms, and whether instantaneously as in the case of bodies perfectly hard, or in time as in that of others. The case of the lead ball resting and pressing on soft clay, without penetrating it, mentioned above in art. 45, accounts for the action and shock not being so violent, or for its not producing in certain cases so much effect in certain respects, when it is gradual and in time, as when it is instantaneous, though the forces in both cases are equal on the whole.

53. It is entirely owing to the yielding of the substances of the bodies that the changes in their state are effected gradually and in time in place of instantaneously on their collisions; and to these changes being gradual that the bodies continue to act on each other in altering one another's forms, and in changing one another's states as to motion and rest, till such time as the velocity thus acquired by the quiescent body is equal to the velocity thus diminished remaining in the other body; or that the moving body loses but half of its original velocity by the impact, from the quiescent body having acquired a velocity equal to the remaining half, by the time of its having lost the other half of its original velocity; the action being gradual, and effecting the changes in the forms of the bodies, and the changes in

their

their states as to motion and rest equally during each particular instant of its operation, the bodies all along resisting both these kinds of changes with equal force and effect. The effects being double in the former cases of elastic bodies, to what they are in the latter of non-elastic bodies, when the velocities or relative velocities and the masses are equal in both cases, does not proceed however from the forces being in the former cases as the squares of the velocities, and in the latter as the velocities, but from the acting forces being actually double in the former cases of what they are in the latter, from a new power, the elastic or restituent, coming into action in these cases; a force which experiments prove precisely to equal in each of these cases the impressive force or that part of the percussive which acts in altering the forms of the bodies. And, since there is also experimental or intuitive proof of the most satisfactory kind that this restituent force in cases of collision acting in conjunction with that part of the percussive force whereby motion is generated in the one body, and destroyed in the other by the impact, precisely doubles the effects as to the quantities of motion generated and destroyed in these cases, no doubt can possibly be entertained with regard to that part of the percussive force by which the impressions in the forms of the bodies is made, being precisely equal to the other part of it, whereby motion is generated in the one body and destroyed in the other by the impact, this latter part being necessarily equal to the restituent or elastic, as producing precisely but one half of the effect when not acting in conjunction with it that is produced by their conjoined action, and as the restituent is also in these cases precisely equal to the impressive or the other half of the percussive: so that the effect would be precisely double with respect to the quantities of motion generated in the one body and destroyed in the other, of what it is in cases of impressible non-elastic bodies, if the bodies in place of being impressible were perfectly hard admitting of no alterations in their forms, and the whole of the percussive force was therefore exerted on the impact in altering their states of motion and rest relatively to each other.

54. Thus then it appears, that the phenomena which take place on the collisions of elastic bodies, and on the collisions of yielding non-elastic bodies, not only ascertain with precision the quantities of force in these cases whereby the alterations in the states of the bodies as to motion and rest are

effected,

effected, but also the quantities of force whereby the alterations in the forms of the bodies are produced; and thereby give the greatest possible stability to the preceding theory of percussion, by establishing its validity on the firm and permanent basis of intuitive or experimental certainty. And hence also it is evident, that the impressions or alterations which take place in the forms of bodies in cases of percussion are not, though the quantity of motion in the bodies may be no way diminished by their production but be the same after the impact as before it, effects without adequate and assignable causes; and that there is no occasion for having recourse to the principle of the forces being as the squares of the velocities, to account for these effects in a rational and satisfactory manner.

55. There is no loss of motion in any case of collision, when one of the bodies is not fixed or stationary, and when their motions are not more or less in opposition to each other; and no gain of motion except in certain cases of the collisions of elastic bodies, which now come to be considered.

56. In every case of percussion or impulse, the production of motion in the quiescent body has hitherto been attributed and ascribed solely to the action of the moving or striking body on it; this body has ever been regarded as the cause, and the only cause of the motion generated by the impact in the quiescent; but by what means it should be capable of producing in another body, or in other bodies, a quantity of motion and degree of moment or motive power greater, and admitting of being augmented in an indefinite degree, than it actually possesses itself; or how it should engender a much greater quantity of motion by the impact in other bodies than it is itself possessed of before the impact, and than it loses by it, has hitherto baffled investigation, and indeed it is a difficulty, the resolution of which has never, in as far as I know, been attempted—except in attributing this effect to the elastic or restituent power, though there is decisive experimental proof of its being so far from being capable of augmenting motion, as to be incapable of supporting it or preserving it entire when generated, from the elasticity never being perfect—it never having been so much as suspected that motion may be generated by, what is seemingly its bane, resistance to motion; and that the elastic power is only the agent or instrument in these cases by means of which this power acts in the generation of motion or moment: yet, strange and paradoxical as it may appear, such is

the

the fact; and no fact can be better ascertained, as must be sufficiently manifest from an analysis and due consideration of the circumstances.

57. For, if these are taken in review as they successively occur, and a just appreciation is made of the respective values and operations, it must be concluded that the moving or striking body is not the only agent, and its motion or momentum the only power or cause by which the effect is produced; but, on the contrary, that no more than precisely one half of the motion produced by the impact can justly be attributed to its operation, the other half being justly due to that of the quiescent body, the action between the bodies in this case as in others being reciprocal and equal. That the reaction or resistance to motion of the quiescent body equals the action and urgency to motion of the moving body on it will no doubt readily be admitted, but perhaps it may not so readily be admitted that this reaction and resistance to motion in the quiescent body is the power which causes the one half of the motion on the impact. The truth of this proposition will be best proved and illustrated, by stating the following facts or cases, and attending to their circumstances, which are not less conducive to the illustration of the preceding doctrine than to the establishing of this, viz. first case, That of one elastic body impinging on another equal elastic body at rest. In this case, it is well known that the bodies on the collision change their states, that which was in motion losing all its motion, and that which was at rest acquiring a velocity equal to that the other has lost. By what means have these changes been effected? For the solution of this question, it is necessary to attend first to what takes place in a similar case when the bodies are unelastic. In this case, it is well known that the only effects of the impact are the impressions or alterations in the forms of the bodies, and their moving in contact after it in the same direction, and with half the velocity of the striking body before it; and it is sufficiently obvious that the resistance or reaction of the quiescent body produces no effects in this case besides altering the form of the striking body and reducing its velocity by one half, so that in this case it destroys motion in place of being a cause of the production of it. This, however, is not the case when the bodies are elastic; then a new power comes into action, the elastic, expansive, or restituent, through the agency of which the reaction, or the action proceeding from *resistance to motion*, is enabled to operate with full

effect

effect in producing motion ; and in consequence of this resistance to motion in the body at rest, or of the compression produced by its means in the form of the striking body, the elastic or restituent power of that body comes into action, and by exerting an energy or force precisely equal to that of the compressing, or to that force by which the compression or alteration in the form of the body was produced, generates in the quiescent body a velocity and quantity of motion in the direction of the striking body, precisely double of what it would have had after the impact, if the bodies had been unelastic ; at the same time that the elastic, or restituent power of the quiescent body coming into action, in consequence of the alteration impressed on its form, from the action of the striking body on it, and operating with a force precisely equal to that by which the impression was produced, destroys in the striking body the whole of its motion, or all the motion that would have remained in it after the impact, if the bodies or balls had been unelastic ; so that in this case the bodies on the impact change states, the striking body losing all its motion, and the quiescent acquiring a quantity of motion, and degree of velocity, equal to what the striking has lost.

58. This, when properly attended to, is on several accounts, a very interesting and instructive experiment, since it proves in the clearest manner, that in the case of the collision of equal non-elastic bodies, precisely one half of the force whereby the bodies act upon each other, from their being in different states, is employed in altering their respective forms, and the other half of it only in altering their several states of modification as to motion and rest, and that the quantity of motion generated in the one body and destroyed in the other by the impact, is precisely double of what it is in this case when the bodies are unelastic, and consequently that the restituent force is precisely equal to the impressive, or that by which the impressions or alterations in the forms of the bodies is made ; it is likewise manifest from this, that the quantity of motion in the bodies is the same both in the case of elastic and of non-elastic bodies, and the same in both after the impact that it is before it, and consequently that in these cases there is no gain or loss of motion by the impact on the whole. It also clearly proves what the effect would be in this case, if the bodies, in place of being impressive, were perfectly hard, since it is sufficiently manifest from it, that the result would be precisely the same as in the case of perfectly

fectly elastic bodies, and that the only difference in the process by which the result is produced would be, that in the case of perfectly hard bodies, the action and effect would have been instantaneous, or by one single operation, in place of by first impressing the forms of the bodies, and then restoring them again, as in the case of perfectly elastic bodies.

59. It will now be proper to state this one other fact or case, and nothing further will, I imagine, be required for establishing the truth of this doctrine on the firm basis of experimental proof, viz. that of an elastic body in motion, impinging on another elastic body of double its mass at rest, or on a succession of these in geometrical progression in contact, each immediately succeeding body being of double the mass of the immediately preceding. In the former case, when the bodies were equal, yielding, and non-elastic, the striking body loses but one half of its velocity, or quantity of motion, on the collision; but in this case, if the bodies or balls were non-elastic, the striking, in place of losing one half only of its quantity of motion on the impact, would lose two-thirds of it, in encountering a proportional resistance to motion in the quiescent ball, from its being of twice the mass, in place of being, as in the former case, of equal mass with the striking body, and it would generate by that means a quantity of motion in the quiescent ball on the collision, equal to what it loses by it, or to two-thirds of what it possessed before the impact, and both balls would proceed after it in the same direction, with a velocity equal to one-third of that the striking ball possessed before the collision, so that the quantity of motion in the balls, notwithstanding these changes in their respective states, would be the same after the impact as before it. But if we suppose the balls perfectly elastic, the restituent power equalling the impressive, the case would be quite altered; thus if we suppose the quantity of motion in the striking ball divided into three equal parts, or that it moves before the collision with a velocity equal three, after the impact, if the balls were non-elastic, they would move with a velocity equal one, from the striking body having lost two-thirds of its quantity of motion, and the quiescent of double its mass having acquired a quantity of motion equal to what it has lost, and thereby a velocity equal to one-third of that of the striking ball before the impact, and the quantity of motion after the impact would be the same as before it, from the moving mass

being

being three times as great, though the velocity is only one-third of what it was before the impact; but when the balls are elastic, the result, in this case, is well known to be the generation of a quantity of motion, and a velocity in the direction of the striking ball, in the quiescent ball, by the impact, precisely double of what is generated in it by the same means when the bodies are non-elastic; and therefore, on the above data, a velocity in it equal to two, and a quantity of motion equal to four, being a quantity of motion in it greater by one-third of the original motion, than the original motion in the balls before the impact; so that there is a gain of motion in this case in the direction of the moving ball before the stroke equal to one-third of the original quantity; at the same time that there is also a gain of motion equal to another third of that quantity, in the opposite direction from the striking ball being reflected on the impact, with one-third of the velocity it possessed before it, so that there actually is a gain of two-thirds on the whole, the motions of both bodies being positive, though in opposite directions and though the motion of their common centre of gravity is not affected by this gain of motion, as they do not counteract and destroy each other. Now the motion thus generated on this increase of motion can proceed from nothing but the increase of resistance to motion; for the only difference between this case and the former, when the balls were equal and there was no gain of motion, is that the quiescent ball, from being in this case of double the mass of the striking, resists motion with more force and effect and by that resistance destroys two-thirds, in place of one-half only, as in the former case, of the quantity of motion in the striking ball, when the balls are non-elastic; and it is manifestly this increase of resistance or reaction that is the cause of that increase of compression or alterations in the forms of the balls whereby that increase of the restituent or elastic power, by which it is measured and through the instrumentality of which this increase of motion is produced, is brought into action; since no other cause comes into act or can be assigned, and since it is in every case in precise proportion or conformity to it, and therefore is necessarily determined by it, the compression in the quiescent ball being always precisely as the quantity of motion lost by the striking on the impact, and the compression in the striking being always the same as in the quiescent, from the action and reaction being equal; and hence it is, that in the above case, the restituent

power,

power, equal the compressing in the quiescent ball and therefore equal to two or the quantity of motion lost by the striking ball, operates on the striking ball in destroying the remaining motion in it equal one, and in generating in it a retrograde motion also equal one, while the restituent power of the striking ball, partly from the remaining motion in that ball and partly from its resistance to motion in a contrary direction after having acquired a state of rest from the destruction of its original motion, operates in generating a quantity of motion in the quiescent ball equal to two, in addition to the two it had before, making the quantity of motion in it in all equal to four; so that this effect is owing in the first instance to the resistance of the quiescent ball to motion, and in the second to the resistance of the striking ball to motion in a contrary direction to that in which it originally moved, since if it were not for these resistances or counteractions the elastic or restituent power would produce no other effect on the balls, than simply restoring their forms from the impressions produced in them by the impact, or by the resistance of the quiescent ball to motion. If the ball which was in this case quiescent, whose mass is equal to two, now becomes the striking, and acts upon another quiescent of twice its mass, or with a mass equal to four, with the velocity and quantity of motion thus acquired, it is manifest there will, by this means, be a further gain, or generation of motion, in the same proportion as before, and that in this manner, making the ball, whose mass is 4, act on one whose mass is 8, that of 8 on one of 16, and so in succession, this generation or gain of motion may be carried to any extent required. If the quantity of motion in the striking ball is 4, and the mass of the quiescent three times that of the striking, then on the impact, the bodies being elastic, the quiescent would acquire a quantity of motion equal to 6, being a gain of 2, equal $\frac{1}{2}$ the original quantity, and the striking would be reflected with 2, also equal $\frac{1}{2}$ of it, so that the original motion would, on the whole, be doubled. If the quantity of motion in the striking ball is 6, and the mass of the quiescent 5, then on impact the quantity of motion in the quiescent would be 10, being a gain of $\frac{2}{3}$ more than the original quantity, and the striking would be reflected with 4 more, also equal $\frac{2}{3}$, so that the original quantity would not only be doubled, but there would besides be a gain of $\frac{1}{3}$ more; and so of other cases. This shews how ill-founded that doctrine is which teaches that the quantity of motion or of mechanic action in the universe always con-

tinues

tinues the same, and that there can be no generation or destruction of motion by percussion while the state of motion or rest of the centre of gravity of the percussive bodies remains the same; were this the case, there would be no loss or destruction of motion when two equal non-elastic bodies moving from any distance with equal velocities in direct opposition to each other encounter and thereby cease to move any longer, since in this case the state and situation of their common centre of gravity is not affected. The above facts prove that the seemingly mysterious result of the generation of motion or moment by rest, or of mechanic moment or power being in certain cases generated in place of expended by means of mechanic action, and that even in so great a degree that the effect, as in the case of a series of elastic bodies increasing in a geometrical progression of great extent, may become almost indefinitely greater than its primary cause, or than the moment or quantity of motion of the very small elastic body by whose agency in impinging against the smallest body of the series this surprising effect is produced, is not an effect without an adequate and an assignable cause, but such as can be rationally and justly accounted for on the above principles, without having recourse to the unfounded hypothesis of the forces being as the squares of the velocities.

60. I am acquainted with no direct and decisive experiment whereby the supposed generation or gain of motion and force in cases of the resolution of forces is proved, and if there is actually ever such generation or gain of motion and force in these cases I imagine it can be only when the bodies are elastic, and then only on the principle just developed.

61. That there actually is and necessarily must be loss of motion, and thereby of moment or force, in the composition of motions or forces must be sufficiently manifest, when it is considered, that in composition the compounding motions or forces always necessarily act more or less in opposition to each other, and thereby necessarily more or less destroy each other; so that if they were equal to two contiguous sides of a parallelogram, they must now become equal to its diagonal only; and hence it appears that this loss of force is not an effect without an adequate and assignable cause, and how very unapplicable the principle of the forces being as the squares of the velocities is to these cases, since according to that principle there should in those cases be no loss of motion or force.

62. Thus

62. Thus then it appears that the principle of the forces being as the squares of the velocities fails with regard to every case of mechanic action of whatever kind it may be, and it is therefore to be regretted that so much time and talent should have been unprofitably wasted in making intricate calculations for the purpose of determining, in cases of percussion the times of action, with the intention of thereby determining the forces in these cases. Every determinate degree of force must necessarily be capable of producing only a certain determinate degree of action, whether the time of that action is long or short; and it is utterly impossible to assign any just reason why forces, confessedly as the velocities when acting instantaneously, should, when acting in time, from being opposed by soft yielding substances, become in a duplicate ratio of the velocities.

63. Though the mechanical force or power is in every case precisely as the mass multiplied into the velocity, and though the total amount of the resistances overcome or the effects produced are in every case precisely as the degree of mechanic force which comes into action or is employed in producing them, yet the effects produced in different cases will differ from each other even when precisely the same degree or quantity of mechanic force comes into action in each case in producing these effects, from differences in the modes in which that degree of mechanic force may be employed and applied in producing them. Thus, for instance, though the moments or mechanic forces of two balls, each of the same magnitude, whereof the density or mass of the one is double that of the other, moving with velocities inversely as their respective densities, and though the total amount of the resistances overcome by them upon impact are precisely the same, as for instance, when they strike against the wall of a house or fortification, or the side, &c. of a ship, yet the effects, produced by the one will differ much from the effects produced by the other, as the wall or yielding body impinged upon would receive only half the shock but be penetrated to twice the depth by the ball moving with double the velocity of the other that it is by that other; while the ball of double the density moving with but half the velocity of the other will penetrate to half the depth only but will give the wall or opposing body double the shock upon impact that the other does; and so in proportion will the differences of the effects produced be in other cases according to the particular circumstances of
each

each particular case; and hence it is manifest that the effects produced by the same mechanic force may differ from each other, and yet the resistances or forces overcome in producing them be the same or equal in both cases. It is on the knowledge of facts such as these that the knowledge of the most effectual modes of employing and applying any given degree of mechanic power or force for the production and attainment of any required object or end must in a great degree necessarily depend. Thus, if it is required to batter down a wall or other obstacle by shaking and shattering it to fragments, bodies of great mass moving with small velocities, as the battering rams of the ancients or very weighty balls discharged from cannon with small velocities, must necessarily be employed for that purpose; whereas if it is required to penetrate the wall or opposing body in place of beating it down or demolishing it, much lighter balls or bodies moving with proportionally greater velocities must necessarily be employed for producing that effect; these effects however are limited, and to produce them the velocities can be carried to a certain degree only of celerity or of slowness.

63. Those machines which have been denominated the mechanic powers are only contrivances for condensing or concentrating the quantity of power applied, so that it shall act in a narrower sphere or space, whereby it is enabled to operate upon the obstacle or opposing body with a proportionally diminished velocity and yet with the same intensity; or, in other words, for diminishing the resistance without diminishing the power, by diminishing the velocity and thereby the counteraction of the load or opposing body, while the velocity of the power and thereby the force with which it acts remains the same; the velocity with which the power acts on the obstacle being diminished by these contrivances without diminishing the velocity of the power itself, and the obstacle resisting *ceteris paribus* with proportionally the less force the less the velocity impressed or with which it is urged. And hence when the moments or quantities of motion in the power and load are equal to each other, a state of equilibrium must, according to the preceding principles as well as to experiment and fact, necessarily take place*.

* Attempts have been made to account for the action of the mechanic powers on other principles by Archimedes, Newton, M'Lauren, and others. See an account of Sir Isaac Newton's Philosophical Discoveries by Colin M'Lauren, book 2, chap. 3, § 3—11: see also Hamilton's Philosophical Essays, 1, &c.

64. Though

64. Though by the employment of these machines what is gained in power is lost in time, and though it is regarded as an established principle that in mechanics there is no gain of power without a proportional loss of time, yet there are several mechanical contrivances and machines by means of which there is a gain of velocity as well as of power. Thus in dragging any weighty body along there is a gain not only in power but in velocity also by placing it on a sledge, as not only a greater weight may be drawn by that means, but also in less time than before by the same strength or force applied; and if placed on a wheel carriage, and particularly a wheel carriage furnished with springs, or on a wheel carriage and rail-way, these effects are encreased in a very great degree; in the case of compression there is also a gain both in power and in time by giving the compressing body the form of a roller, &c.

ESSAY

ESSAY V.

OF FIRE AND TEMPERATURE.

---

1. MANY different opinions have been entertained by philosophers with regard to the nature and properties of fire, of light, of heat, and of cold. The antients regarded fire, or heat, terms often used indiscriminately, either as a particular substance, or as a quality having no substantial existence: some of them regarding it as the one, and some as the other. The same has been the case with respect to most of the moderns; while others of them, and these conspicuous for superior abilities, the mechanical philosophers, have regarded it neither as the one nor the other, but merely as an effect:—an effect of a certain motion, excited mechanically in the minute particles of substances of any kind, solid or liquid, and they have supported this opinion by many ingenious experiments and arguments. Bacon, in an express Treatise, *De Forma Calidi*, from a particular enumeration of the several phenomena and effects of heat, deduces several general properties of it; and hence he defines heat " an expansive undulatory " motion in the minute particles of a body; by which they tend, with some " rapidity towards the circumference, and at the same time incline a little " upwards." And Boyle observes, that when a piece of iron becomes red hot by hammering, " there is nothing to make it so, except the forcible " motion of the hammer impressing a vehement and variously determined " agitation on the small parts of the iron." Sir Isaac Newton also supports this system. " Fire," according to his conception of it, " being only a body, " so much ignited as to emit light copiously; and not any particular body " originally endowed with the properties of producing the sensations of heat

" and

" and light, and the other effects which accompany ignition and combus-
" tion: for what else, (says he), is red hot iron but fire? And what else is a
" burning charcoal but red hot wood; or flame itself, but red hot smoke?
" Flame is only the volatile part of the fuel heated red hot so as to shine;
" and hence it is such bodies only as are volatile, that is, as emit a copious
" fume, that will flame; nor will they flame longer than they have fume to
" burn.   In distilling hot spirits, if the head of the still be taken off, the
" ascending vapours will catch fire from a candle and turn into flame. And in
" the same manner several bodies much heated by friction, attrition, fermen-
" tion or the like, will emit lucid fumes, which if they be copious enough, and
" the heat sufficiently great, will be flame; and the reason why fused metals
" do not flame, is the smallness of their fume; this is evident, because
" splinter which fumes most copiously, does likewise flame. Add, that all
" flaming bodies, oil, tallow, wax, wood, pitch, sulphur, &c. by flaming,
" waste and vanish into burning smoke. And do not all fixed bodies, when
" heated to a certain degree, emit light, and shine? And is not this emission
" performed by the vibrating motion of their parts? and do not all bodies,
" which abound with terrestrial and sulphureous parts, emit light as often
" as these parts are sufficiently agitated, whether that agitation be made by
" external fire, or by friction, or percussion, or putrefaction, or by any other
" cause?—Thus, sea water in a storm; quicksilver agitated in vacuo; the
" back of a cat, or the neck of a horse, obliquely rubbed in a dark place;
" wood, flesh, and fish, while they putrify; vapours from putrifying waters,
" usually called ignes fatui; stacks of moist hay or corn; glow-worms;
" amber and diamonds by rubbing; fragments of steel struck off with a flint,
" &c. all emit light. Are not gross bodies and light convertible into one
" another? and may not bodies receive much of their activity from the
" particles of light which enter their composition? I know no body less apt
" to shine than water; and yet water by frequent distillations, changes into
" fixed earth, which by a sufficient heat may be made to shine like other
" bodies, and may not the attraction of the parts of matter be changed into
" repulsion, when these parts become infinitely small, and assume the
" character of fire?—

It has also been observed, that " we frequently find the effects of fire pro-
" duced where no visible fire appeared. Thus the fingers are easily burnt
" by

" by an iron heated below the degree of ignition, or so as to be no ways red
" hot or fiery: whence it follows, that the eye is no judge of fire. So like-
" wise the touch gives no positive notice of any degree of fire below the na-
" tural heat of the body, or any so great as to destroy the organ. Again, the
" effects of fire are often produced without any manifest signs of burning,
" melting, &c. as in evaporation, &c. If this method of exclusion and re-
" jection were pursued to its due length, we should perhaps find no criterion,
" infallible mark, or characteristic of fire in general, but that of a particular
" motion struggling among the minute parts of bodies and tending to throw
" them off at the surface. If this should prove the case, then such a motion
" will be the form and essence of fire; and which being present, makes
" fire also present; and which being absent, makes fire also absent: whence
" to produce fire, and to produce this motion in bodies, will be one and the
" same thing."*

2. The opinion of Boerhaave with regard to fire or heat did not differ
essentially from that of the above mentioned philosophers; since, according
to his notion, it was also an effect only, and likewise the effect of motion
in minute particles, so that the only difference between them consisted in
the supposition by the former of heat or fire being the result of motion in
the minute particles of any kind of substance whatever; and in the supposition by the latter of heat or fire being the consequence of motion in the
minute particles of one particular kind of substance only: which kind he
represented as being universally diffused. This difference in their opinions,
however, gave rise to long and violent disputes between the mechanical
and chemical philosophers, which terminated at last, through the deference
paid to the principles of Newton, though he himself did not take any very
active part in the dispute, in favour of the mechanical.

3. That celebrated chemist Macquer, following the principles of Stahl,
considers fire in two different views; first as it enters into the composition
of several bodies, of which it is a principle or constituent part, forming the
inflammable principle, or what has been called the phlogiston of these
bodies; and secondly, as being pure, free, and not entering into any compound, but acting sensibly and strongly upon all natural bodies, and pro-

* Encyclopedia Britannica, 1st. Edit. Art. Fire, p. 252.

D D

ducing

ducing effects as a powerful agent in all chemical operations. It is in the first of these views only that he considers it in the Article Phlogiston of his Chemical Dictionary, in which he observes, " the great error of the ancient " chemists was, in not sufficiently distinguishing this principle from other " more compound bodies, which indeed contain much of it, but of which " it is only a constituent part. For instance, they confound it with oil, " and with sulphur, the names of which substances were indiscriminately " given to it, though neither oil nor sulphur be the phlogiston of the modern, " but are only substances into the composition of which a great quantity of " this principle enters."

" On the other hand, as oil, sulphur, and other inflammable matters, " differ so much from each other that they cannot be considered as the " same thing, probably the ancients, who sometimes gave it one, and some- " times another, of the names of these inflammable compounds, mistook " its unity and identity; that is, they did not know that one only inflam- " mable principle exists, always the same, always similar to itself, either " in oils, or in sulphur, or in coals, in a word in any combustible whatever. " We owe the discovery of these important truths to modern chemists, and " particularly to the illustrious Stahl."

" Phlogiston ought to be considered as elementary fire, combined and " rendered one of the principles of combustible bodies."

4. It is in the latter view only that he considers it in the Article Fire of his Chemical Dictionary. In which he observes that, " In fact, all sub- " stances whatever, which are placed in any given degree of heat, and " obliged to remain there, acquire precisely the same degree of heat. " This fact has been ascertained by instruments fit for measuring the degrees " of heat."

" The effects which the fire produces, or rather heated bodies, upon our " senses, are sensations of heat and light; but these sensations are not ex- " cited but when the fire is in a certain quantity; for every known body " contains a certain portion of *uncombined* fire, and yet not any body " which is not lighted or strongly heated excites in us any sensation of heat " or light."

" We ought also to remark, that although all bodies penetrated with " much fire are necessarily hot and luminous; heat, and not light, is the
" only

" only certain sign of the presence of fire. The reason of this is, that bo-
" dies may be very luminous, without any change being induced in any of
" their essential qualities in these two contrary states; whereas, the differ-
" ence of more or less heat produces in all bodies alterations in their pro-
" perties very sensible and proportionable to the difference of heat."

" These considerations have induced some philosophers to imagine, that
" light is a being which indeed is rendered sensible by fire, but distinct and
" different from it. According to this opinion, heat is only a property of
" fire; whereas, light is a distinct and independent substance. This opinion
" appears to be even demonstrated, when we consider that light may be
" decomposed by refraction, as Newton's experiments shew; and that it is
" not, as pure fire is, capable of pervading all bodies, is proved by the
" opacity of many bodies, and by the reflection of light."

5. This opinion of light and fire being distinct and independent substances has been adopted in whole or in part by several of the most distinguished chemists of our time, as Scheele, Lavoisier, &c. The celebrated
Dr. Black, of Edinburgh----to whom the science of chemistry owes so
much, from his discoveries of fixed air, &c. which gave rise to the discoveries of the other different known kinds of airs or gases, and to all our
knowledge respecting them and respecting the nature and properties of
calcarious substances, &c.---taught that that which causes the sensation of
heat, and which expands, fuses, evaporates, &c. bodies, is a substance of a
particular kind, to which he gave the name of matter of heat, not only to
distinguish it from the matter of light, which often, even when pure, produces not sensible heat, but also because he represented the degree of
sensation and effect produced. to be, *ceteris paribus*, directly as the quantity of matter of heat. This matter of heat he taught existed in substances,
without forming a constituent or component part of them, as phlogiston is
supposed to do, and in the two different states of being either sensible or
latent; it being sensible, or producing sensible effects only, when in motion, or proceeding from one body to another, and then the body from
which it proceeds is regarded as hot; and latent, when it remains in any
body fixed and stationary, however great the quantity of it that body may
contain, without acting on, or affecting other bodies; so that this doctrine,
in this respect, differs in little from that of preceding chemists with regard

to heat, as also making it depend on motion in a particular substance, except in not regarding that substance as either essentially motive, or as forming an element or constituent part of combustible substances. From the fact, long known, of evaporation producing the sensation of cold, and from the discovery of the degree of coldness thus produced being, *ceteris paribus*, as the degree of evaporation; and the experiment first made by his colleague in the university, Doctor Cullen, of placing ether and water within the receiver of an air pump and then exhausting the air from within it, whence it appeared that the expansion of the ether in this case, in consequence of being freed from the pressure of the atmosphere, caused not only the contiguous water to become so cold as to freeze, but also the ether itself to become much colder than it was before; as well as from other experiments purposely made for ascertaining this fact, &c. he inferred and taught that the *capacity* of even the same substance for acquiring and retaining matter of heat without any alteration being induced in its temperature was different, according to the different states of that substance as to solidity, liquidity, and aerial; its capacity being much increased in its liquid state above what it was in its solid, and in its aerial above what it was in its liquid:— and that different substances, when in the same states as to solidity, liquidity, and aerial, have nevertheless different capacities for matter of heat; which differences he attempted to ascertain and specify in many cases, and from the whole to deduce a just theory, and useful practical inferences. Of the essence, elements, or constituent principles, of that substance he calls matter of heat he gives no account. This doctrine, sometimes slightly modified, has been very generally adopted, and has for a considerable time past been the prevailing one. The French chemists, with the intention of avoiding periphrastic expressions, have substituted the term *caloric* for that of *matter of heat*; and in this they have been generally followed. " In this manner," says that eminent chemist Lavoisier, in the much admired work, his Elements of Chemistry, Part I. chap. 1, page 65, of Kerr's Translation, " we must understand the following expression, in-
" troduced by the English philosophers, who have given us the first precise
" ideas upon this subject—*the capacity of bodies for containing the matter of*
" *heat.* As comparisons with sensible objects are of great use in assisting
" us to form distinct notions of abstract ideas, I shall endeavour to illustrate
" this

" this by instancing the phenomena which take place between water and
" bodies which are wetted and penetrated by it, with a few reflections.

" If equal pieces of different kinds of wood, suppose cubes of one foot
" each, be immersed in water, the fluid gradually insinuates itself into
" their pores, and the pieces of wood are augmented both in weight and
" magnitude: each species of wood will imbibe a different quantity of
" water; the lighter and more porus woods will admit a larger, the com-
" pact and closer grained will admit of a lesser quantity; for the propor-
" tional quantities of water imbibed by the pieces will depend upon the
" nature of the constituent particles of the wood, and upon the greater
" or lesser affinity subsisting between them and water; very resinous wood,
" for instance, though it may be at the same time very porus, will admit
" but little water. We may therefore say, that the different kinds of wood
" possess different capacities for receiving water; we may even determine,
" by means of the augmentation of their weights, what quantity of water
" they have actually absorbed; but as we are ignorant how much water
" they contained, previous to immersion, we cannot determine the absolute
" quantity they contain, after being taken out of the water.

" The same circumstances undoubtedly take place with bodies that are
" immersed in caloric; taking into consideration, however, that water is
" an incompressible fluid, whereas caloric is on the contrary endowed with
" very great elasticity; or, in other words, the particles of caloric have a
" great tendency to separate from each other, when forced by any other
" power to approach; this difference must of necessity occasion very con-
" siderable diversities in the results of experiments made upon these two
" substances.

" Having established these clear and simple propositions, it would be
" very easy to explain the ideas which ought to be affixed to the following
" expressions, which are by no means synonimous, but possess each a strict
" and determined meaning, as in the following definitions:

" *Free caloric* is that which is not combined in any manner with any
" other body. But, as we live in a system to the matter of which caloric
" has a very strong adhesion, we are never able to obtain it in the state
" of absolute freedom.

" *Combined caloric* is that which is fixed in bodies by affinity or elective
" attraction,

" attraction, so as to form part of the substance of the body, even part of
" its solidity.

" By the expression *specific caloric* of bodies, we understand the respec-
" tive quantities of caloric requisite for raising a number of bodies of the
" same weight to an equal degree of temperature. This proportional
" quantity of caloric depends on the distance between the constituent par-
" ticles of bodies, and their greater or lesser degrees of cohesion, and this
" distance, or rather the space or void resulting from it, is as I have already
" observed called the *capacity of bodies for containing caloric.*

" *Heat* considered as a sensation, or in other words sensible heat, is
" only the effect produced upon our sentient organs, by the motion or
" passage of caloric, disengaged from surrounding bodies. In general we
" receive impressions only in consequence of motion, and it might be esta-
" blished as an axiom, *That*, WITHOUT MOTION THERE IS NO SENSATION.
" This general principle applies very accurately to the sensations of heat
" and cold : when we touch a cold body the caloric, which always tends to
" become in equilibrio in all bodies, passes from our hand into the body
" we touch, which gives us the feeling or sensation of cold. The direct
" contrary happens, when we touch a warm body, the caloric then, in
" passing from the body into the hand, produces the sensation of heat.
" If the hand and the body touched be of the same temperature, or very
" nearly so, we receive no impression either of heat or cold, because there
" is no motion or passage of caloric, and thus no sensation can take place
" without some corresponding motion to occasion it.

" When the thermometer rises it shews that free caloric is entering into
" the surrounding bodies; the thermometer, which is one of these, receives
" its share in proportion to its mass and to the capacity which it possesses
" for containing caloric. The change therefore which takes place upon
" the thermometer only announces a change of place of the caloric in these
" bodies, of which the thermometer forms one part; it only indicates the
" portion of caloric received, without being a measure of the whole quan-
" tity disengaged, displaced, or absorbed."

Soon after he adds, " It remains before finishing this article to say a few
" words concerning the cause of the elasticity of gases, and of liquids in
" the state of vapour. It is by no means difficult to perceive that this
" elasticity

" elasticity depends upon that of caloric, which seems to be the most emi-
" nently elastic body in nature. Nothing is more readily conceivable
" than that one body should become elastic by entering into combination
" with another body possessed of that quality."

6. These theories were succeeded but not superseded by that of the late
Dr. Scheele, so famous for the many important discoveries with which he
enriched chemical science, and which have conduced so much to its elucidation and further improvement. According to Dr. Scheele's theory, as
given in his Treatise upon Fire, heat is generated by and consists of a combination of empyreal air, the pure air of Dr. Priestly, with phlogiston,
light of a combination of heat with phlogiston, and inflammable air of a
combination of light with phlogiston. This theory though ingenious, and
supported by many most accurate and valuable experiments, was embarrassed with so many difficulties as to be adopted but by few, and by none
perhaps to its whole extent, though much approved of in part by the
illustrious Bergman. It differs however from those that preceded it, in the
essential circumstance of not regarding phlogiston as fire, or as pure fire,
whether in a combined or in a free and disengaged state. According to this
theory fire and light must be gravitating substances, since the empyreal air
of which they are supposed by it principally to consist is manifestly so.

7. The present opinion with regard to the matter of fire is that it is composed of and engendered by a combination of heat and light; or rather
of two different distinct powers or substances capable of producing in sentient beings the two different sensations called heat and light, and these
accordingly have been treated of separately in all the late treatises on chemistry under the names of light and caloric; these are supposed to be the
component parts of fire, those into which it is resolvable, and by the combination of which it is produced. But of the elements or component principles of caloric, or of light, no account is attempted in this theory. The
experiments of Count Rumford and others have evinced that certain substances are better conductors of the calorific power than others, and the
knowledge thus acquired has been applied by him to useful economical
purposes. Though cold, according to all the preceding theories, is regarded
in no other point of view than as consisting merely in the absence or privation of heat; yet in the opinion of some it is a real entity, actually existing
in

in nature as an effective, diffusive, substantial agent, and some experiments
are adduced in support of this theory.

8. Such are the opinions which have prevailed at different times respecting the nature and properties of heat, of light, of fire, of temperature, and
of cold, and such is the present state of our knowledge with regard to
them.   Perhaps the observations in this and the immediately succeeding
Essay may prove in some degree conducive towards the further progress
and improvement of this deep and difficult investigation, and to the establishing of doctrines which may not be liable to some of the objections
which are imputable to those at present adopted.

9. That which affects the human mind with the sensations we call heat,
light, and colour, attended more or less with those of pleasure or pain, and
which expands, fuses, evaporates, and dissipates bodies we call fire.   We
are sensible of these effects, but with respect to the nature of the cause, or
of the power itself by which they are produced and to which we give the
name of fire, we are entirely ignorant, except in as far as its existence, and
certain of its properties, may be rationally inferred from phenomena: heat,
light, and colour, being merely sensations in the mind, and not any thing
existing in that form in that whereby they are produced.   We have however
sufficient reasons for believing that the power by which these sensations are
produced has an existence perfectly independent of that relation to us
whereby they are produced, and might exist though no sentient being
existed ; that any power though existing absolutely, or without any existing
relation, would nevertheless differ from non-entity in being capable of
certain modifications without being essentially altered, and of relation if
other relative substances should be created ; and that it is the primary qualities, or that in any thing which may exist independent of relation and from
which relations may under proper circumstances proceed, that seems to
constitute its real nature or essence.

10. It is however only through the mediums of sensation, reflection, and
reason, that we can have any knowledge of any thing whatever, whether
power, matter, or property, for that which is insensible to us or affects us
not, must as has been already observed be to us as nothing, and hence our
knowledge must be relative only, and confined merely to those things
which either directly or indirectly affect our senses :—it is from the *relative*
                                                                        only

only that we can deduce the *absolute* existence of anything, and that only in a limited sense:—it is through the *sensible* only that we can form any rational conception of the *real* essence.

11. The elementary or chemical powers of substances properly so called, unless that now treated of may be regarded as one of them, seem never to come under the cognizance of our senses in an uncombined and separate state as single and distinct powers, for when they subsist in such a state its duration is too evanescent to be to us perceptible, as it seems to take place only in the act of instantaneously passing from one combination to another, so that they can affect our senses only when they are in a state of combination. The mechanic power and most others not strictly chemical, as gravity, elasticity, magnetism, &c. affect the senses not directly or immediately, but through the medium of matter only, and therefore their existence and properties can only be inferred, and that merely from the sensible effects produced by the material agent or instrument. This however is not the case with the power now treated of, which in many cases affects our senses directly and immediately, without the intervention or the agency of other matter, or without being in a state of combination with it, as well as when in a state of combination with it, and the phenomena produced by it both in this pure and in a combined state are such as seem to warrant the following conclusions, or enumerations of its qualities, viz.

12. First, From those changes of state in the mind, which are accompanied with those sensations we denominate heat, light, and colour, being evidently effects, it may justly be inferred that they must necessarily have an adequate cause, and it is to this cause or power whereby these effects are produced that we give the name of fire.

13. Secondly, From observing that we never experience these sensations, or that these effects never take place but under particular circumstances, as when the external organs of sense are exposed to the influence of particular bodies, as the sun, &c. it may rationally be inferred that that power has an actual existence, and either resides in or proceeds from those bodies, which, on that account, we denominate fiery and luminous.

14. Thirdly, From these bodies or the powers they possess not being affected by any alterations in the sensitive faculties of any animated beings, a lighted candle continuing to burn and yield heat and light, or that at

E E

least

least which is capable of producing these sensations in sentient beings, till it is consumed, even when not acting on or being perceived by any being whatever, it may justly be inferred that that power whereby these sensations may be produced has an existence perfectly independent of that relation or of animal sensation.

15. Fourthly, From the manifest extension of the effects it may justly be inferred that the power whereby they are produced must necessarily be extended.

Fifthly, From the various phenomena in which the effects seem to be divided and modified, and from the known methods of artificially modifying the direction and intensity of its action, and dividing it so as to affect different things, and different parts of the same thing in preference to others, and thereby of producing different effects by its means under circumstances otherwise the same, it may rationally be inferred that the power by which these effects are produced is divisable and modifiable.

Sixthly, From its being capable of being modified in various respects without being essentially altered, and from its also being capable of subsisting in vacuo, or in the absence of every other known substance, and therefore of itself, as proved by an experiment of Newton's and by several others since, it may justly be inferred that this power is a substance.

16. Seventhly, From the known facts of light and heat diffusing themselves equally and indiscriminately in all directions from an ignited body as from a centre, and that even in vacuo, and from their dilating or expanding and thereby enlarging the dimensions of every body, solid or fluid, with which they combine, or rather to whose parts or particles they cohere, and that in exact proportion to the additional cohering quantity of the igneous substance, it may justly be inferred that the parts or particles of fire or of this igneous substance are essentially repulsive of each other.

17. Eighthly, From its penetrating through the pores of even the densest bodies, and hence from its being impossible to confine it in any great quantity or in a dense contracted state mechanically or forcibly in vessels of any other substances, it may rationally be concluded that its integrant parts or particles must necessarily be indefinitely minute.

18. Ninthly, From this minuteness, and this mutually repulsive power, of its particles, as well as from its dilating and penetrating qualities, and the

well

well known fact of its being the cause of fluidity in every other substance that is palpable to sense, it may justly be inferred that it necessarily must be in its own nature essentially fluid, and therefore that its particles are spheres, and that those of no other known substances are so, since no other known substance is essentially fluid, and therefore that the ancient chemists possessed in this what they so much coveted, an alkahest or universal solvent. That water is not essentially fluid is evident from its freezing on a partial deprivation of its igneous fluid, and that its particles are not spheres is manifest from the manner in which they arrange themselves in chrystallizing or freezing.

19. Tenthly, From the well ascertained facts that the absorption of igneous fluid, however great in quantity, by any gravitating body, adds nothing to the weight of that body, and that any emission of it from any such body diminishes not its weight, it must necessarily be inferred that fire or the igneous fluid possesses not gravity. By the term gravitating, attractive of itself seems in general to be meant; thus matter is said to gravitate because matter is attractive of matter, or because material bodies mutually attract each other; but if this is a proper meaning of the term gravity as seems to be the case, fire cannot possibly gravitate, since in place of being attractive it is repulsive of itself, and since if attractive of itself it should rather gravitate to the fiery and luminous body from which it originally proceeded, or to the sun, than to this earth, as the sun contains it in much greater quantity than this earth does. It however does not diminish the gravity or the attraction of any body to the earth with which it combines, or communicates not absolute levity to it, but only diminishes its specific gravity, by expanding and enlarging its dimensions, or its gravity relatively to its magnitude, or to the magnitude of any other body of the same kind possessing a proportionally less quantity of it and therefore not so much expanded. It is the quantity of gravitating matter only, and of no other kind of matter in a body or space—for a vacuum of gravitating matter may for any thing that is known to the contrary be a plenum of other matter—that can be known by the weight of that body or space.

The term gravity properly expresses that mutual attraction, whether proximate or remote, which takes place between bodies or substances

whether

whether homogeneous or heterogeneous, which are each *essentially* attractive, or attractive of itself, or of which the homogeneous integrant parts or molecules, particles, and masses, are attractive of each other, and which reciprocal attraction is in every case in direct proportion to the attracting masses; and hence that reciprocal attraction which takes place between substances which are *essentially repulsive*, or repulsive of themselves, as fire, &c. and other substances which are *essentially attractive*, or attractive of themselves, is not properly gravity, or of that kind properly denominated gravitating; and hence neither fire nor any other substances repulsive of themselves, notwithstanding of their attraction to gravitating matter, can with propriety be regarded as being possessed of gravity, or as being gravitating substances.

20. Eleventhly, From its possessing magnitude or bulk, from its being palpable to sense or capable of affecting animated beings and thereby of producing sensations in them through the material organs of sense, from its entering the pores and occupying and enlarging the interstices of gravitating matter and thereby expanding it, from its resisting and being resisted by it, or from its capability of acting and reacting on it, and from its powerfully resisting compression and thereby occupying space to the exclusion of other material substances, it may with strict justice be inferred that fire or the igneous fluid is actually solid, dense, or material. Sir Isaac Newton seems to think that that only is dense, or solid and material, which weighs or gravitates, and that that which is not gravitating is not matter, and hence in estimating the *mass or quantity of matter* in bodies, he says (Princ. Def. 1.) " I have no regard in this place to a *medium*, if any such " there is, that freely pervades the interstices between the parts of bodies, " &c." But substances, whether gravitating or not, possessing the above enumerated qualities must necessarily be material; besides the igneous fluid seems to be capable of penetrating gravitating bodies by means of their pores or the interstices between their integrant particles only, and substances which are not capable of mutual free penetration, otherwise than by means of pores, must necessarily be solid or material relatively to each other. According to Sir Isaac Newton (Princ. lib. 3, prop. 8, corol. 3), the sun has one fourth part only of the density of the earth; that is according to his manner of computing density there is only one fourth of gravitating matter in any particular
cular

cular portion of the sun that there is in any equal portion of the earth---from which it seems probable that a portion of the earth contains not more than one-fourth of the quantity of fire or igneous fluid, or of ungravitating matter, that an equal portion of the sun does.

21. Twelfthly, From various phenomena it may be inferred that the igneous matter, though repulsive of itself, is attractive of and capable of combination with gravitating matter ; or rather that igneous and gravitating matter are mutually attractive of each other. In certain cases the attraction and cohesion between igneous matter and gravitating bodies is but very feeble and of short duration---thus certain pyropheri, phosphori, &c. readily combine with it and as readily part with it again. In certain other cases where the attraction is stronger, and the combination of a nature more permanent, yet the adhesion of the igneous matter to the gravitating bodies is still but slight, as only filling and expanding their pores, or the vacuities between their particles, and is therefore easily got the better of by mechanical compression and other means. This last is the kind of combination between these two different kinds of matter that has been most attended to by philosophical chemists. It is in some respects analagous to that which takes place between water and a spunge ; and as, in these cases, the quantities of igneous matter absorbed by and contained in different bodies are, *ceteris paribus*, in direct proportion to their several *capacities* for containing it, or in a compound ratio of the number and magnitude of the vacuities or pores between their respective particles, the attraction and combination of igneous and gravitating matter have been supposed to be regulated in all cases entirely by that circumstance ; or it hath been supposed that the power in any body of attracting and combining with igneous matter is precisely as its *capacity;* or, in other words, *ceteris paribus*, inversely as its density. In other cases the attraction or cohesion between igneous matter and the particles of gravitating bodies is so very powerful that it seems to form an essential part, though not an element, of these substances or of the particles of the compounds formed by their union, even of their solidity, since the bodies thus formed cannot be compressed by any mechanical means known. Thus in the melting of ice, from its combining with igneous matter, each particle of the ice seems either to have had its form changed to a sphere, or to have acquired a repulsive sphere of igneous matter, from the ice becoming

coming

coming by this means water, or being reduced from a dry and solid to a liquid state ; and the vacuities that were in the ice seem to be diminished in a much greater degree than the particles of the ice are enlarged by this means, notwithstanding the great addition of igneous matter, as the water thus formed is of greater density or specific gravity than the ice of which it is formed ; and the particles or repulsive spheres thus formed are so solid as to be perfectly incompressible by any known mechanical means. The compressions and expansions discovered by Mr. Canton, in the year 1761, to take place under certain circumstances in rain water, were so small, amounting by his account only to a forty-sixth millionth part, as scarcely to admit of distinct perception or accurate measurement, and are such as may reasonably be accounted for from the compressions and expansions of the air and other impurities contained in the water employed : it being impossible by any known means to free water entirely from air and all other heterogeneous matter.

The force of the mutual attraction which takes place between the gravitating and the igneous matter, in the case of water, must necessarily be exceedingly great; since, the force whereby they cohere and are retained in that state must necessarily be superior to that expansive force whereby the gravitating matter shoots into chrystals, forming ice, on being deprived of that igneous matter which retained it in the state of water, and since this expansive force is found by experiment to be exceedingly great. The same is the case with respect to mercury, and probably with respect to all other metallic substances, and even earths, when in a fused or liquid state; and indeed in a great degree with respect to all liquids known; and several bodies in a dry state, or in a state of solidity as opposed to that of liquidity, also contain much igneous matter in an incorporated state, as an ingredient in their respective compositions, as quartz, &c. and even ice itself seems by no means to be destitute of it. But though igneous matter forms an essential and considerable part, a part even of the solidity of most bodies, yet it adds nothing as was before observed to their gravity. And water, notwithstanding the great quantity of igneous matter it contains in its composition, is entirely devoid of elasticity. To those who are of opinion that the igneous fluid is the cause and only cause of elasticity in bodies, and this opinion I imagine is the prevalent one, or who have been deceived

into

into the supposition of water being actually elastic, from certain phenomena which seem to indicate it—as the upward projection of part of the water, when any body falls forcibly and with much velocity into it, and the successive reboundings from it of a flat piece of stone when projected into it, in a direction not deviating much from the horizontal—the truth of this assertion will appear to be at least doubtful; but when it is considered that it must be absurd in the highest degree to infer elasticity where compression cannot be induced ; and that these appearances may, on other principles, be accounted for in a satisfactory manner; all doubt with regard to the non-elasticity of water must necessarily vanish. The upward projection of the water at and near the surface, in the first case mentioned above, is merely the effect of the impulse or propulsion of the water immediately underneath on it, from its being agitated and moved by the action of the rapidly descending body in the fluid, and of its being the nature of such fluids as water to act in all directions equally or with equal force, and with the most sensible effect where most immediately acted upon and where least opposed; and, in the second case, the successive reboundings of the stone from the water is the effect merely of the resistance of a non-elastic gravitating fluid as water to any body moving in it diminishing in direct proportion as the depth of the body from the surface of the fluid diminishes; and of a projectile's always proceeding in that direction in which it is least resisted; whence it successively ascends to the surface and above it, as urged by the force of projection, and then successively descends again on account of its gravity. Mercury is also non-elastic; and the same is the case probably with several other fluids.

22. Thirteenthly. Though igneous matter combines with gravitating bodies, from their mutual attraction, and thereby gradually penetrates and expands these bodies, yet that this combination, however strong, is not chemical may justly be inferred ; since the natures of the proximate principles are not changed by it, and the new products or substances formed by their union possess no chemical qualities but those the proximate principles possessed before, and since no decomposition of either of the principles takes place, and they combine in toto, their respective natures being essentially the same when in a combined as when in an uncombined state. This kind of attraction seems to approach nearer to that of cohesion than

to

to any other kind of attraction; and one of the principal qualities the gravitating bodies acquire from the igneous matter with which they combine is that of becoming more penetrating or solvent than they were before; or that the compound possesses a greater degree of that quality than the gravitating body did before such combination.

23. Fourteenthly. From the repulsive power---from the almost instantaneous diffusion of light to the extent of many miles as sensibly perceived---and from rational deductions from certain astronomical phenomena---it may justly be inferred that a very rapid motion is essential to fire, or the igneous particles, when in a pure and disengaged state. It may also be inferred from several phenomena that the particles proceed in right lines or rays in all directions as they successively disengage themselves from the ignited body as from a centre; and it is when the ignited body is thus discharging that it is said to be in a state of inflammation. Also, from the igneous particles being reflected from bodies capable of reflecting them in rays or right lines, and at angles equal to those of incidence, it may be inferred that these particles move at so very great distances between themselves in the direction of their motion as to have little or no lateral effect on each other, and little or no impulse or pressure but in that direction; since, if otherwise, they would necessarily affect and oppose each other's rectilineal motion both before and after reflection, and would be repelled from the reflecting body not in rays, but, as is the case in other fluids, in undulations verging in successive rings. As this is the only known fluid that possesses these qualities, so it is the only known fluid that can act, and that only when in a pure and uncombined state, upon a plane immersed in it, and opposing the direction of its motion with different inclinations, with forces as the squares of the sines of these inclinations; since no fluid, not possessing these qualities, can possibly act when in motion, or oppose motion when at rest, agreeable to this principle in a perfect manner, though certain gravitating fluids which are rare, elastic, and admit of being formed into partial currents, from particular portions of them being projected in particular directions with force sufficient for penetrating in some degree the general mass, may in a very imperfect manner, and in a very limited degree; as the air in certain cases, particularly in the reflecting of sounds, for though sound, or rather the currents of air by which it is produced, proceeds

from

from the reflecting surface in every direction, yet a greater quantity of it often proceeds from it in some particular directions than in others: with respect to gravitating fluids that are incompressible and unelastic, it must be manifest that they cannot, as not proceeding in rays from their particles being in contact or nearly so, and in cases of this kind necessarily counteracting each other, act on this principle in any manner, or in any degree, and consequently that the resistances with respect to them in these cases must necessarily be not as the squares of the sines, but simply as the sines of the angles of inclination.

24. Fifteenthly, From its having been rationally deduced, from certain well known optical experiments, that if only a 100 igneous particles, proceeding from a point in the surface of the sun, enter the eye in a second of time, they will be more than sufficient to produce an uninterrupted sensation of light in the mind during that period, though these particles, from the prodigious velocity with which they move, may be more than a 1000 miles distant from each other, and therefore leaving room enough for innumerable such other particles to pass through between them in all directions, it may be justly inferred that the sensation of light does not depend so much on the number of igneous particles, as on the velocity with which they move; and it seems probable that no number of them, however great, if at rest relative to motion, or moving slowly, could produce that sensation.

25. Sixteenthly, Though fire, or igneous matter, in a pure or disengaged state, moves in general with prodigious velocity, yet there are many facts from which it may be inferred, that igneous matter, more or less combined with gravitating matter, remains either stationary, and in a certain degree fixed, or moves with a velocity more or less diminished, according as the quantity and density of gravitating matter with which it is combined and loaded is greater or smaller. Thus, that fire seldom disengages itself from any substance with which it may be united, either by means of combustion, compression, or electrical excitation, without instantly combining in part with other matter, particularly with that of the atmosphere, and that it frequently carries part of the matter of the substance from which it detaches itself along with it, is manifest from several circumstances, as in the cases of steam from boiling water, of smoke from a burning candle, and of vapours from other heated substances, and even from the igneous matter

F F proceeding

proceeding from solid bodies in a red heat, which seems often to be loaded
with matter derived partly from the ignited body, and partly from the
atmosphere, as well as from that odour or effluvia emitted along with the
fire on the collision of two pieces of quartz together, &c. and that fire, when
thus combined and clogged with other matter of very different qualities
from its own, necessarily loses much of its activity, &c. and is rendered
incapable of producing many phenomena, and of penetrating many substances it otherwise could have done, or even of passing through such as it
may penetrate, with nearly the same facility and velocity, is also from many
circumstances manifest. When fire is combined and incumbered with so
much other matter, from being detached from the ignited body, as that the
compound assumes the form of smoke or vapour, the fire thus detached
instantly loses the whole force, direction, and velocity of the impulse by
which it was projected, and instead of proceeding in rays from the ignited
body, as from a centre, it expends the whole of its repulsive force in
expanding the matter with which it is combined, whereby the specific
gravity of that matter is diminished, or its relative levity increased, so that
the new compound, or smoke or vapour thus formed, ascends, if surrounded
by the atmosphere, from being specifically lighter than it, in a direction
perpendicular to the horizon. In this state of combination, the fire is
incapable of reflection and refraction by the usual means, and cannot
penetrate glass, otherwise than by being absorbed by it gradually and
slowly, none of it passing through it in the form of light; and it also in
this state comes into *immediate* contact with polished metals, in place of
being reflected by them, whereby it is absorbed by them, and so expands
or heats them, leaving the gravitating matter with which it was combined
adhering to their surfaces. When not so much loaded with gravitating
matter, it is capable of proceeding in the direction of the projecting force,
or in rays proceeding from the ignited body, though still too much combined and incumbered, and with a velocity too slow for to produce in us
at least the sensations of light or colours, though it is in this state capable
of being reflected by a metallic mirror, and of being refracted and decomposed, in part at least, by means of a glass prism, and probably by other
means, so that some small part of it seems to penetrate glass, while the
remainder is imbibed by it, and thereby renders it hot: to igneous matter
in this state, Doctor Scheele gave the name of radiant heat. When combined

bined with a still smaller proportion of other matter, the state of ignition is higher, and it approaches nearer to the qualities of pure fire. It then not only proceeds in rays, is capable of reflection, refraction, &c. but also of exciting in us the sensation we call red; on which account the matter with which it is combined is said to be in a red heat. When in this state, much of it is capable of penetrating a pane of glass, without combining with it, in the form of light, while the remainder is absorbed by it, combines with it, and renders it hot, &c. from which it would appear that some parts of it, in this state, are more incumbered and loaded with other matter, than others, and that the glass operates in this case as a filter for separating them from each other. But after the pores of the glass are much expanded from this absorption, the greater part, if not the whole, passes through it.

26. In treating of this subject, it becomes, on several accounts, necessary to distinguish between fire or igneous matter, when in a pure and disengaged state, as it proceeds from the sun, &c. and when in a state of combination with a greater or smaller proportion of gravitating matter, since in the latter case it often becomes, by means of this combination, more or less fixed, latent, and inactive, with respect to all other bodies but that with which it is combined, and in some cases altogether incapable of acting on or affecting any other; and with a view to perspicuity, and the obviating of circumlocution, it may be proper, when treating of it, to distinguish it, when so combined, and thereby more or less fixed and inactive, by means of an appropriate name from fire properly so called, or from igneous matter in a free and pure state. I shall therefore treat of it in these Essays under the denomination of ignite, which may suffice till some other term better suited to the purpose may be adopted in its stead. Ignite may be so far in a free or disengaged state, as to be capable, under certain circumstances, of affecting other bodies besides those with which it is particularly combined, or of moving from one body to another, when it may be called free ignite, to distinguish it from that which is fixed or latent. Ignite differs essentially from what has been called caloric, which is represented as denoting a substance essentially different from those either of light or of fire, and which is in no case luminous.

27. The ignite formed from the combination of gravitating matter with fire, in some of the above-mentioned cases, possesses not any degree of

gravity

gravity that is sensible to us, nor a sufficient quantity of gravitating matter for producing any sensible effect upon a vacuum or barometer; but this may be the effect only of the quantity of gravitating matter being very small relatively to the space it occupies, or of its particles being very minute and very widely diffused; for many material gravitating substances when in a rare state are insensible to us, and therefore to us as nothing, except, in some instances, by their sensible effects on other matter or things : thus the material effluvia by means of which a dog can follow the tract of his master's footsteps, even some hours after his master's departure from the place where the dog is, has no effect upon us whereby we can become sensible of it, and were it not for the dog its existence would be to us unknown; and it is also probable that neither a vacuum, nor a barometer, would be sensibly affected by the fine effluvia of musk, &c.

28. Seventeenthly, Though the sensation of light depends more upon the velocity than upon the number of igneous particles acting upon the sentient being through the proper organ, it may be inferred from many facts that the very reverse is the case with respect to the sensation of heat; or that the degree of intensity depends more on the number of igneous particles acting on the organs of the sentient being than upon any velocity or motion in them; nay there is reason to believe that it has no dependence whatever upon motion. Indeed, that doctrine which makes heat to be produced by motion alone, or by motion in a particular fluid, seems to be a mere hypothesis unsupported by experience or proof; for, if the sensation of heat in us was produced by the motion of the matter of fire or of ignite in entering and expanding our bodies, that sensation should cease how soon that matter forbore to enter, and the degree of expansion become fixed and stationary, but should commence again as soon as that matter begins to leave our bodies, as being by that means again in motion; the very contrary of this however takes place, for after our bodies have acquired a certain degree of heat, we can retain them for some time, in nearly the same state with respect to heat merely by means of proper coverings, and on the igneous matter's beginning and continuing to leave our bodies we experience the sensation of cold in place of that of heat; so that SEN-SATION does not in all cases depend upon MOTION.

29. Eighteenthly, Though that mutual attraction which takes place be-
                                                                    tween

tween igneous and gravitating matters is not chemical, it may from various phenomena with certainty be inferred to be according to certain determined laws or pre-established affinities. Thus, igneous matter is often manifestly disengaged and separated from certain gravitating material bodies, in whole or in part, either from the gravitating material base with which it is combined having, under the then existing circumstances, a greater affinity to some other gravitating material base than to igneous matter; or from the igneous matter having a greater affinity to some other material base than to that with which it may then be united. Igneous matter, by being attractive of other matter, and repulsive of itself, combines with and separates the integrant particles, or the component parts, from each other of other substances, and thereby either diminishes or annihilates their mutual attraction. The absorption of igneous matter by any body must necessarily, *ceteris paribus*, depend on the attraction between the particles of that body and igneous matter being greater in the then circumstances than the attraction between the particles themselves of which the body is composed; and the greater the attraction between the igneous matter and the gravitating matter of that body, and the less between the particles of the body, the greater, *ceteris paribus*, the power and tendency of the body to absorb igneous matter; at the same time, that the more that is absorbed, the greater must be the distance between the particles of the body, and the greater that distance the less the attraction of aggregation among the particles themselves, this power diminishing as the distance increases in a very high but unknown ratio, and therefore in this case the greater the power and tendency of these particles to attract and combine with more igneous matter. It is the igneous matter contained in a body, before any augmentation of it has taken place, that produces in cases of diminished pressure the expansion of that body, or what has been called the enlargement of its capacity, and thereby its increased tendency to attract and combine with igneous matter; thus, when æther, &c. placed in the receiver of an air-pump, expand on withdrawing the pressure of the atmosphere, it is the igneous matter they contain that expands them, from its repulsive nature, and thereby enables them to attract other igneous matter much more powerfully from contiguous substances than they could before, from the attraction of aggregation between their particles being much diminished or annihilated by the increase of

distance

distance between them thus produced, while their attraction or affinity for igneous matter remains unimpaired or undiminished; and hence these contiguous substances soon produce the effects and exhibit the appearances to which we give the name of cold. The interposition of any other substance, even with which it has but little affinity, between the particles of a body whereby their distance is increased produces the same effects; as of water which increases that distance mechanically by means of the minuteness of its particles, its fluidity, and its gravity; and hence, on the solution of certain salts in water, the absorption of igneous matter by the mixture and the sensible cold produced in contiguous substances.—this is the principle on which the operation of freezing mixtures depends.

30. From these facts it appears that the affinities of different gravitating bodies for igneous matter are, *ceteris paribus*, inversely as the degrees of the attraction of aggregation which takes place among the integrant particles of the several bodies respectively; and, therefore, the quantities of igneous matter absorbable and retainable by gravitating bodies should be said to be, *ceteris paribus*, according to their respective AFFINITIES, rather than according to their respective CAPACITIES for it, especially as there may be vacuities of much capacity between the grains or chrystals of which a body may be constructed, at the same time that the attraction of aggregation between the integrant particles or molecules of which these grains are formed may be of the most powerful kind.

31. It is generally believed that fire is the cause of all fluidity in nature;—that the liquid, the vaporous, and the gazeous or aëriform states of substances all depend on it; and this indeed is the case with respect to the different states of solid, fluid, and vaporous of many substances, but not of all. For though most of the gravitating substances in nature seem severally capable of assuming either the solid, the fluid, or the aëriform states; and though their respective appearances in each of these states seem in general to depend upon the proportions of fire or igneous matter with which they are severally combined, those in a solid state being converted into fluid on being combined with a larger proportion of it, and those in a fluid into an aeriform state from being united with a still larger proportion of it, and conversely; yet this seems not to hold universally: and all the fluidity and elasticity in nature does not seem to be owing to

fire

fire or igneous fluid. For all pure earths, and carbon, are altogether infusible *per se*, or cannot be rendered fluid, by any degree of heat that can be artificially raised; and the higher the temperature to which argil is exposed the more it contracts in volume, and becomes the more compact, solid, and hard, in place of becoming liquid: while many substances which are in a fluid state become solid merely by the application of fire to them, as albumen, &c. without any alteration of their gravity or of specific gravity taking place by that means; and it is also to be observed, that many salts, as the fixed alkalis, concentrated acids, &c. on combining with water and thereby parting with much fire in place of becoming more solid and dense, become more fluid by that means than they were before; and it will be proved in the immediately succeeding Essay that there actually are fluid and elastic substances which owe neither their fluidity nor their elasticity to fire or igneous fluid.

32. That most substances owe their states of fluidity to fire is manifest from nothing further being required in most cases for rendering solid substances fluid than combining them artificially with igneous matter, and nothing further for restoring them to a solid state again than making them disgorge the igneous matter by which they are retained in a fluid. This latter effect may in certain cases be effected even by mechanic compression; and in others by whatever augments the attraction of aggregation among the particles of the substances sufficiently for expelling it from them; and this is sometimes effected merely by the abstracting of water or other gravitating fluid which may keep their particles at a distance from each other, and sometimes by the mixing of two or more gravitating substances together the particles of each of which have greater affinity for those of the others than they have for igneous matter:—these effects take place in the chrystalization of salts, on mixing of concentrated acids with water, or mixing them with certain essential oils when inflammation ensues, and in the slaking or mixing of quicklime with water. In these cases the disengaged igneous matter becomes palpable to sense, and on the mixing of concentrated acids with essential oils and sometimes even in the slaking of lime, in the form of fire, flame, or light; which diffuses itself around by its repulsive power, till being attracted and absorbed by the contiguous substances, the equilibrium of igneous matter and thereby of temperatures

tures between the different gravitating substances according to their respective affinities for it is restored ; while the water or other fluids of the substances from which the igneous matter has thus been expelled assumes on account of its expulsion from them a dry and solid state. Is is on the same principle that igneous matter, when applied in sufficient quantity, produces the discharge again of that aqueous matter from salts, slaked lime, &c. which they had absorbed in chrystalizing or slaking and which is contained in them in a dry and solid state : this aqueous matter having first by that means a portion of igneous matter restored to it equal to that it was deprived of on the chrystalization of the salts or slaking of the lime whereby it became dry and solid, so as thereby to be enabled to assume again the liquid state; and then another portion sufficient for its acquiring the state of steam or vapour, whereby, its specific gravity being diminished, it evaporates separating from the more fixed substances. The water in this case, when in a dry and solid state, cannot with propriety be called ice; as being in intimate combination with other gravitating matter to which it has more affinity under the then circumstances than it has to igneous matter, and by that means less tendency for attracting and imbibing it, and thereby of producing the effects of cold in other substances, than water in the dry, solid, and uncombined state of ice has.

33. The degree of coldness in any body may not depend on the partial deprivation, or on the smallness of the quantity, of fire or of ignite in that body, but on the degree of attraction or affinity it has under the then circumstances for either of these; for a body may possess little or no fire or ignite, and yet not produce the effects to which we give the name of cold, from its having no attraction or affinity for fire or ignite:—the attraction of aggregation of its particles exceeding their attraction for fire. In like manner the degree of heat, or at least the power of producing the effects to which we give that name, in any body, does not depend so much on the quantity of fire or ignite it contains, as on the quantity it parts with; for a body may contain a great deal of it without producing the sensation of heat in contiguous sentient beings or the other effects of it on contiguous inanimated matter, from its attraction for it being so great as to prevent its parting with any of it. And not only the degree of attraction of aggregation among the particles of a body, and the quantity

of

of fire contained in it, but also the degree of repulsive force among the particles themselves of the fire or of the ignite contained in that body, as depending on their degree of purity and condensation, is also to be taken into account in appreciating these effects or the powers of the bodies for producing them. Ignite seems to be diffused through all matter; and, by means of its innate repulsive power, perhaps through all nature: even that which we regard as vacuum, or vacuums of gravitating matter, not being devoid of it.

34. The ignite in any body or bodies is inactive or latent with respect to any other body or bodies having under the then circumstances neither more nor less attraction for ignite than those have with which it is then in combination, so that there is in this case an equilibrium or attraction, that of aggregation and that for ignite balancing in each body. It is in this kind of equilibrium among bodies that *equality of temperature* properly consists; and it is *difference in this respect* among them that properly constitutes what is called *difference of temperature* in bodies; and in cases of the same or equal temperature, the ignite in each particular body is not only fixed and latent with respect to all the other bodies, but also with respect to that particular body itself, except in as far as it may retain it in a state of expansion, or of fluidity, or may, if the body is a sentient being, produce in it a permanent sensation of heat. But when the integrant particles of any particular body or bodies have a greater or less attraction for ignite than the particles of the surrounding bodies have, then that circumstance renders that body of a lower or higher temperature than these other bodies; as, in the first case, it must necessarily attract and imbibe ignite from them, and thereby produce the effects and exhibit the appearances of greater coldness, or of being what is called of a lower temperature than these contiguous bodies are: and, in the last case, the ignite must necessarily be drawn off by the other bodies having a greater affinity for it, whereby it must necessarily appear to emit, diffuse, and communicate ignite to them, thereby producing the sensations and other effects to which we give the names of heat, light, fire, &c. and therefore be of what is called a higher temperature than the other contiguous bodies, which in place of emitting fire and thereby producing these effects, on the contrary attract and imbibe it, producing effects the very reverse. The degrees of expansion produced

by

by fire in different bodies are, *ceteris paribus*, as the quantities of fire or of ignite they respectively contain. The degree of the sensation of heat produced by it is, *ceteris paribus*, as the quantity of fire or of ignite contained in and expanding the organ of sensation, and thereby affecting the sentient principle. And the powers of bodies to produce the sensations and other effects to which we give the names of hot and of cold are, under the proper circumstances, *ceteris paribus*, according as the quantities of fire or of ignite they respectively contain is more or less than is sufficient for keeping them in an equilibrium of temperature with the contiguous substances, or with the organ of sensation to which they are applied.

35. The fire that is disengaged on the combination of certain acids, alkalis, &c. with water has hitherto been supposed to proceed principally if not entirely from the water; but the erroneousness of this opinion is proved beyond dispute by the fact, well established from experiments often repeated, of these salts dissolving ice, and thereby converting it into water, with nearly the same rapidity that a red hot stone would do, and that merely by means of the fire contained in their own compositions, and which is imbibed so eagerly by the ice, that the combination, in place of evolving fire, imbibes it so powerfully as do produce in contiguous beings the sensations and other effects of intense cold; while the mixture, or compound of salt and water, thus formed when the process is completed, is, *ceteris paribus*, precisely of the same temperature as it is when formed by simply mixing the same salt with water, and when fire has been emitted during the process:—so that it is manifest that it is from the salt and not from the water that the fire in these cases proceeds; and from these facts it appears that an acid and ice, on being mixed together, do not contain between them a sufficiency of fire for their perfect combination in a fluid state, or for the mixtures acquiring and retaining that state; but that an acid and water, on mixture, are between them possessed of a superfluity of fire, or contain more of it than is necessary for their retaining a fluid state. That the superfluity of fire, in the one case, is discharged by the emission of it from the acid, and not from the water, is proved by the water's losing none of its fluidity by the process, which would necessarily happen if it was deprived of any of that fire which is essential to the state of water; and the deficiency of fire, in the other case,

is

is therefore manifestly supplied by the attraction of it from contiguous substances by the acid, from its being reduced much below the equilibrium of temperature of these substances, on its imparting a sufficiency of its fire to the ice for transforming it into the state of water, while the ice thus transformed contains no more of it than is precisely sufficient for retaining it in that state: so that it is not to the acid's imparting a stronger power to the ice of attracting fire than it possessed before, but to the acid itself having acquired a stronger power of attracting fire from other substances from its having parted with much of what it possessed to the ice, that fire is absorbed from the contiguous substances during the process of the intimate mixing and combining of these ingredients together by means of their mutual attraction. Acids, alkalis, lime, &c. in many cases produce nearly the same effects as fire; from which it is probable that they contain a large proportion of fire in their respective compositions as a proximate principle in corpuscular combination with their other proximate principles.

36. Combinations, and affinities, in their natural state, and more especially chemical ones, seem to be much under the influence of, if not entirely to depend upon and be regulated by, temperature; all *changes of combination*, mechanical excepted, and consequently all chemical action, depending in the first instance on *changes of temperature* :---so that temperature, as an agent or instrument of the first Cause, might in some respects, perhaps, justly be regarded as the *primum mobile*, or the immediate efficient cause of all action in nature---in as far at least as action depends on changes of combinations---were it not known to be itself an effect, and an effect of a natural or secondary cause. It is only at certain degrees of temperature that certain combinations can take place; and these degrees are different for different combinations: those substances which unite together in preference to others with which they are severally in combination, from a certain change in temperature determining that circumstance, on a still further change of temperature separate from each other again, to combine with other substances to which under this degree of temperature they have greater affinity; and so of other cases. And, hence, if there were no changes of temperature, or if temperature was always to remain invariable and the same, nature would continue in one and the same state of com-

bination,

bination, from there then being an equilibrium or balancing of attractions; and from there being nothing in that case to decompose, alter, or affect the combinations then subsisting, or those attractions and affinities whereby they were generated and are maintained; for no new chemical combinations, and no new modifications, otherwise than by mechanical means—as by the mechanically mixing of acids with alkalis, &c.—could then take place, and even these in that event would also soon cease. But though there could in this case be no changes of state, there would still be action from gravitation, cohesion, and other powers, and especially from that mutual attraction subsisting between the elementary or constituent powers of nature. Changes of temperature are much influenced by and depending upon changes of place and of aspect; as on those produced by the annual and diurnal motions of the planets and their satellites. And, thus, CHANGING OF PLACE, OR MOTION, though neither A POWER, nor properly a CAUSE, is the OCCASION of many or most of the changes which take place in nature, as being the means of bringing different bodies, and thereby different powers, into action which were not so before, and of the same powers acting in different manners and on different substances or bodies, or on different parts of the same body from what they did before.

37. Nineteenthly. That the particles of fire are solid or material, and in some circumstances may be regarded as inert, and that they are capable, though destitute of gravity, of acting mechanically or by means of impulse, and that in many cases with most astonishing force and violence, is incontestibly proved by many facts familiar to our experience. The addition however of igneous matter to a gravitating body, be the quantity ever so great, adds nothing to the mechanic power, more than to the gravity of the body: thus a ball of metal in motion will not be more or less resisted on impinging against a similar ball at rest, from the ball at rest possessing a larger or smaller portion of igneous matter in a latent state than the impinging ball does; or, even from being of a higher or lower temperature, or from possessing more or less of it in a sensible state, provided the masses or quantities of gravitating matter in each ball remain the same. It would seem from this that the mechanic action of gravitating matter on gravitating matter was no way affected by combinations with igneous matter provided its state as to solidity or fluidity remains the same. But

we

we must not thence conclude that mechanic power and action is peculiar to gravitating matter, or that it results from gravity, or as many have done, or that gravity and it are the same: for mechanic power is evidently possessed by igneous matter, &c. as well as by gravitating, and it takes place even between different kinds of matter; besides mechanic power, when a body is at rest, as was observed in the last Essay, resists motion equally in all directions, and excites it in none, which is not the case with gravity; and, when a body is in motion, it resists any alteration in the velocity and direction of that body, whatever that velocity or direction may be; and even any increase of velocity in the direction in which the body may be urged and moved by means of its gravity with as much force as in any other direction.

38. Pure fire, or fire in a state of light, seems to be but little attracted by the matter of diaphanous bodies in passing through their pores, as it does not combine with it and is only refracted by it; probably owing to the great velocity with which it moves, and more particularly to each of these bodies being of equal density throughout, and to those pores being uniformly arranged: with perfectly reflecting bodies it does not combine at all, and does not seem to be any otherwise affected by them than in being reflected. And radiant ignite, or radiant heat or calorific rays, are also reflected by polished metallic surfaces when incident upon them; and it would seem, from an experiment of Professor Leslie's, though that inference has not been deduced from it, that they are reflected by the polished surfaces of metallic plates, even when not incident or acting immediately upon these surfaces, but upon the opposite and unpolished sides or surfaces of these plates, and after having passed through the substance of the metal from the unpolished side or surface on which they immediately act to the polished side or surface by which they are reflected and thereby retained within the substance of the metal, as being prevented by this means from escaping by that surface:—whether or not this reflection is any way influenced by or dependent on the external air, or external light, &c. there are no experiments to determine. As neither fire nor ignite are capable of penetrating unreflecting opaque gravitating bodies by means of their pores, but when moving slowly, or of combining with, and thereby expanding them and diffusing themselves through them, otherwise than gradually and

slowly,

slowly, and as the combination thus effected is not properly chemical, it must follow as a necessary consequence, that if, from any cause, igneous matter expands itself, while opposed and confined by gravitating matter, with much greater velocity than that whereby it is capable of penetrating it by its pores, or of combining with and expanding that matter, and thereby of diffusing itself and in part penetrating through it, and with much greater force than that which the mechanic resistance from the mutual attraction of the particles of that matter opposes to its expansion, the opposing matter must either be rent asunder, or be shattered to fragments and be thrown to a considerable distance in all directions, by its action on it :— that it not only can penetrate through its pores by acting upon and expanding it gradually and slowly, but also that it can rend it asunder, or propel it in all directions, by acting upon it suddenly and with a violence that admits not of combination or gradual penetration through pores, are facts well known and experimentally ascertained ; and hence it appears that fire, though destitute of gravity, is yet capable of mechanic impulse ; or that there may be impulse or action that is not CHEMICAL in substances devoid of gravity.

39. Twentiethly. That light, or rather that which produces the sensations of light and colours and also the sensation of heat, is fire—though these different sensations are not always excited by it at the same time in equal degrees as depending on the differences of its states as to quantity and modification ; and though in some cases the light with which the heat is accompanied, and in others the heat with which the light is attended, as in that of the moon, the glow-worm, rotten wood, putrifying fish, pyrophori, &c. is sometimes so weak, as to be incapable of sensibly affecting the organs of human beings—is proved by there being no known means of generating light but by generating fire; by the high temperature of the tropical regions of the earth ; and by the greatest degree of heat producible by art being that procurable by a concentration of the solar rays. These effects seemingly so discordant as the production of the sensations of heat and of light by means of the same power may be accounted for by the one sensation, that of heat, depending on the quantity, number, or density of the particles or rays of the igneous matter ; while the other, that of light, depends more on the velocity with which these particles forming the rays move than on their number or quantity; by the human organs of vision by whose agency

the

the sensation of light is produced being more easily affected or more sensible than those of feeling whereby the sensations of heat are experienced; and by the appeal being made to these only, though there can be no doubt that other beings, and even certain animals, of more delicate organs and greater sensibility, would experience both of these sensations of light and of heat at the same time, in many cases where one of them only is sensible to us. According to a computation of the learned Dr. Henry Pemberton the density of the rays or of the light of the sun exceeds that of the moon more than 190,000 times, and there are experiments from which it may be inferred to be even much greater; and hence it can be matter of no surprise that the light or rays from the moon, even when concentrated by art, should produce in us no sensible degree of heat.

40. The greater heat in the confines of the red ray than in those of the violet ray of the prismatic spectrum, as discovered by that justly celebrated astronomer Dr. Herschell, may perhaps be owing partly to the rays or igneous matter being more intense, dense, and concentrated near the red rays than near the violet; partly from their being nearer the centre of what would have been the luminous spot, or the spot on which the light or the whole of the rays, if they had not been refracted by the prism, would have fallen; and partly from the rays which fall near this spot being less refracted, diffused, and dissipated, and acting more directly than those which fall at a greater distance from it :—and that this is the fact is proved by the rays which fall beyond the red end of the spectrum, not only producing the sensible effects of heat, but also being at the same time, when collected by a lens, visible in the form of fire of a faint red colour. The different coloured rays of light must likewise necessarily heat the body on which they fall in forming the spectrum in different degrees according to their several different intensities and modes of action, and the parts of the body thus heated must communicate heat or fire to the contiguous air, which fire combining with part of it and of the other substances floating in it or on which it acts must thereby become ignite, which though in this case invisible, may yet be radiant: it is also to be observed that violet light from being the most reflectible as well as the most refrangible, must even *ceteris paribus* affect the thermometer much less than red light which is the least reflectible. In the distinction made between light and radiant ignite,

or

or what has been called radiant heat or calorific rays, reference is made to human vision only as a standard : vision is relative, and though radiant heat is insensible to us, it probably may not be so to vultures, cats, &c.

41. Twenty-firstly. That that modification of fire to which we give the name of light is the cause of vision is proved by there being no vision but by its means; daily experience evincing that there cannot be privation of light without there being a privation of vision at the same time. And from all the phenomena of vision it may justly be inferred that fire, when in the state of light, or more properly when in that state whereby it produces on animated beings the sensation to which we give the name of light, proceeds in rays or right lines, and is reflected at angles equal to those of incidence by such substances as reflect it, and that it proceeds not in undulations, by means of vibrations excited in it, since this is manifest even in the simplest kinds of these, as in the visible perception of objects by means of a mirror. In this case the mirror itself, if perfect, as reflecting all the light that falls on it and emitting none, is altogether invisible to us, and it is the objects only from which the light proceeds to it, and which it reflects at an angle equal to that of incidence upon the eye of the beholder, that is visible; and hence it is that these objects as thus seen by us, or through the agency of a mirror, appear to us from the mode of vision being necessarily determined by the directions in which the rays proceed, through the instrumentality of which the vision is effected, to be in a place and situation not only very different from that in which they actully are, but also from that of the mirror itself, as seeming to be as far on the further side of it as they are in reality on this side of it, and that we see them in that direction only in which the reflected rays of light, proceeding directly or in a right line from the mirror to the eye on being reflected by it at an angle equal to that of their incidence on it, fall upon the eye. These are phenomena and effects too well known and established, as resting on universal experience, to admit of doubt or controversy, and such as could not possibly take place were light propagated by vibrations, and in undulations, as has been supposed by Hook, Euler, and others of great literary eminence, or in any other manner or directions than in those above described of proceeding in rays, and of these rays being reflected at angles equal to those of incidence; indeed, the hypothesis of light being propagated by vibrations, and in undulations, runs directly counter to fact and

experience

experience in every case, is totally inconsistent with the phenomena and effects produced, and is altogether incompetent to their explanation. For, if propagated as thus supposed, it would, contrary to fact and experience, on entering a darkened chamber through a hole in a window shutter necessarily diffuse itself in undulations equally through the room in place of proceeding in rays; and on entering an angular or curved tube move through it without experiencing any deficiency of quantity or intensity, and when through it diffuse itself equally in all directions:---were this the case there could be no shadows, and indeed no darkness, and light could not be permanently separated by refraction into its several separate distinct prismatic colours, as on this hypothesis these would necessarily diffuse themselves through each other again immediately on separation.

42. Twenty-secondly. From the preceding facts and reasonings it follows as necessary consequences. First, That there is but one kind of fire in nature;—solar fire, electrical fire, and the fire of combustion, sometimes called culinary, being all identical or essentially the same. Secondly, That the planet we inhabit is affected by and contains no fire but what is ultimately derived from the sun and stars, its great and original source. And that though the fire it contains is generally latent and insensible, from being generally in a state of combination with gravitating matter, yet it is by various different means liberated from these combinations, and thereby evolved and exhibited in its own proper form in a free and disengaged state. These means are mixture, compression, percussion, friction or attrition, electricity, and combustion. The two last of these will be treated of in the immediately succeeding Essay; and that of mixture has in a great degree been treated of already, when treating of temperature, in describing the great increase of temperature proceeding from the great disengagement and evolution of fire on the mixing of different substances together the gravitating bases of which have greater attraction or affinity to each other than they have to the portions of fire with which they are severally combined, and which disengage themselves from that fire in uniting together in consequence of this superior attraction:---the evolution of fire in these cases being merely the effect of affinities or electrical attractions. And it appears from the large quantities of fire evolved in proportion to their volume on the mixing of certain

tain substances together that the proportion of fire which enters into the composition of some substances is extremely great; pure concentrated acid, pure fixed alkalis, and pure lime in particular, contain such very large proportions of it that they seem in many cases to operate in the same manner and on the same principle that bodies in a high state of ignition do; and to owe their causticity, or burning and destructive quality, in a great degree at least to this cause; though it may no doubt partly be owing to the strong affinity of these bodies for moisture, &c.

43. Fire may be evolved or expelled from certain substances by mere mechanical compression; and not only from those in a fluid or aeriform state, but also from bodies in a solid state which are elastic and contain much fire in their composition, especially when the compression is sudden as in cases of percussion. This is the case on the collision of two pieces of quartz, two pieces of flint, or two pieces of felt-spar—and probably of two pieces of diamond—&c. together; and of flint and steel: in this last case combustion is produced, in the small particles of metal which fly off from the mass, by the fire evolved on the collision; and in the case of the collision of two pieces of quartz the small particles which are detached from them, which resemble the eggs of flies, seem to have been deprived by the collision of part of the fire they naturally contained.

Fire is evolved by hammering or repeated percussions, and by friction or attrition, partly on the above principle; and partly from the vibratory motion induced by these means, in the body hammered or rubbed, by the alternate compressions and expansions of it, from the action of the hammer or of the protuberances of the rubbing substance on it, and from the action of its own elasticity in recovering from these successive compressions during the intervals between the strokes of the hammer or the operations of the protuberances. That the vibratory motion excited by hammering or friction is not excited in the body hammered only, as in the rod of iron that may be hammered on an anvil, but also in the anvil itself on which it rests, &c. and not in any particular part only of any body or mass that is subjected to friction, but in a certain degree either in the whole of the body or mass, or in more or less of it according to its size and circumstances, though that body and those particular parts to which the hammer or friction is immediately
applied

applied are most affected, or experience the greatest compressions and expansions, are facts fully ascertained and well known ; that a small body requires a much smaller quantity of fire to raise it to a high temperature than a large body, and a small part of the same body than the whole of it, are also facts well established and well known ; and that many elastic bodies, indeed all that owe their elasticity to fire, on compression evolve fire, and on expansion absorb it, and absorb it from the contiguous substances, are likewise facts no less certain and well known. And these are facts which are such as are sufficient to account for the phenomena and effects in these cases; as clearly pointing out the sources from which the fire is procured whereby the ignition, &c. is produced; and the manner and means by which it is produced; these effects being manifestly a necessary consequence of those frequently repeated and successive emissions and absorptions of fire by the body in consequence of the repeated compressions and expansions produced in it by the hammer or friction ; and of the fire thus disengaged collecting principally at those places where the vibrations and consequently expansions are greatest, that is at those parts where the hammer or friction more immediately acts; whereby these small bodies, or small parts of the bodies, on which the hammer or friction immediately acts, which, from their smallness require but a small quantity of fire to raise them to a high temperature, become ignited. In all the above cases fire is evolved in vacuo the same as in air.—

And Thirdly, From the preceding facts and reasonings it follows as a necessary consequence that cold---or rather that that by which those sensations, contractions, and other effects, which are attributed to cold are produced—in place of being a diffusive substantial agent possessing qualities peculiar to itself, whereby it produces these effects, is nothing in reality but that power which bodies---possessing less fire or ignite in a loosely adhering state relatively to others, in the then circumstances, according to their respective affinities for it---possess of attracting part of it from these others, whereby those effects are produced in these others---as the sensation of coldness, &c.---which are attributed to the agency of an imaginary SUBSTANCE OR BEING denominated COLD:---and hence it is that the bodies producing these effects, or possessing this frigorific power, have been denominated cold bodies, and have been and are regarded as cold of nature or cold in themselves.

To describe the various different manners and means whereby fire is, and may be applied which practical utility---as to the facilitating, promoting, and improving of manufactures and the arts---or to describe the various different ways by which fire may be generated or extinguished, and the various different means by which it may be so modified and directed, as to be rendered subservient to the will and conducive to the purposes of man, falls not within my plan, as it is a subject which has been successfully treated of by others, and now seems to be in general well understood.

ESSAY VI.

OF CHEMISTRY, ELECTRICITY, AND MAGNETISM.

———

INTRODUCTION.

1. CHEMISTRY is that science which treats of those changes which either spontaneously take place in nature, or which may be effected by art, whereby substances are altered not only in mode but in essence also; and of which the object is the investigation and discovery, experimentally and practically by the method of analysis, of the constituent principles of bodies; and also, experimentally and practically by the method of synthesis, of the several modes and manners of their respective compositions: as well as the investigation and discovery of the principles, or of those mutual relations among created things, which are the physical efficient causes of these changes, or those on which the composition and decomposition, the destructions and renovations, of bodies depend.

2. Chemistry as an art has from the earliest times been known and practised: as a science it is of very recent date. As an art it was carried, or at least that branch of it now named metallurgy, in certain respects to a great degree of perfection by the eastern nations before it was introduced into Greece; for " the writings of Moses (who was born about 1635 years " before Christ), furnishes us with the amplest proof of at how early a " period it was known in Egypt and Phœnicia. He mentions furnaces " for working iron, ores from which it was extracted; and tells us that " swords, knives, axes, and tools for cutting stones, were then made of that " metal. How many ages before the birth of Moses iron may have been
" discovered

" discovered in these countries, we may perhaps conceive, if we reflect,
" that the knowledge of iron was brought over from Phrygia into Greece
" by the Dactyli, who settled in Crete during the reign of Menus I. about
" 1431 years before Christ; yet during the Trojan war, which happened
" 200 years after that period, iron was in such high estimation, that
" Achilles proposed a ball of it as one of his prizes during the games which
" he celebrated in honour of Patroclus.   At that period none of their arms
" were formed of iron.   Now if the Greeks in 200 years had made so little
" progress in an art which they learned from others, how long must it have
" taken the Egyptians, Phrygeans, Chalybes, or whatever nation first dis-
" covered the art of working iron, to have made that progress in it which
" we find they had done in the days of Moses."*   The Greeks had then
no arms or armour but what was made of bronze or a mixture of copper
and tin.

3. The first traces of chemistry as a science, and of its application to
medicine, are to be found in the writings of the Arabians, under the name
of Alchemy; a name since appropriated to the pretended art of transmuting every thing into gold and silver, and of which the origin is doubtful, as the name occurs in the works of Julius Fermicus, who wrote about
the time of Constantine the Great, before the Greeks had any communication with the Arabians.   Whether chemistry as a science originated with
the Arabians, or whether they derived what knowledge they possessed of it,
which seems to have been very limited and imperfect, from their more
enlightened neighbours of the East is not known, though the latter seems
most probable, as we are informed by Abel Farajius that the Arabians
before the time of Mahometanism had no philosophical knowledge, and that
all their literature consisted in the study of their language and poetry.   But,
be that how it may, certain it is that chemistry along with many other arts
and sciences was first introduced into Europe by the Arabians or Moors;
and that in Europe it soon assumed the character to which the term alchemy is now applied, if it possessed it not before; or, if it did in some degree,
from the Arabians having acquired a knowledge of that pretended art from
the Greeks, it was soon carried in Europe to a much higher pitch of extra-

* Thomson's System of Chemistry, vol. i. pages 210 and 211.

vagance

vagance and absurdity, and was for several centuries cultivated by many individuals denominating themselves Adepts with much ardour and assiduity; first from the expectation of discovering by its means what they called the philosopher's stone, which they supposed possessed a power of transmuting certain or all substances into gold; and afterwards of discovering a panacea, or universal medicine, and an elixir of life, capable of subduing and eradicating every disease to which humanity is subjected, and of even conferring upon it the attribute of immortality itself.

4. These expectations proving not only vain, but also ruinous and disgraceful to those who entertained them, partly from the great expense with which their experiments, &c. were attended, and that discredit which results from a prosecution of unsuccessful and vain pursuits—partly from the impostures and frauds practised by some of the adepts, encouraged by that implicit credit which in those ages of ignorance was given to their representations and assertions especially by the avaricious who were eager for enriching themselves by means of those arts the adepts pretended to possess, and from that success which in every age but too often attends the impudent pretensions and confident assertions of quacks and impostors of all descriptions—and partly and principally from the discovery of the art of printing, and that more general diffusion of knowledge, and rapid progress in intellectual improvement which were the almost immediate consequences of it, this pretended science of alchemy, along with those kindred ones of astrology, and magic or witchcraft, towards the end of the 16th century fell into very general disrepute; and, being consigned either to infamy or oblivion, gave way to less aspiring but more attainable, rational, instructive and useful pursuits. And such was the contempt in which they then were held that the very names of alchemy and alchemist were abandoned along with their objects, as having become terms expressive of opprobrium, indicative of folly or of infamy, and those of chemistry and chemist were substituted in their place. To the alchemists nevertheless chemistry is indebted for the discovery of several important facts, for the introduction of several chemical processes into pharmacy, and of several very powerful chemical preparations into medical practice:—thus antimonial preparations were first applied to medicine by Basil Valentine a Benedictine monk at Erford in Germany, the original discoverer of them, who is said to have

been

been born in 1394—mercurial preparations were first introduced into medicine, and applied with great advantage against the venereal disease which
had made its appearance about that time; and for which no effectual remedy
was then known, by that enterprising impostor Theophrastus Paracelsus,
not less distinguished by the profligacy and madness of his conduct than by
his great talents, who was born near Zurich in Switzerland in 1493, and
who raised alchemy to its highest pitch of reputation. And during the
reign of alchemy several of the chemical arts though they were exercised
by people unacquainted with science made considerable progress in improvement; no such thing as chemical science being then known or even
thought of.

5. Happily however about this time some men of observation and philosophical talents applied themselves to collect those chemical facts which
had been discovered by the alchemists and artists, and to arrange them
into classes according to the particular branches of art to which they respectively belonged—to add new facts to those already known by experimental discoveries of their own—and to express themselves with precision
and perspicuity in communicating the knowledge thus acquired to the
public instead of following the method of the alchemists in employing
symbols and figurative ambiguous language, and in studiously expressing
themselves so obscurely and mystically as to be altogether unintelligible.
The principal of these were Agricola, Schlutter, and Henkel, who collected
the facts relative to mines and metallurgy; Neri, Merret, and Kunkel,
who collected and arranged those relating to the arts of making glass,
enamels, imitations of jewels, &c.

6. From these materials or the facts thus collected and arranged by the
above mentioned authors and others men of speculative minds began to attempt rational explanations of chemical processes and results, to form
theories with respect to their mutual relations and dependencies, and thereby to reduce chemistry which before was an art to system and to science.
The first authors who treated of rational chemistry were Tachenius, James
Berner, physician to the King of Poland, and Bobnius a professor at
Leipsic, who all established their theories of chemistry on the reciprocal
actions of acids and alkalis. They were succeeded in this meritorious un-
dertaking by the famous Beccher principal physician to the electors of
                                                                    Mentz

Mentz and of Bavaria, who published his celebrated work entitled Physica Subterranea at Frankfort in 1669. In this work are contained those principles of chemistry which were adopted, and so much simplified, illustrated, and improved by the editor of the Physica Subterranea, the illustrious Ernest Stahl, that they have ever since been distinguished by the name of the Stahlian theory;—a theory that till of late has generally been regarded as incontestibly established and as affording the only sure guide for the conducting of chemical researches.

7. It has already been stated in the introductory part of the Essay on Fire and Temperature, that according to the Stahlian or phlogistic theory of chemistry pure elementary fire enters into *chemical* combination and thereby becomes one of the constituent principles of combustible bodies; and *that* it is to fire thus combined that the name phlogiston is exclusively appropriated.

8. No process of nature has so much engaged the attention of philosophical chemists as that wonderful one of combustion, not only on account of the diffusion of light and heat, and the other surprising phenomena attending it, with the various differences of states and of combinations produced by its means, but also on account of the very great importance of the discovery of the true principles on which it depends as a necessary foundation or indispensable requisite towards the formation of a just and satisfactory theory of chemistry. According to this system, combustion consists in the disengagement at certain temperatures, or when the temperature is high enough for producing that effect, of the phlogiston, inflammable principle or pure elementary fire contained in the several kinds of bodies from the bodies, and continues till the whole of the phlogiston which entered into their composition, and to the containing of which in chemical combination as a constituent, they owed their name of combustibles, is disengaged and dissipated, when what remains of these bodies is no longer combustible from their having been thus deprived of the phlogiston they possessed; and hence substances possessing not phlogiston as a constituent are according to this theory incombustibles. Thus, for instance, when sulphur burns its phlogiston is disengaged and dissipated in its proper form of light and heat, or fire; and what remains is sulphuric acid, an incombustible substance; sulphur therefore is a compound of sulphuric acid and phlogiston.

I I

9. To

9. To prove this theory experimentally both in the way of analysis and in that of synthesis, Stahl first melted a mixture of fixed alkali and sulphur till it became a brittle mass, which after reducing to a powder he put into a flat open vessel and exposed to a gentle fire, when the sulphur a combustible gradually vanished and nothing remained in the vessel but an incombustible compound of sulphuric acid and fixed alkali. This he observes affords a decisive proof in the way of analysis of sulphur being a compound of acid and phlogiston, since on the phlogiston being disengaged from it and dissipated by the gentle heat or increase of temperature applied, nothing remains of it but the acid an incombustible substance. He then put this incombustible compound of sulphuric acid and alkali into a crucible, to which he added an equal weight of some combustible substance as charcoal, and then covering the crucible with another inverted over it he applied a strong heat to it. On allowing it to cool he found the contents to consist of a mixture of sulphur and alkali with the incombustible residuum of the charcoal which had vanished during the process. This artificial generation of sulphur a combustible by the combination of the incombustible acid of the compound with the phlogiston of the charcoal, as is proved by the vanishing of the charcoal and nothing remaining of it in a disengaged state after the process but its incombustible residuum, he observes likewise affords a decisive proof in the way of synthesis of the constituents of sulphur being acid and phlogiston, and also of its being owing to its containing phlogiston that charcoal is combustible, since of the three substances put into the crucible, viz. acid, alkali, and charcoal, one only of them is combustible the charcoal, and two of them have vanished during the process, the acid and the charcoal, and sulphur and the incombustible residuum of charcoal have been found in their stead; a result which could have taken place only in consequence of the charcoal being decomposed in imparting its phlogiston to the acid, and of the acid being converted into sulphur a combustible by combining with the phlogiston of the charcoal. He next decomposed or converted any of the imperfect metals into a calx or metallic earth by placing it in a muffle and applying to it a fire strong enough to raise the temperature sufficiently high for disengaging and dissipating the phlogiston of the metal; and the calx or metallic earth thus produced he reduced again or restored to its pristine metallic

tallic state by mixing it with some combustible as charcoal, and fusing it in a close vessel.

10. These simple but pertinent experiments with the inferences deduced from them afforded at once so beautiful an illustration and a proof seemingly so satisfactory and conclusive of the phlogistic theory that it was generally adopted and deemed to be established on such evidence as admitted not of doubt or controversy, and it continued to be the prevailing system of chemistry till shaken and superseded at last, after a strenuous contest between the supporters of the old and new theories, by that system proposed by the late very ingenious M. Lavoisier.

11. It was objected to the Stahlian system that there are two very important facts attending the process of combustion which it does not account for; and from this it was inferred to be defective, unsatisfactory, and unfounded. These are, first, that the weight of the residuum after the combustion of sulphurs and of metals is greater than that of the sulphurs and metals before having undergone combustion; and, second, that the presence of air is necessary to combustion: and it is to no satisfactory explanation having been given of these two facts, agreeable to the principles of the Stahlian system, that its downfal is principally to be ascribed.

12. It seems surprising that it never occurred to any of the very able and ingenious supporters of the phlogistic system to have obviated these objections by attributing the gain of weight on combustion to a combination taking place in these cases between the calx or incombustible residuum and a portion of the air; and the presence of air being necessary to combustion, to combustion depending upon and being a necessary result of a greater affinity at certain temperatures between the gravitating base or incombustible constituent of the combustible and a portion of the air, than between that base and the phlogiston with which it is in combination in the combustible, whereby that base combines with a portion of the air, and the phlogiston with which it was in union is liberated and diffused in the state of fire whenever the temperature is sufficiently raised for producing these effects, or what is the same thing for producing combustion, since it is in the liberation and diffusion of fire or of light and heat and the conversion of the combustible into an incombustible in combination with a portion of

the

the air that combustion is supposed to consist. This was the theory of combustion that first suggested itself to the author of these Essays about twenty years ago, and though it accounts for the phenomena and effects in a manner at least equally natural, simple, and satisfactory with that of the theory which has superseded the Stahlian, it is many years since he found reason for abandoning it and for adopting that given in this Essay.

13. The theory of combustion that was next in point of time offered to the public was that proposed by that truly eminent chemist the justly celebrated Scheele, in his treatise entitled *Chemical Experiments on Air and Fire*, published in 1777. According to this theory empyreal air, or the pure air of Priestley, consists in a combination of a supposed acid principle or base with a small portion of phlogiston—matter of heat or caloric of a combination of empyreal air with a further portion of phlogiston—and light of matter of heat combined also with an additional portion of phlogiston, &c. as was formerly observed in the introductory part of the last Essay on Fire and Temperature. And hence it is inferred that the heat and light of combustion must necessarily proceed from combinations, resulting from differences of affinities at different temperatures, among the principles of the substances producing the combustion, of different portions either of the acid principle, or of empyreal air, with different portions of phlogiston. This theory though generally acknowledged to be ingenious was not generally adopted. It was not sufficiently explicit with respect to the nature of phlogiston, which it made to differ from fire, from matter of heat, and from light; and it was not accompanied with any formal refutation of the Stahlian the then favourite and prevailing theory of combustion. It was for these reasons rejected without any strict scrutiny having been made with respect to the validity of the facts and reasons on which it was founded, and without its being even ever so much as objected to it, that according to the principles on which it is established, fire, matter of heat and of light, contrary to fact, must all necessarily be gravitating substances, since empyreal air, and inflammable air, which are represented as differing in nothing from matter of heat and of light than in the former containing a smaller and the latter a larger proportion of phlogiston than these do, are both proved by experiment to be gravitating substances; and hence, according

to

to this theory, matter of heat and matter of light should both be gravitating substances also, and of gravities intermediate between those of empyreal and inflammable airs.

14. This was followed by Dr. Crawford's theory of combustion, which was founded upon Dr. Black's doctrine of latent heat. According to this theory, phlogiston is not fire, but a substance which has very little affinity to matter of heat and great affinity to air; and when the phlogiston of the combustible has more affinity to the air than to the solid base with which it is in combination in the combustible from the temperature being so raised as to produce this effect combustion takes place, as consisting in a combination of the phlogiston of the combustible with air, and a disengagement and diffusion of the specific matter of heat, or of the caloric of fluidity, of the air in consequence of this combination. More attention was paid to this theory by the public than had been paid to the immediately preceding one, though it is not more explicit with regard to the nature and the essential characteristics of phlogiston, and though it does not account for the increase of weight acquired by several bodies on combustion.

15. Not long after the publication of this last theory the celebrated Elements of Chemistry by Mr. Lavoisier made their appearance, and in a very short period of time effected nearly a complete revolution in philosophical chemistry. Mr. Lavoisier founds his system of chemistry in the first instance on Dr. Black's doctrine of latent heat, and Mr. Cavendish's discovery of the production of water on the combustion of a mixture of inflammable air with pure air. From this experiment of Mr. Cavendish and from other very ingenious and apt experiments in the way of analysis conceived and executed by himself he concludes not only that water is generated by this process, as Mr. Cavendish and others had done before, but also, in conformity to the doctrines of Dr. Black, that the heat and the light of the combustion is in consequence of the liberation, disengagement, and diffusion of that caloric to which these airs owe their fluidity or aeriform state, on their assuming a liquid on thus combining together and forming water; and he endeavours to determine by experiment and calculation the quantity of caloric disengaged from each of these kinds of air respectively in these cases. To the several airs when deprived of that caloric to which they owed their aeriform state he gives the name of bases

or

or radicals, and to the base of inflammable air he has appropriated the name of hydrogen, as considering it as one of the constituents of water, and to inflammable air the name of hydrogen gas, gas being the name appropriated by him to all permanently elastic aeriform fluids except atmospheric air, of which he still retains the name of air. It having been for some time known not only that the presence of atmospheric air was necessary to combustion, but also that it was to the pure air contained in it that it owed the quality of promoting combustion, and that a great many substances assumed on combustion the character of acids; he concluded, first, that the base of the pure air contained in the atmosphere on the disengagement and diffusion of its caloric of fluidity combined with the combustible substances, during the process of combustion; and he thereby accounted not only for the changes of state induced in these substances by the process, but also for their gain of weight on combustion, which gain he proved to be always precisely equal to the weight of the pure air consumed by it; and, secondly, he concluded that the base of pure air is the acidifying principle of nature, or that principle to combination with which all the acids are indebted for their acid qualities; and on this account he denominated this base oxygen, and the name of the aeriform fluid formed by its combination with caloric he changed to oxygen gas, from those of pure, empyreal, and vital air by which it had formerly been known. When the oxygen which combines with the combustible on combustion is not in sufficient quantity to communicate acid qualities to it, as is the case on the combustion of most of the metals and of several other substances, he gave the name of oxids and not of acids to these products of combustion; and he laid it down as a general law of nature, " that in every case of combustion " oxygen combines with the burning body."

16. According then to this theory of combustion, when a combustible body is raised to a certain temperature it gradually combines with the oxygen of the atmosphere, which during this combination gradually loses that caloric and light with which it was united when in a gaseous state, and it is to the disengagement and diffusion of which that the heat and light attending combustion are exclusively owing, as the change of state in the combustible on combustion is to its combination with oxygen; and that the products of combustion are incombustible from being in consequence of

combustion

combustion already saturated with oxygen. It is not according to this theory with the base of the combustible on its being deprived of phlogiston or any other substance, but with the combustible in its entire state, that the oxygen of the atmosphere combines; and the oxygen gas, but not the combustible, is decomposed by the process:—thus sulphuric acid is formed on the combustion of sulphur by a combination of the sulphur in its intire state with oxygen; oxid of iron on the combustion of iron, by a combination of iron in its intire state with oxygen, &c. In thus accounting for combustion he got rid of that hypothetical entity of dubious nature phlogiston: and hence it is that the Lavoiserian is often denominated the antiphlogistic theory. These principles were easily applied to account for many of the other processes of chemistry, the phenomena attending them, and the effects resulting from them; as the solutions of metals and other combustibles in acids, the revivification of metallic oxids, and the reproduction of sulphur from sulphuric acid, &c. The metal dissolves in an acid from being oxydated by combining with part of the oxygen either of the acid or of the water, and when dissolved is found on separating it from the acid to be oxydated. A metal thus oxydated is revived or precipitated in its metallic state, by another metal having greater affinity to oxygen from its depriving it of that oxygen to which its unmetallic state and dissolution in the acid was owing. A metallic oxid in a dry state is reduced by fusing it in combination with any substance, as charcoal, having more affinity to and therefore depriving it of oxygen. And sulphur, phosphorus, &c. are reproduced by exposing sulphuric, phosphoric, acids, &c. to a great heat in combination with some substance capable, from its great affinity to it under these circumstances, of depriving them of oxygen. And hence being oxygenated has according to this doctrine nearly the same signification with being dephlogisticated, and being deoxygenated with being phlogisticated by the Stahlian.

17. To the base of the phlogisticated air of Priestley, or the foul air of Scheele, he gave the name of azot, and to the air itself that of azotic gas, as being fatal to animal life on respiration, and he discovered that atmospheric air is composed almost entirely of azotic and oxygen gases in the proportion of nearly seventy-nine parts of the former and twenty-one of the latter. According to this system all the elements of the ancients, not only earth

and

and air, but water and fire also, are compound substances; and oxygen, hydrogen, carbon, phosphorus, sulphur, azot, muriatic acid, and the metals, are elements, that is substances indecomposible by any known means. This is a short sketch of this truly ingenious system which is at present, and has for several years past, been almost generally adopted:—in the course of this Essay there will be occasion to treat of different parts of it, in a manner more particularly.

18. Electricity denotes that part of the philosophy of nature which endeavours to investigate the properties of that power or powers, by whose agency these phenomena and effects denominated electrical—from that quality first discovered in ηλεκτρον or amber of attracting and repelling light bodies when excited by friction—are produced. Many different theories have been proposed at different times with the intention of explaining the nature of the electrical power and of accounting rationally and justly for the phenomena and effects it produces. The first was that of the Peripatetics, who supposed these attractions and repulsions to be the effects of a sympathetic power; the next was that of Gilbert, Gassendus, and Sir Kenelm Digby, of these effects being produced by the emission of unctuous effluvia from the excited bodies, which effluvia returned to them again; this last was succeeded by that of the Cartesians, who ascribed these effects to the globules of the first elements being discharged through the pores of the excited substance, and in their return carrying along with them those light bodies in whose pores they were entangled. But all these theories which were formed before the invention of the electrical machine, by Otto Guericke, Burgo-master of Magdeburg, the same who rendered himself so famous by the invention of the air-pump, were rejected soon after the discovery of that machine, and the improvement of it by others, as being then deemed altogether inadequate for explaining the various new and wonderful electrical phenomena which were exhibited by its means, and by the means of other ingenious instruments then contrived and successfully applied to the making of electrical experiments.

19. These theories were succeeded by two others, each of which had its advocates and adherents. These were that first suggested by M. Du Fay—from his having discovered that the phenomena and effects exhibited and produced on the excitation of vitreous bodies differed much from those which

which take place on the excitation of resinous bodies---and which was afterwards much improved by Messrs Symmer, Eeles, &c.----of there being two different and distinct species of electricity or of electrical fire, distinguishable from each other not only by the differences in the appearances they respectively exhibit on excited bodies of the vitreous and of the resinous kinds being severally presented to a pointed conductor as a needle or a wire in the dark, from the one kind of electrical fire assuming in that case that of a pencil of lucid rays, while the other assumes that of a lucid globule like a star, from the one appearing to issue from, and the other to enter into the excited body, and from each seeming to produce effects, the contrary of those produced by the other; but also from each being producible only by the excitation of a substance differing essentially from that by the excitation of which the other is produced, the one being obtainable only by the excitation of vitreous and the other only by that of resinous substances. These supposed different kinds of electrical fire were denominated the vitreous and the resinous electricities from the persuasion of the former being a product of or producible from vitreous bodies only, and the latter from resinous only.

20. The discovery of Mr. Canton that these electricities, denominated the vitreous and the resinous, had no dependance on the substances themselves by the excitation of which they were produced, and that they were not products or properties exclusively appertaining to, or resulting from those particular substances, by the excitation of which they had been first discovered, and from which they had derived their respective names; and that either the one kind or the other could be obtained at pleasure, by the excitation of the same substance by varying the circumstances, as depending *ceteris paribus* on the state of the surface of the substance rubbed or excited, and not on the substance itself---smooth glass yielding the vitreous while rough glass treated in the same manner yields the resinous electricity---had a great effect in bringing this theory into disrepute, and in procuring a more ready acceptance for the other of these theories or mode accounting for the phenomena and effects of electricity in this more improved state of the science.

21. This other theory was that of Dr. Watson and Dr. Franklin, who first suggested the notion of *positive* and *negative,* or *plus* and *minus*, elec-

K K   tricity.

tricity. They concluded from electrical phenomena and effects, and the experiments by means of which they were discovered, that every body in nature possessed a certain quantity of electrical matter, that this natural quantity admitted of being augmented or diminished by means of particular circumstances, and that when augmented in any body that body may with propriety be said to be electrified plus or positively, while when diminished in any body that body may justly be said to be electrified minus or negatively. "When the wire or inside," says Dr. Franklin, " of the " bottle (Leyd. Phial) is electrified positively or plus, the outside of the " bottle is electrified negatively or minus, in exact proportion. The equi- " librium of electric matter in the bottle being thus lost, it cannot be re- " stored by any *inward communication* or contact of the parts; but this must " be done by a communication formed *without* the bottle between the in- " side and the outside, by some conductor touching or approaching both " sides at the same time; in which case the equilibrium is restored with " an inexpressible violence and quickness: or, it may be done by touch- " ing each side alternately; in which case, the equilibrium is restored by " degrees. As no more electrical fire can be thrown into the inside of the " bottle, when all is driven from the outside; so, in a bottle not yet elec- " trified, none can be thrown into the inside, when none can get out at the " outside. The shock to the nerves, or rather convulsion, is occasioned " by the sudden passage of the fire through the body in its way from the " inside to the outside of the bottle."

22. This theory—which has since been known by the appellation of the Franklinian hypothesis—has been very generally approved of and adopted; and it is that which at present is regarded, if not altogether as unexceptionable, as that which at least seems most probable and is most satisfactory. Such are the various theories which at different times have been proposed for explaining and accounting for the causes and phenomena of these important and astonishing effects which electricity produces and exhibits; and such with regard to this youngest sister of the sciences is the present state of philosophical knowledge.

23. Magnetism is that transient power possessed by certain bodies of the ferruginous kind, known by the names of natural and artificial magnets, whereby they, according to circumstances, either attract or repel each other;

and

and whereby they attract or repel iron, and communicate to it, when properly formed and suspended for the purpose as in the cases of the mar-
riner's and the dipping needles, a direction nearly meridional, and in some
degree deviating from a horizontal; and which power is capable of being
produced, destroyed, and restored, in these bodies, by certain known means,
at pleasure. The surprising phenomena of the magnetic attractions and repulsions, which seem to have been known from time immemorial, and the
very great importance of the directive power of the magnet needles in navigation, have excited in a particular manner the attention of philosophers,
and various theories have accordingly been conceived and proposed at
different times for ascertaining and determining the cause of these wonderful
properties of magnets, and for explaining and accounting for the effects
they produce : but such is the obscurity of the subject, the abstruse nature
of this power, and so very difficult is the investigation, that these theories
have hitherto served only to amuse the fancy, as being altogether incompetent to the purposes for which they are intended; and hence it is that the
doctrine of magnetism as treated of by different authors, though abounding
in various important facts, has at present no pretensions whatever for
being regarded as a SCIENCE: these treatises conveying no knowledge
whatever that is properly philosophical, and at the same time such as may
with safety be relied upon ; the theory of magnetism that is most approved
of, that of Aepinus, being only the Franklinian hypothesis of electricity
applied to magnetism, in supposing there is a magnetical fluid---repulsive
of itself and attractive of iron and of no other substance---which is the
cause of all magnetical phenomena and effects, from iron or ferruginous
bodies being sometimes over or under charged with it, or in a positive or negative or a plus or minus state with respect to it; and from the surcharge
of it in magnets attracting the matter of iron, at the same time that it repels
the natural quantity of magnetic fluid the iron may contain, &c.

24. Of Galvinism as a science no notice is taken in these Essays, since it
in reality possesses not any pretensions to be regarded as such; as consisting
evidently in nothing but in the discovery of new ways of producing electricity, by means of which indeed many new, curious, and instructive, electrical phenomena have been and may be exhibited. For a knowledge of
these we are principally indebted to Galvini the original discoverer of

the

the method, from whom it derives its name, Volta of Coma, Nicholson, Wolaston, Davy, Halden, Cruickshank, &c.

CHAP. I.

OF AFFINITY OR CHEMICAL ATTRACTION.

1. THOUGH the natures of chemical action and affinity have already been pointed out in the preceding Essays, viz. in Articles 25, 30 of Essay III., and in Articles 29, 33 of Essay V., yet as it is of the utmost importance in chemical research that these should be precisely determined and well understood, it is proposed in this section to treat of them in a manner somewhat more particular than was done in the preceding Essays.

2. That mutual tendency, or rather the unknown cause of that mutual tendency, to unite and to adhere when united, which universal experience has proved to take place among many of the substances of nature, has by common consent of the civilized part of mankind been denominated attraction; and hence attraction may be defined to be *that power whereby substances unite or tend to unite and adhere together when united.* Attractions have been distinguished into different kinds or genera according to the several differences in the phenomena and modes of operation they respectively exhibit. And these different kinds may be divided into two classes, viz. First, Into those which seem to operate at a distance as well as on contact: as the attraction of gravitation. And, secondly, Into those whose operation seems scarcely to extend beyond contact; as the capillary, cohesive, corpuscular, and chemical or elementary. It is to the attractions of this latter class whose operation is thus limited, that I exclusively appropriate the term affinity. And affinity I distinguish into two species—corpuscular, and chemical or elementary. I have likewise taken the liberty from a conviction of its utility to introduce into the science a distinction between affinity and elective attraction, whether these affinities or elective attractions are chemical or corpuscular.

3. It has already been observed in Essay III. that the physical powers by means of which most of those changes in nature are effected which take

place

place among substances on contact or nearly so may in a general manner, in compliance with custom and the opinions which have hitherto prevailed, be distinguished into the two classes of chemical and mechanical—chemical action consisting in the composition and decomposition, the generation and destruction of substances themselves, and mechanical in the effecting of changes in their modifications only, or in aggregating them, or in dividing and separating them into smaller parts, but not with intire precision, there being another power in nature of very extensive influence and importance which acts only on contact or nearly so, whereby conjunctions and separations of parts are effected which with no propriety can be regarded as either chemical or mechanical, as it differs specifically from either, and seems in some respects to be intermediate between them, since the combinations it effects agree in certain of their qualities with those which are the result of mechanical, and in others of them with those which proceed from chemical combination. This power is the corpuscular.

4. That the corpuscules or integrant parts of bodies tend to unite and adhere in masses when applied to each other; and that substances in a fluid state, even in cases when of different specific gravities, on being mixed together diffuse themselves equally through each other, from the reciprocal attractions of their corpuscules, are facts which admit not of doubt, as being founded on the natures of things and established on and confirmed by universal experience. This species of affinity is denominated corpuscular from its subsisting between the corpuscules or integrant parts of bodies whether homogeneous or heterogeneous when brought into contact, and from its taking effect without any decomposition of these integrant parts or corpuscules taking place. It is manifest that capillary attraction, and that attraction whereby mixture and equal diffusion is effected, as well as those of cohesion, and of aggregation attended with adhesion of parts, on the applying of substances whether homogeneous or heterogeneous to each other, either in a fluid or in a solid state, all depend upon and are necessarily either results or modifications of corpuscular attraction, since the natures of bodies are not essentially affected by the action of either of these, and since they are all found on experience to depend *ceteris paribus* more on the extent of surface and apposition of parts than on the masses; or more on the number of corpuscules that come into immediate action by coming

coming into contact, than on the numbers of them of which the parts, masses, or substances thus mixing, cohering, and aggregating, are compounded and formed; and, indeed, to be in general *ceteris paribus* directly as the surfaces and inversely as the masses. From this it follows as a necessary consequence that *ceteris paribus* the more minute the integrant parts, or the finer the division of the substances mixed together, when these substances are heterogeneous, the more equal and intimate will the mixture or compound be, and the stronger the cohesion of the integrant parts of the several substances with each other.

5. So different in their natures are the corpuscular and chemical affinities or attractions from each other, though the force or degree of intensity of each is *ceteris paribus* directly as the surfaces and inversely as the masses, that they oppose and counteract each other's action and effect, the corpuscular impeding or preventing the operation of the chemical, and the chemical diminishing or destroying that of the corpuscular; and hence, it is often necessary in practical chemistry to weaken or diminish the affinities of the corpuscules for each other by the pulverization, solution, or fusion of the substances they form, to allow the chemical agents or elementary powers of the several different substances to act on each other with proper energy and effect.

6. Corpuscular combination is regarded and represented as being mechanical, and is denominated such. Partly because mixtures, junctions, and separations of heterogeneous substances or ingredients can in certain cases be effected by means merely mechanical, as in the separations of compounds into their ingredients by mere mechanical fracture, sifting, filtration, &c. and because the formation of compounds can be effected by mere mechanical mixture of ingredients. And partly because the qualities of corpuscular compounds, like those merely mechanical, are either intermediate, or partake in proportion to the quantities, of the qualities of the several ingredients which enter into their respective compositions. But though there are certain corpuscular combinations which can be decompounded by known mechanical means, yet there are numerous others which do not admit of being thus decompounded, so intimate is the mixture and so strong the mutual attractions of the integrant parts forming the particles of the compound; and hence it is manifest that the impossibility of decompounding

pounding any combination by known mechanical means cannot afford a sufficient test or criterion of that combination being chemical. And though corpuscular compounds agree with those that are mechanical in possessing qualities which are intermediate of those of their respective proximate principles, or of the substances of which they are compounded, yet the mixture is not nearly so intimate, the diffusion of the corpuscules nearly so equal, and the mutual attraction and cohesion among them is not nearly so strong, in mechanical combination as in corpuscular; while the diffusion, equal mixture, &c. in the mechanical are not the effect of affinity or attraction as they are in the corpuscular; and if there is any cohesion of parts on mechanical mixture it is necessarily corpuscular and not mechanical. Moreover, no elective attractions can take place between the substances, or integrant parts, mixed together, on mechanical combinations as there often does in cases of corpuscular combination; so that corpuscular and mechanical combination differ essentially from each other. And though in both the qualities are intermediate of their respective proximate principles, yet the products of corpuscular affinity, even when formed of the same proximate principles and when they differ from each other only by the differences in the proportions of these principles relatively to each other, are so very dissimilar in qualities from each other, and from those of each of their proximate principles taken severally, as to entitle them in some respect to be regarded as substances differing essentially from each other: thus, ice, water, and steam, all of which are products of the same proximate principles, or of corpuscular combinations of fire with the gravitating base or radicle of ice, only in different proportions, seem to differ in many of their essential qualities not only from each other, but also from those of their proximate principles taken severally; and the affinity between those in ice are so extremely strong that ice has never yet been decompounded mechanically or by any other known means. Besides corpuscular affinities and elective attractions are so far from being mechanical and from having any dependence on mechanical principles, that in place of being *ceteris paribus* directly as the MASSES, without any dependence on the surfaces, as is the case of mechanical powers and forces, they are on the contrary *ceteris paribus*, directly as the SURFACES, and therefore inversely as the masses: even aggregation, though it may be the result of

other

other powers besides the corpuscular and though separable in a certain degree by mechanical means, when the effect of attraction and attended with adhesion of parts is neither mechanical nor the effect of mechanical action.

There are indeed other powers in nature by means of which combinations and separations are effected, which cannot be regarded either as mechanical, corpuscular, or chemical; as that of gravity, and those which influence moral conduct and determine animal action, &c. For these operate at a distance as well as on contact, or at least appear to do so; and their modes of action, which with respect to combinations and separations are very limited, seem to depend on quite different principles from those of mechanical, corpuscular, or chemical action; since they never seem to be the proximate cause either of the generation of substance, or of its resolution into its elements or proximate principles; or to be the cause of mechanic power in substance, though they are often successfully employed to actuate engines and machines as motive powers, or to put into action that mechanic power these possess.

7. It has been common to regard those attractions denominated electrical and magnetical as mechanical; and they have accordingly been treated of as such by the writers on natural philosophy and mechanics:— they are however in these Essays, for reasons to be afterwards assigned, comprehended among the chemical attractions.

7. Though the corpuscules or integrant parts which form by their aggregation the particles and the masses of substances, whether homogeneous or heterogeneous, cannot justly be regarded as *elementary or constituent* parts of these substances, yet they are proximate principles and even *essential* parts of them, since these substances cannot possibly subsist otherwise than by their means and their union:—thus, though the union between the proximate principles of water—fire and ice— is not chemical, yet these principles are essential parts of the compound substance water, since it can exist only by their means and by their union; the same is the case with respect to the proximate principles of that combination of quicklime and water known by the name of slaked lime, of most combinations from solution and from fusion, and indeed of most of those that are really corpuscular.

8. Mechanical

8. Mechanical combinations are distinguishable from corpuscular in as far as they are destitute of all spontaneous or natural adhesion of parts and have no dependence on natural affinities or elective attractions: and when combinations which are not mechanical possess the qualities of their known proximate principles in an intermediate degree, or in proportion to the quantities of each in its composition, it may with certainty be concluded that no saturation or neutralization has taken place between them, and consequently that their union is not chemical but corpuscular. This is the case with solutions of salts, of soaps, and of mucilages in water; of many substances in alkahol, in oils, and in æther; of ice, sulphur, metals, &c. in the igneous fluid; of some substances in acids, and of some in alkalis; and of many substances in the different gasses:—thus, water is generated by combining a certain portion of ice with a certain portion of fire, and it differs from ice and from fire, only in possessing the intermediate qualities of being of a higher temperature than ice and of a lower than the igneous principle, and in not being so solid as ice or so fluid as fire, the only substance that seems to be essentially so, qualities essential to water as water, since if it possessed them not it could not be water. Water combined with a certain additional portion of fire becomes aqueous vapour or steam, a substance also possessing intermediate qualities between its proximate principles water and fire: and so of other cases. And, reciprocally, as either corpuscular or mechanical combination may with certainty be inferred when the qualities of the compound are intermediate of those of its proximate principles, so may chemical union with certainty be inferred when the qualities of the compound, whether generated by a combination of elementary or of integrant parts, in place of being intermediate differ entirely from those of its proximate principles, from the qualities of these having been destroyed and annulled on combination in consequence of their mutual action, saturation, and neutralization. Also when a substance which admits of decomposition by known means, whether the proximate principles of it are known or not, cannot be resolved into others which are palpable to sense, or cannot be decomposed any otherwise than by means of new combinations with other proximate principles whereby new substances are generated differing essentially in their qualities from those it possesses, it may likewise with intire confidence be concluded that the

com-

combination of the principles in this substance is chemical, and neither corpuscular nor mechanical; and likewise that these principles are elementary or constituent parts, and not integrant parts or corpuscles. Salts truly neutral afford a pertinent example and convincing proof of chemical combinations taking place between substances which are not simple but compound, which are not elementary or constituent but corpuscular or integrant; for when two compound substances of different kinds combine togeter *in toto* forming a substance of qualities essentially different from those of either of its proximate principles or generating substances, as is precisely the case in the formation of neutral salts, the new substances thus produced necessarily must be generated by means of new combinations among themselves of the elements or constituent parts of these compound substances which form the proximate principles of the new product, and not by means of combinations of these compounds undecomposed with each other; since, if the latter was the case, the qualities of the new substance thus generated necessarily would be intermediate of those of its proximate principles or generating substances in place of being what they really are in these cases essentially different from them, and it is hence manifest that chemical combination takes place between compound as well as between simple substances. And from the decomposition of these salts by means of elective attractions it is also manifest that compound substances formed of other compound substances or proximate principles chemically combined may be decomposed by separating these substances which form its proximate principles from each other without any changes in the qualities of these proximate principles or substances having been induced by that means: and hence that such separations without change in the qualities of the substances separated is no proof, as has been supposed, of these substances not having been before their separation in a state of chemical union.

9. It must likewise be manifest that an intermediate specific gravity, or any determinate deviation from it, on the combination of two principles or substances can afford no proper indication, though the contrary is supposed, of the kind of union which has taken place between them, as whether it is chemical or not; when it is considered that the specific gravity of the compound often depends much on the particular forms and modes of

arrange-

arrangement of its particles or chrystals, and that from this cause the specific gravity of the compound is sometimes less than that even of one of the proximate principles of which it is formed, and that certain substances become specifically lighter from being deprived of one of their proximate principles, even though that principle of which they are deprived is itself destitute of gravity, as in the case of ice, which is specifically lighter than the water of which it is formed by its being deprived of part of the fire with which it was in combination when in the state of water. And also that it is the *reciprocal* saturation of the principles, and not the saturation of one or of a part of them only, that affords a proof of the combination being chemical; for a substance, as water for instance, may be saturated with many different substances severally or conjunctly without being chemically combined with any or all of them, from these not being at the same time saturated with it or with water; and hence it is that no new qualities result from such combinations but such as are intermediate:— thus a small portion of lime, or of certain salts, will saturate a certain quantity of water, at the same time that that portion of lime or of salt in place of being saturated with water will combine with more of it in almost any proportion.

10. Elective attractions, like affinities, are either corpuscular or chemical. And as affinity is that power whereby substances, and the elements of substances, when in contact or nearly so, unite together, or tend to unite together, in toto or without decomposition or the separation and rejection of any of their parts, and thus adhere when united; so elective attraction is that power whereby certain parts of substances, constituent or integrant, elements or corpuscules, when in contact or nearly so, unite under certain circumstances with a seeming preference or election to certain other substances, or to certain of the integrant or the elementary parts of other substances, to the rejection and exclusion of other substances, or of the other part or parts whether integrant or elementary, with which they were before united, and by their union with which that substance was composed of which they then formed a part; and which substance by their thus separating and detaching themselves from the other part or parts of it now is decomposed. Elective attraction is single or simple, when a substance or integrant part in combination with some other substance or integrant part

dis-

disengages itself from the substance or integrant part with which it is combined and unites itself to some other substance in a free and disengaged state. It is double or compound, when the two proximate principles, whether elements or constituent parts, or the corpuscules or integrant parts of any substance, have greater or superior affinity under the then circumstances to the two proximate principles, elements or corpuscules, of some other substance, each to each respectively, than they have to each other; and in consequence of that superior affinity disengage themselves from their former combinations, and unite and adhere together forming two new compound substances. These elective attractions are chemical when the changes or qualities produced by their means are essential, or when they are between elements or constituent parts; and, when these changes are not essential but immediate only or these attractions not between elements but between integrant parts, corpuscular. There are other and more complex elective attractions, as triple, quadruple, &c. but these have been but little attended to and are but little known.

11. Both solution and fusion differ essentially from dissolution; the two former depending entirely upon affinities, and those of the corpuscular kind only, as has already been in some degree shewn in Essays III. and V., while the latter is the result of elective attractions, and these of the chemical kind, from which result decompositions and the generation of new products, differing essentially from their proximate principles. Many of those intimate mixtures in a liquid state, which are regarded as the results of solution only, are the effects of the joint operations of solution, and of fusion as having much dependence on a high degree of temperature; and solution and fusion differ in nothing from each other but in the differences of the substances, or in the nature of the substances by which they are respectively produced—fire and water. A substance, however large the quantity or mass of it may be relatively to any other, cannot detach, separate, or precipitate that other from a any third substance with which it is in chemical or even corpuscular combination, if that substance has no affinity either chemical or corpuscular to either of those in combination; or, though it has, unless that affinity is considerably stronger for the one than for the other of them, and than their affinity for each other, under the then temperature. And

any

any substance however small in quantity or in mass relatively to any other will separate or precipitate a part in proportion to its quantity of that other substance from its chemical or corpuscular combination with any third substance, if it has considerably greater affinity to that third substance than the other substance with which it is in combination has at the then temperature. It is no doubt difficult to separate a small quantity of any substance from a large quantity of any other substance with which it is either mechanically mixed or chemically or corpuscularly combined, and hence substances seem to be strongly retentive of the last small portions of any other substances with which they have been united; but this is owing to the minute division and wide separation and dispersion of the particles of this small portion equally diffused through the whole of that substance, and to the consequent great extent of surface in proportion to its mass and great attraction of cohesion thence resulting; as well as to the difficulty with which the precipitant can separate and diffuse its particles so as to act upon all the particles of the solvent in combination with all the particles of that minute remaining portion of the substance in combination with it immediately and directly so as to produce that effect; and hence a very high degree of temperature is often required to weaken the cohesion in such cases before a separation can be effected and the affinities become capable of acting with full effect.

12. Chemists, from not discriminating with sufficient precision between those combinations which are strictly chemical and those that are not, have admitted into chemical science certain general rules or axioms with respect to affinities and elective attractions as fundamental principles of the science, which when applied to *chemical* affinities and elective attractions are altogether erroneous and deceitful:—as the following, viz. First, " That substances have great affinity to, and are much disposed to unite, " and that even superabundantly, with any of the elements or proximate " principles of which they are composed." Secondly, " That two substances " having a great affinity to any third substance, have a great affinity to each " other; *quæ sunt eadem uni tertio, sunt eadem inter se.*" And, Thirdly, " That substances having some common principle, or that are of the " same natures, have the greatest affinity to each other." These maxims are indeed applicable in general to *corpuscular* or what has usually been called mechanical combinations, or to compound substances formed by

mere

mere mixture and apposition of integrant parts; such uniting by mixture, &c. superabundantly with any substances of the same kind with those of which they are compounded, or which form their proximate principles; and two substances which are missible in this manner with any third substance, or which have any common principle, or are of the same or nearly the same nature, are generally missible in this manner with each other, and by this means form intermediate substances partaking of the qualities, in proportion to their respective quantities, of the substances of which they are compounded. But the case is precisely the reverse with respect to elementary or chemical affinities and combinations; there being NO elementary or chemical affinity or attraction between elements or principles of the same kind or natures; and, when of different kinds, these affinities are *ceteris paribus* the greater the more opposite and contrary the natures of the elements or proximate principles uniting. And that reciprocal SATURATION of the elements or of the proximate principles which takes place in these combinations is not only a necessary result of the CONTRARIETY of their natures, but also necessarily precludes a superabundance of any of them, except in cases of complicated affinities from three or more elements coming into action at once; at the same time that this reciprocal saturation affords a sure criterion of the combination being elementary and chemical. Hence CONTRARIETY OF NATURE in different substances is inferrible either from their having GREAT AFFINITY for each other, or from the one having little or no affinity to any third substance to which the other has much affinity; though this latter rule with respect to their respective affinities to third substances, may be liable to many exceptions as these affinities may depend on many different causes and combinations when these third substances are *compound;* and, reciprocally, SIMILARITY IN NATURE of different substances is indicated either by their having LITTLE OR NO AFFINITY for each other, or by their having the same or nearly the same affinity to any third substance. These observations may perhaps be the means of furnishing a key for unlocking some of the recesses and disclosing some of the secrets of nature, whereby some of these phenomena may be rationally accounted for which have hitherto eluded all explanation.

CHAP.

CHAP. II.

OF ELECTRICITY.

IT has been ascertained in a manner sufficiently satisfactory by frequently repeated, varied, and accurate experiments, First, That the hitherto unknown powers or causes of those effects which have been denominated electrical can be obtained by various different means, and thereby these effects produced. Secondly, That the same substance or body is often, according to circumstances, either what has been called an electric, or a conductor of electricity; thus glass, of the common temperature and excited by the common means, is an electric; while glass of a higher temperature, and excited by the same means, is a conductor of electricity. Thirdly, That when an electric, on being excited, it produces according to circumstances either positive or negative electricity: thus smooth glass on being excited by friction yields positive electricity, while rough glass on being excited by the same means yields negative. Fourthly, That two different substances, though insulated, cannot be electrified by being rubbed together, or otherwise excited, if they are equally good conductors of electricity; but that, if this is not the case, they will be electrified by these means, and the one will acquire the electricity contrary to that of the other, as is always the case with the cylinder and rubber of the common electrical machine. Fifthly, That when two substances of different conducting powers are excited by being rubbed together, that which conducts the best acquires the negative, and the other the positive electricity. Sixthly, That when two electrics, equal in other respects, having surfaces of unequal roughnesses are rubbed together, that which suffers the greatest friction and thereby acquires the highest temperature, generally that having the roughest surface, acquires the negative and the other the positive electricity. And, seventhly, That no substance or body in its natural state, or not exhibiting any electrical effects, can, of its own intrinsic power, alter its state of electric or conductor; or can exhibit or produce any electrical effects,

effects, otherwise than by means of differences of affinities induced in it from differences of temperature, or other extrinsic causes.

2. All the known phenomena of electricity consist in, or are deducible from those of attraction and repulsion and the effects that in this case naturally result from them; for take away attraction and repulsion, and with them every indication, sign, appearance, or effect of electricity, that is electricity itself, vanishes with them.

3. From these facts it may rationally be inferred that both the generation and destruction of these powers and effects which are denominated electrical, or that electricity is in all cases a consequence of differences of affinities and of the attractions thence resulting; and that these differences of affinities often arise from differences of temperature, from whatever causes these differences of temperature may proceed; as whether from friction, from the application or absorption of fire or of ignite, from condensation or expansion, evaporation, effervescence, &c.

4. Since there seems to be no gravitating body in nature but what may by proper means be rendered electrical, and wherever situated; since the one kind of electricity cannot, by any known means, be excited and produced without the other being produced also; since the electrical effects produced differ so much as, in many cases, to be the very reverse of each other; and since these effects cannot possibly be owing to plenums and vacuums of any one power or substance, or to plus and minus states of what has been called positive electricity—those electrical repulsions and electrical spheres of action whereby gravitating bodies negatively electrified mutually repell, &c. each other, not admitting of being rationally and justly accounted for on that hypothesis, or by a mere privation of all electrical powers and properties in them; it being utterly impossible for bodies which are essentially or of their own natures *attractive* of each other to be rendered mutually *repulsive* merely by being deprived of what is foreign and extraneous to their natures—it may also rationally be inferred that these phenomena and effects cannot be produced in the manner and by the means assumed in the Franklinean hypothesis or theory at present generally adopted, or by the agency of one power only, but necessarily must be results of the agencies of two different and distinct powers. But though they are the effects of two different and distinct powers, these two different

powers

powers are not the vitreous and resinous electricities of M. du Fay, &c. or two different kinds of fire, the one the product of vitreous and the other of resinous substances; as is sufficiently manifest from the experiments of Mr. Canton, &c. which prove that both kinds of electricity may be produced at pleasure by means of either of these kinds of substances, and without either of them being decomposed or any way altered by the process.

5. That each of these powers is self-repellent, or essentially repulsive, is proved by that mutual repulsion which takes place between different bodies charged with either of them. That they are attractive of each other is proved by that mutual attraction which takes place between two bodies of the same or of different kinds when the one is charged with the one kind of electricity and the other with the other, &c. That they are altogether devoid of gravity is proved not only by each being repulsive of itself, but also from no body being more attracted by the earth, or becoming more ponderous for being charged with either of them. And that they are of different and even opposite natures is proved by this, that when they combine together, even though imperfectly, as in the common experiments of applying a positive and a negative plate of any kind, and of equal powers, or a piece of sulphur and a metallic cup possessing equal charges of different electricities, to each other, they so effectually counteract each other as to become altogether incapable of producing electrical phenomena and effects; and, while in this combined and thereby dormant and latent state, to lose all pretensions whatever to being regarded as electricities, as then forming a substance possessing no electrical powers or properties.

As it may be convenient, on various accounts, to appropriate a specific name to the powers or substances whereby electrical appearances and effects are produced, I shall denominate them electrites; and, to distinguish the one from the other, shall for the present, in compliance with the general practice, call the one positive and the other negative, but not with any intention of indicating their respective natures by these distinctive names; the term electrons would have answered equally well were it not that it would seem to imply that it was different kinds of amber that was meant by it.

6. It may likewise rationally be inferred from the above facts, that there

actually

actually exists in nature some substance, generally diffused, which is capable of being decomposed by means of elective attractions or differences of affinities, of which the elements or constituent principles are the electrites; and that the only means of obtaining the electrites, or those powers or substances by which electrical appearances and effects are produced, and thereby of producing these appearances and effects themselves, must be by dissolving the union either between themselves, and thereby decomposing that substance which is generated by their union, or between them and any other elements or substances with which they severally may be in chemical combination, by means of the application of two or more appropriate conductors of different conducting powers at the same time, &c.—by means of the known affinities of the electrites to certain substances;—by means of their affinity to each other;—and by means of other known elective attractions.

7. It is not merely on rational inference, however, that these conclusions rest. They are facts admitting of direct positive proof established on the most unexceptionable, experimental or intuitive evidence; for this substance, generally diffused, may actually be artificially decomposed, and often has been so by various different means, though that circumstance has hitherto eluded observation, and the electrites thereby obtained separate and distinct. Under certain circumstances this may be accomplished merely by the mechanical separation of the gravitating bodies to which they respectively adhere; as in the experiments of separating a positive and a negative plate of any kind and of equal powers from each other, or the metallic cup and sulphur mentioned above from each other. In these cases the different electrites have each evidently greater affinity, under the then circumstances, to the gravitating substances to which they respectively adhere than they have to each other; and on this account their union on the plates or the sulphur and cup being applied to each other seems not to be perfect. Under other circumstances, it may be effected by the joint action of two or more contiguous conductors of different powers: the separation being effected in this case by the more perfect conductor carrying off the negative electrite and the less perfect the positive. These conductors to produce that effect must necessarily have a greater affinity or attraction to these powers, respectively, than these powers, in their then state of combination,

tion, have for each other; and the substances with which these powers are severally combined must have a greater affinity for each other than for these powers; at least, under the circumstances in which these effects take place: so that it is not only necessary for the conductors to be of unequal conducting powers, but that they shall also respectively have greater affinity or attraction, under the then circumstances, to these powers than the powers have to each other, and to the substances with which they are severally in combination; and hence it is that the decomposition of the combinations they form, or the separation of these elementary powers, cannot be obtained by means of one conductor, or what amounts to the same thing of two conductors of equal powers, even when excited by friction, as these are not qualified for or capable of separating them from each other, even when in a state of imperfect combination. The decomposition of this substance, or the separation of these powers from each other, may also be effected by other means to be mentioned hereafter: and though these powers are attractive of each other, the substance generated by their union is highly repulsive of itself; owing, probably, to its being formed of elements each of which is repulsive of itself.

8. Electricity then, it would appear, is the consequence of a particular chemical or elementary decomposition taking place, without any chemical or elementary combination resulting from it; or that it is the result of the decomposition of a particular substance into its elements or constituent principles without any elementary or chemical combinations being the consequence of it, whereby the elements or elementary powers of the substance thus decomposed, contrary to what obtains in all or in most other cases of chemical or elementary decomposition, exist and are exhibited separate and distinct from each other, and yet not in a state of *chemical* combination with any other elements or substances; and as thus existing produce, or are the causes of, all those phenomena and effects denominated electrical.

9. By means of rational deductions from these facts, and from other electrical phenomena and experiments that have been long and are well known, may this substance, generally diffused, of which the elements are the electrites, be discovered and ascertained—though the discovery of it by means of these has never hitherto been attempted from its never hav-

ing

ing been imagined that the production of these powers which are the causes of all electrical phenomena and effects could depend upon the decomposition of any substance whatever—for they not only furnish reasons, as given above, for inferring that electricity is owing to the decomposition of some particular substance, but also indicate the particular substance with sufficient precision for its discovery; at the same time that they afford decisive proofs, both analytical and synthetical, of the substance thus indicated and discovered being composed of and decomposible into the different electrites. Thus, in the experiment referred to above of pouring sulphur in fusion into a metallic or glass cup electricity is produced, and two new substances generated, the different electrites, which become manifest to sense on separating the sulphur and the cup, when cool, from each other, from the sulphur being charged with the one electrite and the cup with the other; and since there are only three substances operated upon, the sulphur, the metal or glass of which the cup is formed, and the fire by means of which the fusion of the sulphur is effected, no others entering into the process or being required for producing the effect, the result being the same in vacuo, it may rationally and justly be inferred, that a decomposition of some of the substances employed in it has taken place; and since two of these substances, the sulphur and the cup, are not only not decomposed, but are no way chemically altered by it, the weight, &c. of each being precisely the same as before, it must necessarily be concluded that it is the only other substance operated upon, the fire, or part of the fire that was required to fuse and maintain the sulphur in a fluid state, that has been decomposed into the two electrites generated by the process which thus manifest themselves.

. That the one electrite in this case is not produced from the cup, and that the other is not a product of the sulphur, is proved by either the one or the other electrite being producible at pleasure by means either of the sulphur or of the cup, according as the sulphur is poured either into a metallic cup, or into a cup of glass or of baked wood; and that either electrite did not form a component part of the sulphur or of the metal or glass, &c. is proved not only by their neither being diminished in weight nor altered in quality or quantity by the process; but also by the electrites being producible by the same process, when melted wax, chocolate fresh from
the

the mill, &c. are substituted for the sulphur, and when any one metal is substituted for any other, or several other substances as sealing wax, glass, baked wood, &c. for the metal, in the process ; and that they are not the product of any of these other substances, and do not result from their decomposition is proved not only by none of them being altered in their chemical qualities by the process, but also by the products being the same in all these different cases by this process ; the same electrites being always produced, however different from each other the several gravitating substances employed in producing them may be in the different experiments and operations for that purpose. And since it is thus decisively proved that they are furnished by none of the various different gravitating substances which may with effect be employed for obtaining them by this process ; since they are invariably generated by it even by means of gravitating substances differing essentially from each other ; and since not furnished by the gravitating substances employed in the process, they necessarily must be by the ungravitating; and as no other ungravitating substance but fire is employed in the several operations, and fire is necessary and common to them all, and the only substance that is so, it follows as an unavoidable consequence that it can be from the fire only that they can be and are produced in these cases.

10. That the production of electricity—from exciting by means of friction a tube, globe, or cylinder, of glass or of sulphur, &c. as in the common electrical machine, &c. when no amalgam is used---is the result of the decomposition of part of the disengaged fire, produced by the friction, into the different electrites, from differences of affinities, and differences of conducting powers, resulting from the differences of temperatures which the free fire thus accumulated produces, must be manifest when it is considered, that the glass, sulphur, or other electric, while its temperature is raised by this means, becomes a conductor of electricity, though not of equal conducting power with the rubber, whereby the one electrite, the positive, comes to be attracted and carried off by the glass or sulphur to the prime conductor of the machine, and the other electrite, the negative, by the rubber, as being the best conductor ; and from the glass or sulphur, &c. ceasing to be a conductor as it cools, and possessing, from the mode of applying the friction, not only different temperatures and different conducting powers in

dif-

different parts of it, and also from its being often in some parts of it, from cooling, a non-conductor, while other parts of it conduct, though with different conducting powers, part of the electrites thus produced, in place of being carried off, remain loosely adhering to those parts of the glass, &c. that have lost or are losing their conducting power. These facts are proved by all the phenomena and effects exhibited and produced in these cases; as by none of the gravitating substances being altered in their weight or chemical qualities; by no other substances besides the gravitating but fire coming into action; from there being evidently new products which can in this case possibly result only from decomposition, and from a decomposition of the fire only, and a decomposition so managed as that no *chemical* combinations take place in consequence of it.

11. In the case of the electrophorus, or of producing electricity from exciting by means of friction a plate of glass coated on one side with rosin or sealing wax, these conjoined electrics on being thus excited become conductors of electricity of different attracting and conducting powers whereby the fire disengaged and collected by the friction is analysed into its elements the different electrites; which electrites on the partial or intire cooling of part or of the whole of the plate become in part disengaged from it, and thereby efficient with respect to other substances and manifest to sense, from the conjoined substances of which the plate is formed losing in that case part or all of their conducting powers; at the same time that they remain charged with the other part or remaining portion of the electrites thus produced, from the one electrite being attached to the glass and the other to the rosin or wax of the plate, and from these substances being impenetrable to them in their cool and non-conducting state. That the electricity is produced in this case also by the decomposition of the fire accumulated by the friction into its constituent principles the electrites, in the manner and by the means above described, is likewise proved by the phenomena and effects: by no other substance coming into action but the fire besides the gravitating substances employed which are evidently not decomposed; by the production of new substances by the process which are not gravitating, and which in this case could possibly result only from decomposition, and from the decomposition of an ungravitating substance, only, since none of the gravitating substances employed in the process are

decom-

decomposed by it and the products of it are ungravitating; and which therefore necessarily must result from the decomposition of the fire, the only ungravitating substance which comes into action in it.

12. The production of electricity merely by the direct application of fire without excitation by friction, to the tourmalin, and to certain other crystalized stones and gems, or by alternately heating and cooling them, affords an apt and beautiful illustration and confirmation of the preceding doctrine; since in these cases it is sufficiently obvious that no other substances or powers come into action but fire and the stone; that electricity may be generated at pleasure, or as often as required, by the mere application of fire under the proper circumstances to the same stone; that the stone is no way altered by the process however often repeated; and that the same stone is at the same time differently affected in different parts of it by the application of the fire to it, whereby these parts acquire different degrees of temperature, and thereby those different attractive and conducting powers by which the decomposition of the fire into its elements the electrites is effected, and the electricity in these cases produced.

13. The production of electricity in an insulated conductor, and indeed by proper management in any substance whatever, by decomposing that fire or ignite it naturally contains into its elements the electrites, merely by the near approach of a body surcharged with either electrite to it—from that electrite with which the body is surcharged attracting that electrite of a contrary kind, and repelling that of the same kind with itself which form the elements or constituting principles of that fire or ignite—furnishes another simple, beautiful, and apt illustration and confirmation of the above doctrine: and in conjunction with the doctrine of the general equilibrium of temperature treated of in the immediately preceding Essay, affords also a sufficiently satisfactory proof of that substance which is decomposable into the different electrites being generally diffused through nature.

14. But if the preceding reasoning is just, and this analysis well founded, nothing further can possibly be required for the generation of fire than an intimate combination of the two electrites with each other in a state of sufficient purity for producing that effect; and that this is actually the case, the long known and common experiments of bringing conductors

from

from the rubber and the prime conductor of the electrical machine within what is called the striking distance of each other, of discharging the Leyden phial, or an electrical battery, &c. furnish the most decisive proof, from fire being in all these cases constantly generated by their union and rendered palpable to sense, and thereby confirm this doctrine of the electrites, and consequently of all the electrical phenomena and effects in nature, being produced by the decomposition of a particular substance, and of that particular substance by the decomposition of which they are produced, and of which they of course form the constituent principles, being fire either in a pure state or in that of ignite: as affording a synthetical proof of it, not less satisfactory, convincing, and conclusive than the analytical by which it was preceded.

15. However inconsistent and irreconcilable the preceding doctrines may be with all the theories hitherto adopted with regard to the natures of fire, and of electricity—as those of fire being an element, of its being a compound of caloric and light, or of its being a compound of an acid principle and phlogiston, &c. those of there being a vitreous and a resinous electricity, and those of there being but one kind of electricity only on the plus and minus states, or plenums and vacuums of which all the phenomena and effects depend:—it is hoped the facts and reasonings on which they are founded, supported, and established, as given above, are so direct and conclusive as necessarily to impress conviction on every unprejudiced mind with regard to their validity, independent of the corroborating circumstances of neither of the electrites being possessed of gravity: of each being as well as the substances they generate essentially repulsive of its own nature, the only quality in which they agree, and which of course is not neutralized and destroyed by their *chemical* combination; of neither of them singly giving any indication of its being possessed of any of the other qualities of fire; or of its being either caloric or light, or capable of producing those sensations and other effects to which the names hot and lucid are appled; and of neither of them possessing the qualities either of vitreous or of resinous substances; or of those which have been attributed to any of those hypothetical entities, the *ungravitating* phlogiston of Becker and Stahl, or the *gravitating* oxygen and hydrogen of Lavoisier.

16. This practical analysis and synthesis of fire affords an experimental,

intuitive,

intuitive, and decisive proof of one kind of matter at least being gene-rated by a combination of powers of opposite natures. Powers which, from their effects, are known actually to exist; and to exist separate and distinct from each other; and that often without being in a state of *chemical* combination with any other element or substance, though generally adhering to some gravitating body when not passing from one gravitating substance to another; which admit of being artificially and practically transferred, &c. from one gravitating body to another, and that in given proportions; and which, in some respects may be regarded as palpable to sense. This is the case that was alluded to when treating of the GE-NESIS of gravitating matter in Essay III. pages 136---141; and it un-doubtedly is such as cannot but be regarded as pertinent and in point, and highly conducive to the support and establishment of the doctrines then advanced.

CHAP. III.

OF WATER AND THE GASSES.

WATER is a substance too well known to require either a definition or de-scription.---Gasses may be defined *exceedingly rare, invisible, gravitating fluids, uncondensable by cold, and indeed permanently elastic;* for though they admit of being condensed and fixed by combining with certain sub-stances from the strong mutual attraction which takes place between them and those substances, yet from being elastic of their own nature they in-stantly expand and recover their former gaseous state on being liberated by an increase of temperature or any other means from that combination and reciprocal attraction:---as on the combination of certain gasses in certain cases with water, as on the combination of carbonic gas with quick-lime, of oxygen gas with mercury in what is called the red calx or oxide of mercury, of certain gasses with other calces or oxides forming fulmi-nating compounds as in fulminating gold, &c. A gas differs from air, or that of which the terrestrial atmosphere consists, not only in airs being condensable in some degree by cold, but also in airs being compounded of different gasses, of vapours and other exhalations, and the other substances

N N which

which may be combined with and volatilized by these :—that the gasses likewise differ essentially from vapours, not only in not being condensable by cold, but in other respects also, will soon appear.

2. The two principal gasses are those which are at present generally known by the names of oxygen gas, and hydrogen gas. Dr. Priestley discovered the first of these on the first day of August 1774, and gave it the name of pure air. It was also discovered soon after by Dr. Scheele, a German chemist residing in Sweden, who, ignorant of the discovery of Dr. Priestley, denominated it empyreal, or fire air.---The properties of the other, then called inflammable air, and which had for long been known to exist in mines and had been procured artificially by Drs. Hook, Mayow, and others, were first investigated and ascertained by Mr. Henry Cavendish. The pure air was then generally obtained by applying heat to certain calces and earths moistened either by nitrous or sulphurous acids, and to minium, mercurial precipitate *per se*, and black calx of manganese. The inflammable air was obtained either by dissolving iron, zinc, or tin, in diluted sulphuric or muriatic acids; or by passing steam or aqueous vapour through red hot tubes containing metallic filings or pounded charcoal. It was discovered, in the summer of the year 1781, by the same Mr. Cavendish, by means of experiments expressly made for that purpose, and by Mr. Watt from the experiments of Dr. Priestley and Mr. Warltire, that on the combustion of pure air with inflammable air a quantity of water was deposited precisely equal in weight with that of the airs or gasses consumed. These experiments and this discovery naturally gave rise to the theory of water being a compound substance---in place of an element as was supposed, even by the chemists, before these experiments were made---formed by a combination of the gravitating bases of pure and inflammable airs with each other :---and this theory was supposed to be synthetically and satisfactorily proved by the experiments of Mr. Cavendish and the conclusions he deduced from them. These experiments were repeated and varied by many other chemists, and were always attended with the same result; and, particularly, by M. Lavoisier, who executed them on a very large scale, and conducted them with great accuracy. He likewise, at the same time, attempted an analytical proof of this theory, in endeavouring to decompose water into these two different kinds of airs,

by

by passing it in steam through red hot tubes containing filings of iron, or charcoal reduced to small pieces. And such was his ingenuity and address that by apt illustration, judicious arrangement, and much specious reasoning, he formed, in all probability entirely unacquainted with those suggestions and conjectures of Dr. Hook of London and Dr. Mayow of Oxford by which his principal conclusions had been anticipated, that seemingly luminous and satisfactory system of chemistry which has conferred so much, and, making allowance for the then state of chemical knowledge, justly merited celebrity on his memory, and to which the system of Stahl and those of all preceding philosophers soon yielded the palm. In this system, the theory of warer being decomposable into the gravitating bases of pure and inflammable airs, called by him oxygen and hydrogen, forms an essential and fundamental part. So rapid and complete was its success, that in a very short period of time all opposition to it, with the exception of that of Dr. Priestley to the rejection of phlogiston and the theory of the decomposition of water, entirely ceased. It was universally adopted; and it now reigns unrivalled with an almost undisputed and seemingly undisputable right.

3. M. Lavoisier trusted chiefly to the third experiment of the 8th chapter of Part First of his Elements for his analytical proof of water being a compound, and not an elementary substance, and of its being resolvable into what he denominated oxygen and hydrogen, and which he regarded as being respectively the gravitating bases of pure air, by him called oxygen gas, and of inflammable air by him called hydrogen gas; the only other elements or constituent principle of each of these being, according to his tables of binary combustions, caloric: light, however, is also in certain cases, for the purpose of according with and explaining by its means the phenomena of combination, allowed by this theory to form either a constituent or a proximate principle of these gasses. This experiment consisted in passing 100 grs. of water in the state of steam through a red hot tube containing 274 grs. of soft iron, in thin plates rolled up spirally, whereby the iron in the tube became in a certain degree calcined, or oxydated as he calls it, being converted by the process into black calx of iron, and is found by that means to have gained 85 grs. of additional

weight;

weight; while 15 grs. of inflammable air is at the same time generated by the process: and the weight of this inflammable air added to the weight gained by the iron being precisely equal to that of the water lost by the process, viz. 100 grs. he attributes this loss of water, and the production of the inflammable air together with the additional weight of the iron, to the decomposition of the water, thus lost, into oxygen and hydrogen; of which the former, according to this theory, combines with the iron generating the oxide and producing the addition of weight, and the other with caloric generating the inflammable air; and he contends that there is no other way of accounting rationally and justly for the phenomena and effects produced by the process.

4. This is the part of the proof adduced on which Dr. Priestley founds his objections to this theory and the system raised upon it, who, on the contrary, maintains that the iron in this case is converted into a calx and acquires the additional weight of 85 grs. not from its combining with 85 grs. of oxygen, but from parting with a portion of its phlogiston, an ungravitating substance, and combining with 85 grs. of the 100 grs. of water lost; while the other 15 grs. of it combining with the phlogiston separated from the iron forms the inflammable air generated by the process.---And of the justness of this representation he regards the experiment whereby he effected the revivification of the calciform iron thus produced into perfect iron and the production of a quantity of water precisely equal to that lost in the former process by melting the calciform iron in inflammable air by means of a burning lens as a sufficient proof. But the result of this experiment, or the reduction of the calx and production of water in this case, accords as well with the theory of the decomposition of water as with this; and may by it, if the premises are admitted, be accounted for in a manner equally satisfactory: for if the calciform iron consists, as supposed proved by the Lavoiserian system, of iron in its intire state combined with 85 grs. of oxygen, one of the elements of water, and the inflammable air of hydrogen, the only other element of it, combined with caloric only; on the melting of the calciform iron in inflammable air and the consequent combination of the oxygen of the calx with the hydrogen of the inflammable air, the calciform iron necessarily must resume its former state and appearance

pearance of iron or be revived, and a portion of water equal to what was lost in converting the iron into the form of a calx or oxide necessarily must be produced.

5. But it be may justly objected to both these ways of accounting for these phenomena and effects, that though seemingly satisfactory, neither of them is so without admitting the truth of the premises on which it is founded, and thereby assuming in them that which is required to be proved; as in that of Priestley, the actual existence of phlogiston, &c. and in that Lavoisier, the actual existence of oxygen and of hydrogen, and the compositions of pure and inflammable airs, and of water, by their respective combinations with caloric, and with each other; and that the calciform iron is formed of a combination of iron in its intire state with oxygen or the base of pure air; and as these assumptions are such as can not be admitted without proof, they necessarily involve both in insuperable difficulties.

6. There are however other experiments of Dr. Priestley's, some of which were made many years posterior to the above—for he engaged in this controversy immediately on the Lavoiserian theory first being made public, and continued in it till his death, conducting it all along with that liberal, candid, and truly philosophical spirit, which has ever distinguished those who have the advancement of science only for their object—which appear to me, though they have never been fortunate enough to have been generally regarded in that point of view, to prove decisively that it is not oxygen, but water in its entire state, that enters into the composition of black calx, or black oxide as it is at present called, of iron; and indeed into all the metallic calces, though in some cases containing pure air, &c. in solution: and indeed also to prove not only that water forms the gravitating base of these airs or gasses, but likewsse that it enters into their composition as a constituent principle, though neither caloric nor light, as generally believed, nor phlogiston as he supposes, should on a thorough investigation of their respective natures prove to be the other constituent principle of either of them; and likewise that water in an intire state enters into the composition of all the other gasses, though in several of them not as the only gravitating substance.

7. The experiments above alluded to are, First, Having moistened

filings

filings or grains of iron, copper, zinc, and other metals, and also pieces of charcoal with water, and having exposed them severally in vacuo to the influence of the solar rays drawn to a focus by means of a powerful burning lens; he always obtained pure inflammable air, and no other kind of air, except when charcoal or impure iron containing charcoal was employed, that heavy inflammable air, or inflammable air holding carbon in solution was obtained in place of pure inflammable air; and that when any pure air had in this case found admission that a proportional quantity of fixed air or carbonic gas was produced: when no water was present he found that no air or gas of any kind could be produced by subjecting metals or charcoal to the influence of the concentrated solar rays, and that the quantities produced when they were moistened with water were always in proportion to the quantities of water with which they were moistened. Second, Having exposed filings, &c. of metals and pieces of charcoal severally to concentrated rays of solar light in a glass vessel filled with pure air, combustion took place, the pure air was consumed, the metals assumed the appearances of calces or oxides and acquired an increase of weight equal to that of the air consumed, and no kind of air or gas was produced to supply the place of the pure air consumed, except when charcoal was used when an equal volume of fixed air was produced, or when impure iron was employed when fixed air in smaller quantity was generated. And, Third, Having exposed in vacuo a mixture of the black calx or oxide of iron thus produced with pounded charcoal which had been subjected to as great a heat as would have expelled from it all the air that heat could expel to the influence of solar rays concentrated by the same powerful lens, a large quantity of heavy inflammable air, and no pure air, or fixed air, or any other kind of air or gas whatever was produced; and no combustion ensued.

8. These experiments appear to me to prove clearly, First, That it is not with oxygen, or any constituent part of water, but with water in its entire state that the calx is in combination. For, the result or product is the same when charcoal moistened with water, as in experiment 1st, as when charcoal mixed with the black calx of iron, as in experiment 3d, is exposed to the action of the concentrated solar rays, it being heavy inflammable air in both cases; and if it had been either with oxygen, or with

oxygen

oxygen gas, or pure air in a condensed state, that the calx had been in combination, in place of with water, the necessary consequences would have been, that either pure air would have been evolved, or fixed air would have been produced, as in experiment 1st, when some pure air found admission; or combustion would have ensued, as in experiment 2d, when charcoal placed in pure air was acted upon by the concentrated solar rays; and that the production of heavy inflammable air only, the same product that is obtained by exposing moistened charcoal to heat, could not possibly have been the result: but since none of these consequences ensue on exposing a mixture of the calx with charcoal to the action of the concentrated solar rays, and the production of heavy inflammable air, as in the case of exposing charcoal moistened with water to heat, actually is the only result, it follows as necessary consequences, that it cannot possibly be with oxygen or with oxygen gas, but must be with water in its intire state that the calx is in combination, and that it is to this combination with water that the metal in the state of a calx owes its additional weight. And, Secondly, That it is water in its intire state that constitutes the gravitating base of pure and inflammable airs, or as they are now called oxygen and hydrogen gasses, whatever their other elements may be. For pure inflammable air can be artificially generated not only by exposing grains of zinc, &c. moistened with water to the action of concentrated solar rays; but also by exposing to the same action dry grains of certain metals intimately mixed with any of certain other metals in a calciform state from having been subjected to a high degree of temperature by means of concentrating solar rays in a glass vessel filled with pure air, which could not possibly be the case if water in its intire state did not form the gravitating base of the pure air by means of which the metal was calcined, as well as of the inflammable air generated by means of these calces, which differs in no respect from that obtained by the same process by the direct application of moisture or water to zinc, &c. It also follows from the above facts that if oxygen is the gravitating base of pure air, or what is called oxygen gas, it necessarily must be the gravitating base of inflammable air, or what is called hydrogen gas, likewise, since that which formed the gravitating base of the pure air employed in this case and to combination with which the calces or oxides owed their increase of weight, must necessarily form that of the inflammable air generated by the process, and to the loss of which the

loss

loss of the increase of weight in the calces is owing, also :—a consequence equally fatal to the Lavoiserian theory of the decomposition of water, with that of water in its intire state forming the gravitating bases of these gasses, and of being that to which metallic calces owe their additional weight. Dr. Priestley having failed in his attempts to support the phlogistic system of chemistry, that degree of attention was not bestowed on his well conceived and well conducted experiments which they justly merited, whence those conclusions of so much importance towards the attainment of a just theory of chemical and physical science, which are justly deducible from them, escaped observation.

10. Messrs. Van Troostwyk and Dieman, assisted by Mr. Cuthbertson, found that when electrical explosions were made to pass through water, oxygen and hydrogen gasses were produced; effects they attributed to a decomposition of water by the electric spark.* These experiments were afterwards repeated by Dr. Pearson, assisted by Mr. Cuthbertson, with the same results, who also imputed them to the same cause.† Since the discovery of the galvinic methods of producing electricity, attempts have been made to decompose water by means of the pile of Volta, and the trough of Cruickshank; and having succeeded in generating pure and inflammable airs by placing wires proceeding from the poles either of the pile or the trough in a vessel adapted to the purpose containing water, it has been naturally concluded, as being conformable to the chemical principles at present regarded as established, that that part of the water which appears to have been lost in these processes has been decomposed by them; that water is thus decomposable; and that galvinism or electricity is the power by whose agency this decomposition is and may be effected; and these conclusions were regarded as confirmed by the generation of these airs or gasses, by placing wires proceeding from the prime conductor and the cushion of an excited electrical machine in water. The generation of these gasses by means of galvinism, and several other important galvinical effects, were the discoveries of Messrs. Nicholson, Cruickshank, Davy, Henry, and Haldane; and the generation of these gasses by placing wires proceeding from the common electrical machine in water was the discovery of Dr. Wollaston.

* Journal de Phys. xxxv. 369.
† Nicholson's Journal, i. 242.

11. If,

11. If, however, the preceding deductions and conclusions from the experiments of Dr. Priestley are allowed to be logical and just; and if the very important fact announced in the immediately preceding chapter of FIRE being a compound in place of an elementary substance, of which the elements or constituent principles are the electrites, is admitted to be well founded and fully established; these conclusions and this fact must necessarily make these operations and results be viewed in a very different light from what they have hitherto been, and the several effects produced be attributed to causes and agencies very different from those at present assumed as producing them; and in place of affording any proof, as supposed by the ingenious chemists by whom these experiments were made, of water being decomposed in these cases, and of the gasses produced being generated by the combination of the elements of water with caloric, or with caloric and light, as affording, on the contrary, a synthetic proof, not less satisfactory than the analytical proof already adduced, of the generation of the gasses produced being a consequence of combinations of the different electrites with water. For it follows as necessary consequences, if the fact of fire being decomposable into the electrites is fully proved, and if that of water not being decomposable by any known means and in its intire state forming the gravitating base of pure and inflammable airs is also established on indubitable evidence *(but not otherwise, as in that case these effects may be owing to the cause commonly assigned, or to others unknown)* that a combination of the positive electrite with water must form pure air, and of the negative electrite with water inflammable air; and that this is actually the case these experiments, though of themselves altogether incompetent to the establishing of the above facts and conclusions, furnish, after these facts are established, perfectly satisfactory synthetic proof; and it also necessarily follows that, in the experiment of Mr. Cavendish, of inflaming a mixture of pure and inflammable airs by means of the electric spark, it was not water, as supposed, but fire that was generated; and that the weight of the water deposited on the inflammation must necessarily be precisely equal to that of the airs consumed by it, since no other gravitating principle or ponderating substance enters into their compositions or is employed in the process.

12. The invalidity of the theory of the composition and decomposition of water, as deduced from the experiments of Mr. Cavendish and M. Lavoi-

sier,

sier, may likewise be proved by rational deduction from the incompetency of the powers assumed to produce the effects attributed to them, or of the premises to sanction the conclusions, and this proof, though apogogical, and therefore not intirely satisfactory and conclusive, must yet operate with considerable influence in corroborating the direct proofs formerly adduced. Thus, if pure air or oxygen gas consists of oxygen, one of the elements of water, combined with caloric; and inflammable air or hydrogen gas of hydrogen, the other element of water, and caloric; the decomposition of the water and consequent generation of these gasses must necessarily be effected either by the caloric acting on the water in two different and even opposite ways at once; or by the elements of water, oxygen and hydrogen, having at a high temperature, severally, more affinity to caloric than, under these circumstances, they have to each other; but the first of these modes of operation being impossible in the nature of things, it would be absurd to suppose it could be the cause of these effects; and that the second is not the cause of them is proved by the production of steam and not of these gasses being the result of its operation.

13. That the electrites do not of themselves form any kind of gasses is evident from their not possessing gravity, or any of the other sensible qualities of these; and that they neither contain water in their respective compositions, nor are capable of generating it by their union, is also manifest from their not possessing gravity, &c. and from no water being produced on their combining together.

14. From the proofs adduced, it is presumed it may now with intire confidence be concluded, First, That fire is decomposible into the electrites, and is generated by their combination. Secondly, That water is not decomposible; or, at least, that it has never yet been chemically decomposed by any known means; unless its being resolved into fire and ice, by depriving it of its fire of fluidity, or a large portion of that fire with which its gravitating base, or that of ice, is in corpuscular combination, should be regarded as such, which cannot with propriety, since no other changes in the essential qualities take place in this case but what proceed merely from difference of temperature, and the gravitating base of water or of ice is not known to exist in nature in a separate distinct state, either as a material substance, or as a power or immaterial substance; all that is known

of

of it being that it possesses gravity, and that it has great affinity to fire
with which it forms either ice, water, or steam, according to certain determinate circumstances; and that it has also great affinity to certain other
substances, particularly the electrites with which it forms gasses. Thirdly,
That the differences of these gasses is not owing to differences in their gravitating bases, but to differences in the ungravitating principles which
enter into their respective compositions. Fourthly, That they are generated of combinations of the ELECTRITES with water. And, Fifthly, That
neither the gaseous form assumed by the water in the generation of the
gasses, nor their PERMANENT ELASTICITY when generated, is the effect
of FIRE, or of increase of temperature, but are owing intirely to the ELEC-
TRITES combined with the water in their several compositions. Gasses may,
indeed, in certain cases, have their elasticity increased by increase of temperature, but that increase of elasticity, in as far as it depends upon
increase of temperature, is not permanent, unless that increase of elasticity
is the consequence merely of the gas being liberated by the increase of
temperature from any attraction to any other substance which retained
it in a more or less contracted or condensed state.

15. These conclusions, if just, are fatal as well to the phlogistic system
of Stahl, as to those chemical systems which have succeeded it; for, if
just, the existence of those nominal entities, phlogiston, oxygen, and hydrogen, which never came under the cognizance of our senses, cannot be
rationally inferred from phenomena; and, this being the case, the properties attributed to them can justly be regarded only as mere gratuitous
assumptions; they themselves as having no actual existence in nature;
and, however ingeniously conceived and well adapted for explaining many
of the phenomena of nature, or however splendid and seemingly luminous
and instructive the theories or superstructures erected on such foundations
may be, they can justly be regarded only as the baseless fabrics of a vision
having no existence but in the imaginations of those who are capable " of
" bodying forth the forms of things unknown," and " of giving to aery
" nothing a local habitation and a name."

But however conducive the discovery of the truths developed in Essay V.,
and in this and the preceding chapters of this Essay, and the system of
chemical philosophy naturally resulting from them, may eventually prove

towards

towards the advancement of science, as opening a new, extensive, and hitherto unexplored field of inquiry to philosophical investigation, which seems to promise ample returns to those who cultivate it—the CHEMICAL agencies and combinations of the electrites—as tending to obviate difficulties, subdue prejudices, and conduct that inquiry by a path less devious and less exposed to error than that in which it has hitherto proceeded, and as affording fundamental principles, less exceptionable perhaps, by means of which many facts and phenomena may be rationally and justly accounted for which hitherto have been regarded as inexplicable, it cannot be without regret, without a considerable degree of sorrow and reluctance, that the mind can abandon those principles and supposed discoveries it has been used to contemplate with pleasure, and on the knowledge of which it has prided itself, those systems the beauty of which, from the seemingly almost wonderful conformity of their conclusions with the phenomena of nature, it, with reason, has been accustomed to admire, in common with that ingenuity which could have conceived systems which apparently accord so well with the real state of nature. Some minds are incapable, however cogent the reasons adduced in favour of new discoveries, to relinquish theories to which they have been much attached; and, even, to those minds which are possessed of strength enough to conquer such prejudices, and of candour and magnanimity enough to acknowledge it, the gay prospects presented by the advantages that may result from the new discoveries can, from being clouded and obscured by the recollection of these discoveries proving fatal to their favourite opinions and doctrines, afford but little gratification, as being productive of a mixed sensation only, a pleasure alloyed with pain, such as might be experienced on leaving our native home and the friends and companions of our youth, to enjoy some honourable and lucrative employment in a distant land—a sensation " like the memory of joys that are past, pleasant, and mournful to the soul."

16. From the above facts and reasonings it is manifest, that the electrites are capable of, and actually do produce in nature, two kinds of action, electrical and chemical; on the first of these kinds depends all those attractions and repulsions from which the phenomena denominated electrical result, and which neither depend upon nor produce chemical
composition

composition or decomposition: on the other depends those chemical compositions and decompositions which are effected by the *agency of the electrites*, or by means of those affinities and elective attractions which subsist between them and other elements and substances.

17. There are not only many reasons for inferring, but also evident and direct proof from facts and phenomena, that the electrites abound and are very generally diffused through nature, and that they have very important parts assigned them to perform in the maintenance of the course of nature, or in that continued regular succession of changes, of decompositions and recompositions, of dissolutions and renovations, on which the preservation of the universe in its present state depends : and that, perhaps, not so much as electrical as chemical agents, not only as being constituent parts of fire, but also as combining with most, and under certain circumstances perhaps with all, gravitating substances, and under the proper circumstances forming such an incorporating union with them, from being completely saturated and neutralized, as to lose all their particular electrical powers and properties, and to form an element or constituent part of the new product or substance thus generated, and in being capable, from their possessing different affinities under different circumstances, of passing from one gravitating base to another, and thereby of entering into a wondrous variety of different combinations whence a wondrous variety of different substances necessarily or naturally result.

The Author of these Essays—as regarding opinion unsupported by proof not as science but conjecture, however fortunate or happy such conjecture may eventually prove, and as having no desire to claim as discoveries conjectures or opinions not properly supported—delayed publicly announcing his electrical and chemical theories, long since rationally deduced from electrical phenomena and effects when Galvanism had made but little progress and was but little known, till such time as he could substantiate his assertions by establishing them on facts and reasonings sufficiently valid, and could reduce his principles, supported by suitable proofs, to a regular and systematic form, proper for being introduced into this work as a component part of a connected whole. In consequence of this delay he has been anticipated with regard to the *public annunciation* at least of some of the principles he adopts by Dr. G. S. Gibbes, an eminent physician of Bath, who, in Nicholson's Journal for June 1804, through the medium of Mr. Wilkinson, states it as his opinions or conjectures, rather than as established facts and discoveries, as they are far from being self-evident and no proof of them is attempted, that water is an elementary substance and is not decomposable ; that water enters into the composition of the gasses, and

into

into combination with metallic oxides ; and that there are two different Galvanic powers which on uniting generate fire, and on severally combining with water form with it pure and inflammable airs.—The publication of these opinions seems to have produced no impression whatever on the public, and to have had no influence on chemical theory ; since they do not appear to have been taken notice of by any one of the very numerous writers on chemical science, since first announced, now four years ago, either as approving of them or as controverting them.   Nor is that to be wondered at ; since these opinions were brought before the public altogether unsupported by proof and reasoning, and were controverted when announced even by the very person by whom they were announced.—That fire is generated, or at least exhibited, on bringing the wires proceeding from the opposite poles of the Galvanic pile near each other, and pure and inflammable airs on placing these wires in water, are facts which have now for a considerable time been known, and which are not of Dr. Gibbes' discovery ; and the opinions that water is not decomposable, and that it enters into the compositions of airs and calces, is only the doctrine of Dr. Priestley, and if he failed, by means of many well conceived and well conducted experiments, and many ingenious arguments, to convince the public and effect a revolution in chemical science, it could not reasonably be expected that the mere assertions of any individual, however respectable, unsupported either by proof or reasoning could be productive of that effect.

In Nicholson's Journal of March last, 1808, a letter from Dr. Gibbes himself addressed to Mr. Nicholson made its appearance ; in which, after alluding to the annunciation of his opinions in a former journal, he adds.   " I now take the liberty of sending some further observations on the same subject, " which lead me to conclude, that my former opinions were well founded."—These observations consist partly in making the same or similar assertions as in the former communication, and partly in attempting a proof of there being two different Galvanic powers, and of pure air being formed by the combination of one of these powers with water and inflammable air by the combination of the other of them with water. This proof is preceded and prefaced by the following articles, viz. 1st. " I contend, that in no one experi- " ment have we the least evidence, that the ponderable parts of oxygen and hydrogen air are substances " differing from each other, or in any respect particular substances; or that water is a compound re- " sulting from these two substances."—And 2d, " It is asserted, that the phenomena of Galvanism, " like electricity, are owing to the presence or absence of one and the same fluid, which constitute the " positive and negative sides."—From this last article it might be inferred that it is Dr. Gibbes's opinion that there is but one Galvanic fluid producing by its presence or absence all the Galvanic phenomena, were it not for the preceding assertions, and the supposed proof of there being two which immediately follows, and which seems to imply that it is one of Dr. Gibbes's opinions, that electric power differs from Galvanic ; and that though electricity is owing to the presence or absence of one and the same power, yet that is not the case with Galvanism.—In the first of these articles the expression " *I contend*" can mean only *I assert*, for no refutation is so much as attempted of any one of the various experiments of Messrs. Cavendish, Watt, Lavoisier, &c. from which the decomposition of water into oxygen and hydrogen has been inferred, nor any proof whatever offered of water being a simple elementary substance indecomposable by art:—these assumed facts must be admitted on mere assertion, and all the experiments and reasonings on this subject of the most eminent chemists, of those ingenious philosophers to whom the world is indebted for so many important discoveries, and who have so successfully employed their time and their talents in the improvement of this science, must without refutation, ceremony, or reserve, be abandoned; and those doctrines which Dr. Priestley laboured so long and with so much assiduity and ability in vain to establish must without proof be adopted, on the authority merely of
the

the above sweeping clause : a mode of procedure which truly may be entitled *short work with the chemists*, and which some of those who adopt and maintain the Lavoiserian system of chemistry may perhaps not think very respectful, though certainly nothing disrespectful could have been intended by it.

The proof adduced immediately follows these Articles, and is thus stated. viz. " If two bodies acting " upon a third produce different effects, the bodies themselves must be different."

" A different power is conducted into the water by the two ends of the Galvanic battery; for as the " two pieces of platina remain unaltered, the effect on the water in the galvanic experiment must be " produced by two different powers, to which the pieces of platina merely act as conductors. The " simple fact is then, that the one platina wire produces when placed in water one particular air ; and the " other platina wire, placed under similar circumstances, a different one : the two powers therefore, " conducted by the platina wires must be different."

" Bodies in assuming an aeriform state require the union of different other bodies to constitute those " characters which distinguish them; therefore these two different airs must have received from the two " platina wires two different powers, to enable them, since water is concerned in the production of " both, to assume two different aeriform states. The two airs so formed have certainly distinguishing " characters ; for the one supports combustion, and the other is a combustible body."

" Water then is by the union of these two Galvanic powers transformed into two aeriform bodies, in " which reside all the requisite circumstances of inflammation and combustion. Upon this combustion " water is reproduced, and the two Galvanic powers form fire : fire therefore is composed of the two " Galvanic powers."

This, however, in place of being a proof is in reality a mere *petitio principii* assuming in the premises that which is required to be proved, viz. First, The indecomposability of water, which is here assumed as granted on the authority merely of the above sweeping clause without proof; for the unaltered state of the platina wires by the process, and the natures of the airs generated from the water by it being different, certainly afford no evidence whatever, or even any indication of the indecomposability of water. Secondly, That fire is decomposable into two different Galvanic powers, likewise assumed without proof: no analysis of fire being so much as attempted; for the unaltered state of the platina wires by the process furnishes no evidence of it ; and saying that the airs generated by it are different because there are different Galvanic powers, and that there are different Galvanic powers because the airs generated are different, is only arguing in a circle and proving nothing. And, Thirdly, That the two different airs generated in those cases are produced by two different elements of the Galvanic fluid or fire acting on water a third substance, and not by two different elements of water acting on the Galvanic fluid or fire a third substance, though it is manifest that if water is decomposable, and that it is not is in this case neither proved nor attempted to be proved, its decomposition may be effected by means of any substance, as the Galvanic fluid or fire, with which its elements severally may under certain circumstances have greater affinity than under these circumstances they have with each other and hence the two substances or airs may by these processes be produced differing not only essentially from each other but also from those substances, water and the Galvanic fluid, from which they are generated:—and though no proof is adduced, or so much as attempted, of the production of the airs in these cases not being thus effected, an omission no doubt owing to no such proof having been known, this omission may now however easily be supplied from this Essay.

A proof of the *indecomposability* of water by any known means; and a proof of fire being actually *analysable*

analysable into two different Galvanic powers, are absolutely and indispensably necessary before these opinions or conclusions are rationally and justly deducible from the Galvanic phenomena: before it can logically and legitimately be concluded that there actually are two different Galvanic powers, that the fire exhibited in these experiments is owing to their union, and that the two different airs generated is the result of their respective combinations with water.—For the exhibition of fire in these cases may be in consequence merely of its liberation from some combination which retained it in a latent state; or of its passing from one combination or one body to another, agreeable to the generally received opinion; or, perhaps, even of its liberation from the Galvanic fluid from that fluid being much condensed by being concentrated or drawn to a point by means of the conducting wire; or it may be owing to some other un-unknown cause. It may or it may not be owing to the cause here assigned, for any that is here advanced, as no proof is brought either of its being owing to that cause, or of its not being owing to some other cause: the circumstance of the platina wires which conduct the Galvanic fluid or fire into the water not being altered by conducting it into the water furnishes no proof either of its decomposition in this case or of its being decomposable; and the simple circumstance of fire being exhibited in some of these experiments does not afford any satisfactory proof of its being generated in these cases, and generated by an union of these merely hypothetical entities, two different Galvanic powers, the existence of which is here not proved but assumed only; and it is not enough to say, that fire is composed of two Galvanic powers because it is composed of two Galvanic powers; or, as otherwise expressed, " the two Galvanic " powers form fire; fire therefore is composed of the two Galvanic powers;" as this is only an identical proposition from which there is nothing to be learned.

Though this work carries with it more than mere presumptive proof of its author having formed these electrical and chemical opinions and principles it contains prior to the discovery by the British chemists of the Galvanical methods of generating the gasses, and though it seems impossible for any one who reads this work with attention to entertain any doubt of its originality, and of the author's principles being intirely the result of his own investigations and discoveries, had it not been from the insufficiency and indeed intire failure of the above attempted proof, the author of these essays should not have been disposed to dispute with Dr. Gibbes equality, at least, of claim to these discoveries; not only from his entertaining no doubt of there having been some solid grounds, some sufficient reasons, though these reasons had not been adduced, for the adoption of these opinions; but also, as is usual in such cases, from his giving the author of them credit for an extent of knowledge, and depth of discernment, much superior to that which falls to the lot of the generality of the human race. But since the reasons advanced are altogether insufficient for establishing the facts they are brought to support, since there is a total failure in the proof adduced, these opinions can justly be regarded as vague conjectures only; and, as such, any priority of claim to them cannot be worth the contending for; more especially, as it is probable that such conjectures have not been peculiar to Dr. Gibbes and the author of these Essays, but that they have been entertained by others also; at least, since the publication of the Galvanic methods of producing the gasses, as these methods and the phenomena attending them naturally lead to them.

From the above mentioned publication, it would appear that Dr. Gibbes had changed the opinion he entertained with regard to the nature of metallic calces, as announced by Mr. Wilkinson, when he says, " The same reasoning holds good with respect to the Galvanic property of the negative end of the pile, " as in the instance of metallic calces being reducible to their metallic state; and we account for this " by saying, that the oxidated or positive state of the metal is destroyed by its being saturated with the " hydrogeneous or negative power of the pile. In short, bodies are burnt by the power or principle
" which

" which comes from the one end of the pile, and unburnt by the power or principle which comes from " the other end of the pile."—As it would appear from this that he now regards metallic calces to be metals in their intire state in combination with positive Galvanism; and that the calces resume their former metallic state, or are revived when the oxygated or positive state of the metal is " destroyed by its " being saturated with the hydrogenous or negative power of the pile," in place of regarding them as metallic substances in combination either with water, or with gasses of which water forms a component part. In this last extract Dr. Gibbes's opinions with regard to combustion are likewise stated, viz. that the one Galvanic power burns, and the other unburns, or that the one burns substances and the other unburns them; opinions however which neither originated with Dr. Gibbes, nor are peculiar to him, for that inflammable air has, ever since its discovery, been regarded as a combustible substance, its name sufficiently evinces; and that pure air is a supporter of combustion has for a considerable time been the prevailing opinion.

CHAP.

CHAP. IV.

OF THE NOMENCLATURE EMPLOYED IN THIS ESSAY.

SINCE the perfection of a science must necessarily precede the perfection of its language, it cannot, from the very defective state of human knowledge (and the imperfection of most of the sciences), be matter of surprise, that the language of science is, in many cases, inadequate to the purposes for which it is intended;—that it is often too periphrastical, and is, even, sometimes exceedingly improper, the terms employed seeming to convey and imply meanings neither just, nor applicable with advantage or propriety to the substances, powers, or properties, to which they are respectively appropriated: a circumstance productive of very pernicious consequences, as having a direct and powerful tendency to mislead the judgement, to produce erroneous conclusions and delusive theories, and to terminate in the adoption of doctrines having, in reality, no foundation in reason or nature.—And since, in the present imperfect state of human knowledge, the employing of terms of no meaning, or of no other meaning than what they derive from this exclusive appropriation of them, to denote or signify substances or qualities the natures of which are not properly understood, is on these accounts preferable to employing terms for that purpose expressive of properties which those substances, they are employed to signify and denote, are, according to the prevailing but perhaps erroneous theory of the day, supposed to possess; I have in this Essay, with the intention of obviating the inconveniences and bad consequences necessarily resulting from the use of terms expressive of meanings which a further progress in knowlege may not sanction, been induced to employ new terms, having no meaning but what they owe to this application of them, to signify and express certain of those substances, powers, or qualities, which act the most important and distinguished parts in the sciences of electricity, chemistry, and magnetism:—Thus, I employ the terms mona and avona to signify and denote the electrites, or two elements or constituent principles of fire; and hence for the expressions resinous

elec-

electricity, and negative electricity, or rather for that substance or power they are meant to signify or express, I every where in the sequel of this Essay, &c. substitute the term mona; and for the expressions vitreous electricity, or positive electricity, the term avona:—and hence are derived the adjectives monic, and avonic; and the verbs to monate, monated, monating, and to avonate, avonated, avonating.

Agreeable then to this mode of nomenclature, or of denominating the different electrics by the terms mona and avona, that substance hitherto known by the names of inflammable air, and hydrogen gas, assumes the appellation of mona gas, or monic gas;—and that known by the names of pure air, empyreal air, and oxygen gas, that of avona gas, or avonic gas: also that which has been called oxygenated muriatic acid is expressed, according to this mode, avonated muriatic acid; or, more briefly, avo-muriatic acid.—And, for the reasons assigned above, the term cora, a word of easy pronunciation and of no particular signification till thus appropriated, is substituted for the term azot, and the expression cora gas, for that of azotic gas; an alteration the more requisite from the manifest impropriety of employing the term azotic to express this particular kind of gas exclusively, since several of the other gasses, on being respired, are equally fatal with it to animal life.—From this term the adjective coric, and the verb to corate, corated, corating, are derivable; and, from the adoption of it and of the other terms mentioned above, the compound term cora avona comes to signify and denote the compound radical of nitric acid; and cora mona that of volatile alkali.—The terms sulpha, phospha, carbo, are appropriated to express and denote the radical of sulphur, and of, what is at present called, sulphuric acid; of phosphorus, and of what is called phosphoric acid; and of carbon, and of what is called carbonic acid, respectively:—and, hence, these acids come to be severally denominated the sulphic, the phosphic, and the carbic, acids.—The adoption of any particular appellations for the several radicals of the other acids; and, of course, any new nomenclature of these acids, may with propriety be deferred till these radicals are better known.—I appropriate the term calx to denote any solid gravitating substance that is neither water, nor saline, nor is soluble in water; and which appears not, from experiment, to contain any mona in its composition, and which nevertheless admits of chemical combina-

tion

tion with it:—hence, quick-lime is not, according to this mode of nomenclature, a calx. And, as I am of opinion that the terms Lixa, Trona, and
Ammona, as proposed by the late Dr. Black, may be substituted with
advantage for those of potash, or vegetable alkali, of fossil alkali or soda,
and of volatile alkali or ammoniac respectively, I have accordingly adopted them.

As the elementary or constituent parts of fire, mona and avona, are electrites only when not in chemical combination either with each other, or
with any other substance, the term electrites is applicable to them with
propriety, only, when they are in that state, and not when they are in a
state of chemical combination, or are operating as chemical agents, and
producing chemical effects; on which account it becomes necessary to
denominate them by some general appellation which may be applicable
to them in every state; I shall therefore in the sequel of this Essay denominate them Pyrogens, a term which may answer the purpose well enough
till a better may be substituted for it, retaining and using at the same time
the term electrite to distinguish and denominate them when not in a state
of chemical combination and when possessing and producing electrical
powers and effects.

CHAP. V.

OF COMBUSTION.

1. COMBUSTION differs essentially from ignition. And, indeed, there is
frequently not only ignition but inflammation also without combustion:
bodies often producing those effects, and exhibiting those appearances, to
which the terms ignition and inflammation are severally applied, without
these bodies being in a state of combustion; as in the first case appearing
often in what is called a red or a white heat, and producing the sensation
and other effects of heat; and in the other case in that of acual inflammation, as emitting and discharging fire in large quantities, and in a very
pure and highly luminous state. This is the case with bodies raised to a
                                                                    high

high degree of temperature by the application of fire to them, which when the fire by which they were heated is withdrawn, soon cool again, and become the same as they were before the application of the fire to them, no essential or chemical alteration having taken place in them in consequence of the process; this is also the case on the inflammation, or the discharge from condensation, or any other cause, of that fire from bodies which they retained in a state of corpuscular combination only, and part with in the form of fire, or of heat, light, and flame, without their being chemically affected by that means; and this is likewise the case in the inflammations of particular bodies from their emitting those rays of light, or that radiant and luminous fire, at a certain degree of temperature, which at another degree of it they had imbibed on being exposed to the action of such rays or radiant and luminous fire; as the natural and artificial pyrophori:---ignitions and inflammations from the above causes take place in vacuo the same as in air.

2. Combustion consists not merely in an emission of fire from bodies, but in an emission of fire from them accompanied with a *chemical* decomposition of those bodies. That combustion is not owing to the phlogiston of Becker and Stahl, according to whose theory of combustion, phlogiston is nothing but pure fire in a state of *chemical* combination, with certain gravitating substances which by their union with it are rendered combustible, and combustion only a liberation and discharge of the phlogiston of the combustible substances by means of an increase of temperature, is proved by no instance of *chemical* combination, strictly and properly so called, between fire and any gravitating substance being known, all known combinations of these being corpuscular only and their qualities intermediate of those of their proximate principles; and from the corpuscular combinations of gravitating substances with phlogiston or fire not rendering these substances combustible; as in the case of water, which though formed by a corpuscular combination of ice with fire is not combustible.

3. It is manifest that combustion can not be owing to the causes assigned for it in the Lavoiserian System of Chemistry, if there is actually no such substance in nature as oxygen, one of the supposed elements of water and the supposed gravitating base of avona gas, as has been attempted to be proved in the preceding chapters of this Essay; for, if

that

that is the case, that which exists not can not, in combustion, as this system assumes, combine with the combustible forming the product, and occasion the increase of weight: and, if it is not with caloric and light, or even with fire, that the gravitating bases of the gasses is in combination, but with the pyrogens, and that it is to the pyrogens they owe their elasticity, as has also been attempted to be proved in the preceding chapters, the fire exhibited and produced on combustion can not be owing, as this system pretends, to any discharge of caloric and light from the avona gas of the atmosphere, on its gravitating base condensing in combining with the combustible forming the product.

4. There are numerous other facts besides those already adduced which afford the most decisive proofs of the doctrines advanced in the preceding chapters of this Essay being well founded, and of the incompetency of the Lavoiserian Theory for accounting justly for the cause and phenomena of combustion; as, First, That the gasses, even avona gas, that to the condensation of which the caloric and light evolved on combustion is by that theory ascribed, are, by means of that reciprocal attraction which subsists between them and certain other gravitating substances condensable even to solidity, or seeming solidity, without evolving caloric or light; which could not be the case if it was to caloric and light that they owed their elasticity and gaseous state, and it was to the discharge of that caloric and light on their being deprived of that state by condensation that the fire of combustion is owing. Second, Fire is often evolved on condensation where there is no reason for suspecting the presence of any gas; as on the condensation of vapour or steam, but that is not combustion or the fire of combustion. Third, The product of combustion is often a gas, and a gas of more weight and of equal volume with the avona gas consumed by it; as on the combustion of charcoal in avona gas. Fourth, Caloric is often emitted in large quantities in cases where gasses in place of being condensed are generated in abundance; as on the dissolving of certain metals in certain acids under certain circumstances. And, Fifth, Avona gas produces and promotes combustion as much when in a condensed as when in an uncondensed state; as when forming a proximate principle of avomuriatic or nitric acids, or of nitre or other neutral salts containing these, or of certain fulminating powders, as fulminating gold, common gun powder, &c.

From

From the terms avona gas and oxygen gas denoting the same substance, and also from mona gas and hydrogen gas being terms expressive of the same substance, and from the term gas being common to all these expressions, it may perhaps be imagined by some that the terms mona and avona, and the terms hydrogen and oxygen, are respectively only different names for the same substances; but this is far from being the case, mona differs essentially from hydrogen, the first denotes the ungravitating principle combined with the gravitating base of the gas, while the other denotes the supposed gravitating base combined with the caloric and light, or the supposed ungravitating principle, to which the gas owes its elasticity and gaseous state; and in the same manner avona differs essentially from oxygen; the former denoting the ungravitating principle of the gas, while the latter denotes its supposed gravitating base.

5. Since combustion then consists in the generation and dissipation of fire from a change of chemical combinations, whereby the substances undergoing it are consumed, or more properly converted into others essentially different, the chemical principles already developed are fully sufficient for accounting for the phenomena it exhibits, and the effects it produces; and for affording a just and satisfactory theory of the whole of this very important, and hitherto abstruse and seemingly mysterious process of nature. For it follows from these as a necessary consequence that combustion can take place only between gravitating substances in chemical combination with the pyrogens, or elements of fire; and between those only of which part are combined with the one pyrogen and part with the other, whether these substances possessing different pyrogens as proximate principles exist separately as distinct bodies, or in corpuscular or even chemical combination with other substances, if their different pyrogens are not in chemical combination with each other from each under the then circumstances having greater affinity to its respective gravitating base than they have for each other, forming one body or substance only; and that combustion is the result of differences of affinities, from differences of temperature, &c. induced in the proximate principles of these bodies or substances, whereby they form new chemical combinations, and consists merely in the chemical or corpuscular combinations of the gravitating bases of these substances together, according as these gravitating bases are either sub-

stances

stances of different kinds or substances of the same kind, and in the chemical combination at the same time of the different pyrogens forming the other proximate principles of these substances with each other generating the fire of combustion, which diffusing itself in all directions is soon dissipated and disappears except in cases of continued combustion.

6. These changes of chemical combination in which combustion consists are sometimes the effect of single or simple affinities, as when the gravitating bases of the different bodies are substances of the same kind, as in the combustion of a mixture of avona and mona gasses, which happens but seldom; but otherwise of a play of affinities or of double or compound affinities, the gravitating bases having, under the then circumstances, greater affinity for each other than each has for its respective pyrogen, and the different pyrogens having at the same time greater affinity for each other than each has for its respective gravitating base. And hence it may with intire confidence be concluded that every gravitating substance which is not combustible alone, and which is combustible only when in contact or mixture with some other gravitating substance known to contain avona as one of its proximate principles, are themselves possessed of mona as one of their constituent parts or proximate principles; and, conversely, that gravitating substances which are combustible only in conjunction with other gravitating substances known to contain mona in their composition, are themselves possessed of avona, or the other pyrogen, as one of their constituent principles.

7. These facts naturally suggest an easy, and in general sure test or criterion for determining by trial whether any particular gravitating body is possessed of a pyrogen as one of its principles or not; and, when possessed of one, its nature and kind: thus, on exposing any substance to a high degree of temperature in contact with air, or avona gas, its being possessed or not of mona as a constituent principle will be discovered and determined by its proving combustible or not under these circumstances; while by exposing any particular substance to a high degree of temperature in conjunction with any body proved by the above experiment to contain mona as a constituent principle, as by exposing black calx of iron in conjunction with charcoal or phosphorus, its being possessed or not of avona as a proximate principle will be discovered and determined by its proving combustible or

not

not under these circumstances; and even when it contains it not as an element, but as an element of the avona gas or other substance, only, with which it may be in combination. Continued combustion results from the particles of the combustibles not acquiring all at once the requisite degree of temperature but successively and gradually; and from their not coming all at once in that state into immediate contact with the air but successively and gradually as those particles by which they were covered are successively and gradually dissipated or consumed.

8. The substances in nature divide themselves into the two great classes or orders of COMBUSTIBLES and INCOMBUSTIBLES. And the first of these into three genera, viz. First, Those that are combustible from containing mona in their composition. Secondly, Those that are so from containing avona in their composition. And, Thirdly, Those that are so from containing both mona and avona, the two different elements of fire but not in a state of chemical combination with each other, in their composition. This last genus, from the circumstance of containing both the elements of fire in their composition, are combustible in vacuo, in the different gasses, and even under water, mercury, &c. phenomena and effects hitherto unaccounted for, and regarded as inexplicable; and which, indeed, are inexplicable on any other theory of combustion.

From the principles established in Essay V. and in this and the preceding chapters of this Essay, explanations and just theories flow as from their source with respect to many of the most important and seemingly most mysterious of the chemical, electrical, and magnetical phenomena, operations, and effects.

END OF VOL. I.

www.ingramcontent.com/pod-product-compliance
Lightning Source LLC
Chambersburg PA
CBHW062036090426
42740CB00016B/2921